The Political Economy of Independent Ukraine

The Political Economy of Independent Ukraine

Hans van Zon
Research Professor in Central and Eastern European Studies
University of Sunderland

First published in Great Britain 2000 by
MACMILLAN PRESS LTD
Houndmills, Basingstoke, Hampshire RG21 6XS and London
Companies and representatives throughout the world

A catalogue record for this book is available from the British Library.

ISBN 0–333–78301–8

First published in the United States of America 2000 by
ST. MARTIN'S PRESS, LLC,
Scholarly and Reference Division,
175 Fifth Avenue, New York, N.Y. 10010

ISBN 0–312–23593–3

Library of Congress Cataloging-in-Publication Data
Zon, Hans van, 1949–
The political economy of independent Ukraine / Hans van Zon.
p. cm.
Includes bibliographical references (p.) and index.
ISBN 0–312–23593–3
1. Ukraine—Economic conditions—1991– 2. Ukraine—Economic policy—1991–
3. Post-communism—Ukraine. I. Title.

HC340.19 .Z4 2000
338.9477—dc21

00–036911

This book is printed on paper suitable for recycling and made from fully managed and sustained
forest sources.

10   9   8   7   6   5   4   3   2   1
09   08   07   06   05   04   03   02   01   00

Printed and bound in Great Britain by
Antony Rowe Ltd, Chippenham, Wiltshire

For Anna

Contents

List of Figures, Schemes and Tables

Acknowledgements

I would like to thank Marten van Meurs and Jens Hölscher who commented on draft versions of this book. I would also like to thank the State Engineering Academy in Zaporizhzhya. The ACE programme of the Commission of the EU provided support for field research during 1996 and 1997 in Zaporizhzhya.

1
Introduction

When Ukraine gained independence in 1991, many Ukrainians assumed that the country would perform relatively well if the ties with Russia could be severed. Most nationalists were convinced that Ukraine, a country of 51.9 million inhabitants in 1991 (49.8 in late 1999), was exploited by Russia and that, with independence, the new country would be able to profit from its rich natural resources. These beliefs were fuelled by a report from Deutsche Bank (1991) that gave Ukraine the best economic development prospects of all the ex-Soviet republics. In particular, the country's rich soil and its expertise in machine building and heavy metallurgy were mentioned as great assets. These factors, together with the lack of faith in the ability of the authorities in Moscow to govern for the benefit of Ukraine, especially after the aborted coup of 1991, led the Russian-speaking half of the population to support independence.

In 1999, eight years after the proclamation of independence, the transition to a market economy and parliamentary democracy, the Ukrainian economy and society were in a disastrous state. Registered industrial production in Ukraine had declined to less than one-quarter of its pre-independence level and (registered) agricultural production had more than halved since independence. Per capita GDP, based on purchasing power parity, fell to US$2000 in 1998, half that of Russia (US$3950), and between that of India and China.[1] Ukraine is the only transition country to have known nine consecutive years of economic decline. At the turn of the millennium the economy is not yet on a growth path and stabilized, privatization is far from complete and the overwhelming majority of the population is living below the official poverty line. One of the major achievements of the Ukrainian government has been the consolidation of the Ukrainian state. However, even this accomplishment is fragile given the country's economic dependence upon Russia and the large disgruntled Russian minority.

Ukraine has one of the worst economic records of all transition countries. In the 1997 Transition Report from the European Bank for Reconstruction and Development, in which progress towards a market economy was assessed, Ukraine was rated 23 on the transition index, which encompassed 25 countries.[2] In the Global Competitiveness Report 1999, under the heading 'overall competitiveness' Ukraine occupied position 58 out of 59 states. Even compared with Russia, the economic situation is gloomy.

What is the background to this abysmal economic record and where is the Ukrainian economy heading? To what extent can the economic performance be blamed on transitional or external factors or is it related to more structural factors? In this respect the question arises as to what kind of socio-economic system is emerging in the Ukraine. Why shouldn't a market economy develop and attain a critical mass as in many Central European countries? Why can reform forces not gain the upper hand? Why is the vicious downward economic spiral perpetuated? What constitutes the blocking mechanisms in the Ukrainian economy? Is the continuing economic disintegration and decline simply a reflection of a phase difference, compared to more advanced transition countries?

Many observers of contemporary Ukraine, especially those attached to international organizations advising the Ukrainian government, make the naive assumption that Ukraine has only one option, namely to move further on the continuum from public and plan to private and market and accomplish the transition to democracy. They assume that the medicine of the market will prove to be irresistible for policy-makers in Kyiv and that, sooner or later, lagging Ukraine will follow other transition economies in their transition from plan to market. In this respect, every step the Ukrainian government takes to comply with recommendations from the International Monetary Fund (IMF) is considered a step towards introducing a market economy.

In this book, the transition process is seen as open-ended.

Many factors influence the economic performance of Ukraine. Some factors are external and transitional, such as (i) the economic impact of the dissolution of the Soviet Union, leading to a loss of trading partners for Ukraine; (ii) Ukraine had to pay more for Russian energy; and (iii) the dislocations inherited from Soviet times (emphasis on heavy industry, no rational spatial division of labour). For example, Ukraine is dependent on energy imports from other former Soviet republics for

40 per cent of its energy consumption. Energy costs have increased rapidly, from 15 per cent of the world market price to the world market level between 1991 and 1995. There are historical legacies in the distorted economic structure, with an emphasis on heavy industry, a small service sector and a large but neglected agricultural sector. There are also deep-rooted attitudes that are inappropriate under present circumstances. There are demographic factors: Ukraine has a comparatively large proportion of pensioners.[3] There is the environmental legacy, with its associated economic costs. For example, all enterprises until recently paid a Chernobyl tax.[4]

Another factor is the changeover to a different economic system, that has caused in all transitional economies a recession related to systemic change. One problem for Ukraine is the low level of economic competence of Ukrainian politicians and public servants. Here it is relevant to distinguish between the impact of government policies and the constraints posed by the economic system. Policy-makers are limited in the range of choices they can make because of the constraints imposed by the inherited institutional framework.

In this book the focus will be on the question of what economic system is emerging in Ukraine. As the socio-economic situation is still very fluid and both Ukrainian society and the economy are faced with major change, methodological problems arise in answering this question.

First of all, no theories exist that can adequately explain the transition process. Therefore an inductive approach is used, starting from analysing concrete behaviour of economic actors and arriving at generalizations on that basis. In conceptualizing transition, an eclectic approach towards theory is used, to generate a theoretical framework for better understanding the political economy of Ukrainian transition. It will be a 'disciplined eclecticism', i.e. 'the controlled and systematic use of complementary ideas drawn from different orientations'.[5]

The emphasis is not so much on actors or structures but rather on the structural constraints faced by economic agents. It is about to what extent actors in the Ukrainian economy are trapped by the past.

A multidisciplinary approach is used. For example, the assumption is that in order to understand the process of economic policy-making and policy implementation it is essential to understand how questions of power and influence are resolved in the Ukrainian polity. It is argued that an understanding of a set of deep-rooted social practices is necessary for understanding why people in Ukraine accept the way in which they are ruled and the way they work. The economic system in Ukraine, even more so than in developed capitalist countries, is socially embedded and cannot be understood outside its social and political context.

The main thesis is that economic and social development in Ukraine is blocked by a set of parasitic mechanisms at all levels of the economy that prevent profitable and productive value-added economic activities to emerge. This has led to the emergence of an economic system that devours its own economic base. Ukraine has developed into a blocked and paralysed society.

The parasitic mechanisms developed under Soviet rule, when 'beating the system' by extracting and redistributing resources from the state and spreading disregard for the public good, created the foundations for the grab and run practices in independent Ukraine.

In Chapter 2 the legacy of the pre-Soviet and Soviet past is analysed. The fact that Ukraine has almost no previous experience of a market economy and has, for the most part, been part of a despotically ruled empire, constitutes a liability in the transition to a market economy. The most important obstacles inherited from the Soviet period do not appear to lie in the distorted economic structure but rather in ingrained social practices and institutional weaknesses. In particular, the gradual process of privatization of the state proved to be a phenomenon that paralysed the economy. The forced industrialization and urbanization of the Ukrainian peasant society has led to a partial modernization. The communists neglected the complex social fabric of industrial society. The Soviet economy missed the complicated horizontal organizational differentiation, so characteristic of modern industrial economies. With the demise of Soviet socialism, a world that was hitherto hidden came to the fore.

Chapter 3 analyses the Byzantine labyrinth of the Ukrainian polity. The transformation from a developmental to a predatory state is linked to the rent-seeking inclinations of a ruling élite that sees the state primarily as a feeding ground. Many elements of the institutional set-up of the centrally planned economy are still in place. Division of competencies between executive, legislative and judiciary power is unusually diffuse. Many state institutions produce legislative and quasi-legislative acts that are often not published. This has created a legal jungle and has given the bureaucracy a high discretionary power.

The state bureaucracy is a paralysing and major antireform force. Corruption is rampant and bureaucrats often consider themselves free to exploit their domain for private purposes.

Although the base of the redistributive state is subject to erosion, and there are conflicting interests between feuding factions of the ruling élite, no powerful reform constituency is discernible. The impact of international pressure groups upon the Ukrainian polity is mixed. In many respects, IMF policies have strengthened the predatory ruling élite.

Economic reform is analysed in Chapter 4. It appears that the concept of 'reform' is used by the Ukrainian government to denote improvement of the present system rather than market-oriented reform, although the legal infrastructure for market-oriented reform has certainly improved. Although hyperinflation has come under control since 1995, monetary stabilization had a fragile basis. Advances in one field were usually cancelled out by failures in others, and by mid-2000, the state still intervened heavily in the sphere of production. Huge resources are still channelled from the value-adding to the value-subtracting sectors of the economy.

In Chapter 5, changes in the area of production are examined from a macro-perspective. The economic structure of Ukraine was fundamentally transformed during the 1990s, as a result of differential decline rather than deliberate government policies. The share of high-value-added production as a proportion of total production decreased sharply, whereas value-subtracting industries like heavy metallurgy and coal increased their share.

The prospects for heavy metallurgy are gloomy because production outlays are obsolete and energy intensiveness of production is very high. Huge fortunes have been made in the energy sector, mainly related to the trading of energy. Although restructuring of the coal industry is progressing, albeit slowly, large subsidies are still channelled into this sector. The development of agriculture and the food processing industry is held back by semi-feudal relationships, the farmers being squeezed by government, middlemen and local administrations.

Chapter 6 shows that hardly any strategic adjustment has occurred in industrial enterprises. This is related to a lack of incentives to restructure. Privatization of state-owned enterprises has had, in most cases, little impact on corporate governance. If industrial enterprises have changed the way they operate, it was often in order to protect against market forces.

Chapter 7 looks at the development of international economic relations. With independence, the institutional framework for foreign economic relations had to be developed from scratch. The share of trade with OECD countries is small while that of the former socialist states is still overwhelming. The commodity composition of exports has become very susceptible to price fluctuations on the world market and is very dependent on exports from value-subtracting industries such as steel and chemicals. Import competition has destroyed enterprises rather than stimulating them to perform better, related to the deficient incentive structure in Ukraine. Direct foreign investment is minimal. Internationalization did not include productive activities. Capital flight meant a drain of resources from the Ukrainian economy.

The inclusion of Ukraine in the world economy has been one-sided, ephemeral and asymmetrical. Although dependent on assistance from international financial institutions, the Ukrainian economy is still to a large extent disassociated from the world economy.

Chapter 8 examines regional and local economies. Regional economies in terms of territorially coherent groupings of related industries are rare in Ukraine. Regional policies have hardly developed at the provincial level. The frequent heavy reliance of regions and localities on one industrial sector hampers industrial restructuring. This is especially the case for company towns. Provincial administrations focus their energies on extracting resources from the centre, i.e. redistribution, rather than fostering endogenous development potential. The centralized redistributive state keeps the provinces dependent upon its subsidies and uses these subsidies as an instrument of control and cohesion.

In Chapter 9 social change is analysed as far as is relevant for economic development. Attitudes such as lack of initiative and lack of accountability, which are rooted in the socialist past, constitute a brake on economic development. It is shown that social practices which developed under socialism, such as 'beating the system' by extracting resources from the state sector and a tolerant attitude towards parasitic activities, have had a negative impact upon economic development since Ukraine's independence. Generalized distrust hampered cooperation for the public good. It seems that a combination of centralized state structures and a weak civil society breeds hierarchical clientelistic networks that undermine the creation of a public–private divide as it exists in Western Europe and North America.

Although human skills, in terms of educational levels, are considerable, organizational capital is at a very low level. The low level of self-organization of society allowed a predatory state to develop and a parasitic bureaucracy to act with impunity. Deep social divisions were able to develop due to the passivity of the general population.

Chapter 10 analyses the emerging economic system and alternative development paths. Although at first sight, the Ukrainian economy resembles an archipelago of economic sub-systems that are barely linked, the state with its redistributive mechanisms and paralysing bureaucracy provides a framework that keeps the economy interconnected. The large shadow economy is linked through criminal networks to the state sector. Lawlessness and criminalization of the economy increases transaction costs enormously. Although capitalist elements have emerged in Ukraine, they are largely parasitic upon the (quasi) state sector.

Given the structural constraints and the weakness of agents that act for change, development prospects for the Ukrainian economy are gloomy, both in the short and medium term.

This book analyses the political economy of Ukraine, stating that the roots of the economic decline are social and political in nature and that the emerged socio-economic formation is characterized by generalized parasitism. Here, Ukraine is not unique and similar cases can be found elsewhere in the post-Soviet and developing world.

In the case of economic reforms, there is a crucial role for administrative reform, to change the role of the state from suffocating and predatory to facilitative and developmental. This scenario presupposes a government that is willing to act for the common good. A reform of the state apparatus may further the transformation of social practices in such a way that they sustain modernization of society and the economy. It may lead to the emergence of governance mechanisms at all levels that may foster economic development.

2
Independence: Euphoria and Disillusionment

This chapter discusses aspects of Ukrainian history relevant to under-standing economic transition in the 1990s. The processes of extraction from a centrally planned economy and formation of a new socio-economic system are put in a historical context.

Pre-socialist legacies

Visitors to Ukraine will see the marked contrast between Eastern and Western Ukraine. This contrast is not only related to different eco-nomic and national characteristics, the East being more industrialized and Russsian-speaking and the West being more rural and Ukrainian, but also to attitudes. The population of Western Ukraine is more open to reform than that of Eastern Ukraine. This is due to the fact that part of Western Ukraine was only incorporated into the Soviet Union during the Second World War and was previously part of Poland, Czechoslovakia, Hungary, Romania and the Austrian–Hungarian monarchy.[1] As a result, this part of Western Ukraine has had less expe-rience of socialism and has experienced the civilizational impact of the Austrian Empire. This experience is still reflected in the collective memory in some provinces of Western Ukraine.

Although the multicultural mosaic that constituted early century Ukraine, in its present borders, has disappeared, the multiple layers of different regional historical configurations are still discernible.

The majority of Ukraine has for a long time been part of the Russian Empire and Russian-speaking. Up until the 17th century it was subject to numerous invasions and raids. Russia has never known classical European feudalism, with its decentralized power structures, nor the experiences of Renaissance and Enlightenment. Slavery was only abolished in 1861, and since then Russia has remained a despotically ruled empire.[2] Private property, protected and respected in Western Europe, did not exist in Russia up to the late 19th century, nor did a sizable Russian bourgeoisie. The industrialization that started in the late 19th century was mainly furthered by the state and foreign industrialists. Economic development was hampered by the activities of an absolutist bureaucracy. State control and oppressive taxation severely handicapped the growth of a modern economy, but private property became more secure.

All this means that in most of Ukraine there is no collective memory of capitalist and democratic institutions. The pre-socialist legacy upon which one can build is, for the majority of Ukraine, the Tsarist legacy.

Soviet Ukraine: forced industrialization of a peasant society

On the eve of the October revolution, Ukraine was largely a peasant society. Industry had only developed in the Donbas region, in South-Eastern Ukraine, with the help of foreign investors.

The forced industrialization of Ukraine began with the first Five Year Plans (1928–38). Initially, the industrialization of Soviet Ukraine was based on the development of heavy industry in the Donbas region, with its deposits of iron ore and coal. Later, the machine building industry was developed and integrated into the Soviet industrial complex.

Over-integration, or planned over-dependence, of the republic's economies was a deliberate policy of the planners in Moscow. Ukraine was not allowed to develop consumer goods industries on its territory. According to an account from the early 1950s:

> The crying need of the Ukrainians was for consumer goods. Odessa and Kharkiv requested that they might be given the power to build textile mills to supply the needs of the local population. The request was denied...The iron and steel cities requested that they might be given permission to build factories to complete the fabrication of certain delicate types of machinery. The request was refused because it was to be only in the Moscow area that such articles were to be made.[3]

As a result Ukraine became increasingly dependent on other Soviet republics, in particular with regard to a range of consumer goods.

Imbalances emerged not only between light and heavy industry, but also between consumer-oriented heavy industry and the capital-intensive military-industrial complex.

Most products were shipped to other republics for further manufacturing. Estimates of the number of all industrial enterprises in Ukraine that were controlled by the all-Union ministries vary from 57 per cent to 90 per cent.[4] These ministries hardly communicated with each other and each ministry tried to attain the largest possible autonomy, organizing supplies as much as possible within their own domain. Therefore, the Soviet economy could be considered as a mono-ministerial branch economy. It was far from a single market. Goods were produced step by step in a highly specialized, highly coordinated series of plants, dispersed across the 15 Soviet republics. This resulted in serious misallocation of resources. On independence, the fixed capital structure left little flexibility in product reorientation.

Economic interdependence between the Soviet republics was much greater than in single markets of comparable size. For example, inter-republican trade was at a much higher level than that between EU states.[5]

The Soviet Union consisted of republics (such as Ukraine) and regions. These administrative units did not have their own 'economies'. Regional and republican authorities did not have much leverage in economic affairs. It was the ministries in Moscow that planned the inputs and outputs of most enterprises. In the vertically structured branch-ministerial economy there was hardly room for horizontal communication between enterprises.

Ukraine felt neglected because in 1990 it received only 12 per cent of national investments while its share of national production was 17 per cent.[6] Expenditure on the development of basic research in Ukraine in 1990 was 6.3 rubles per capita, while in Russia it was 25.5 rubles; per capita expenditure on culture in Ukraine was 3.8 rubles, in Russia 12.8; and per capita investment on housing was 94 and 145 rubles, respectively.[7]

Stalin built upon the most backward elements of peasant society such as its mythology, with the deification of the state and its leader, its authoritarianism, and in some ways, its organization of production. The enterprise organization in some ways resembled the dependency relationships within the estates. The workers were in many respects tied to the enterprise and the relationship between management and workers assumed a quasi-feudal character. For example, for most of the

Soviet period, workers in the kolchozes and sovchozes could not obtain internal passports allowing them to travel within the Soviet Union. A major result of Stalinist industrialization was that the social texture of society, as it had developed in Tsarist times, was largely destroyed and that instead, a totalitarian system was created in which there was no place for autonomous initiatives. All spontaneity, an important prerequisite for technological innovation, was crushed.

However, there was some technological innovation, as a result of the mobilization of huge resources, mainly in the military sector. Eighty per cent of spending on research and development was for the military.[8] Direct military employment was 9.3 million in the former Soviet Union, and the associated civilian workforce was 13.8 million. Over half the industrial assets of Ukraine were designed to produce heavy and military equipment.

The character of the centrally planned economic system was that of a war economy, in which everything was subordinated to the needs of the state that was preparing for war.

Before the October revolution, Ukraine had by far the most fertile soils of the Russian Empire and produced most of the grain exported by Russia. However, the collectivization campaign destroyed the productive potential of the countryside. Private farming was crushed.

More so than other republics, Ukraine suffered from forced collectivization during the 1930s. Approximately 2 million Ukrainian peasants lost their lives due to starvation, while millions were deported to Siberia. Collectivization pushed many peasants to the towns, which grew rapidly.[9]

For Soviet leaders, strict control over Ukraine was of particular importance as it was the second largest republic of the Soviet Union. Ukrainian nationalism was seen as a great threat to the cohesion of the Soviet state. With the industrialization of Ukraine there was a massive influx of Russians – the number of Russians in the total Ukrainian population rose from 7 per cent in 1926 to 22 per cent in 1989.[10]

The second wave of Stalinist repression, during the late 1940s and early 1950s, hit Ukraine harder, especially the newly incorporated Western Ukraine, than other parts of the Soviet Union. For most of the 1960s and 1970s the Ukrainian dissident movement was crushed in several waves of police repression.

This background of fierce repression helps explain the docile attitude of the Ukrainian population and the extraordinary emphasis in

Ukrainian politics today upon consensus and the avoidance of open conflict.

The importance attached by the Soviet leadership to having Ukraine under control may explain the fact that Ukraine hardly participated in reforms initiated by the Kremlin and implemented in other republics. For example, Ukraine was shielded from Perestroika and Glasnost because it was governed during the second half of the 1980s by a Brezhnevist leadership. Ukraine was also shielded from foreign influences to a greater extent than other republics. Up until independence, Ukraine was completey isolated. Because of this isolation few within the élite or the population at large were aware of the magnitude of the economic and political crisis. As a result, the Ukrainian élite was unprepared for reforms and was unwilling to implement them.

The nationalist movement had never been very influential in Ukraine because the Ukrainian élite was Russian-speaking. Even today, almost half of Ukrainian citizens speak Russian at home.[11] Under Soviet rule the Ukrainian language became marginalized in public life.

The hidden disintegration of Soviet socialism in Ukraine

Sociological research shows that the number of 'bad workers' has gradually increased since the early 1960s. Surveys by V. Iadov among young workers, carried out in 1962 and 1976, revealed a decline in labour ethos. During the late Brezhnev period, social scientists agreed on an estimate of 30–40 per cent as the share of workers whose discipline was very low, even by Brezhnev's standards.[12]

Increasing labour shortage contributed to low labour ethos and discipline. Workers dismissed for malfunctioning could easily find a job elsewhere, sometimes with a higher salary. Corruption, the spread of the informal economy and theft of state property, as well as nepotism, contributed to the decline in labour ethos, because good work and working for the public good became less rewarded and was often punished.

Concomitant with the phenomenon described above has been, since the late 1950s, the gradual loss of the state's authority. The gradual privatization of the state, which was accelerated under the reign of Brezhnev and encompassed the use of public functions for private purposes, led to the undermining of the economic and the political system. Since the mid-1950s the performance of individuals has become less rewarded while loyalty has gained in importance. In the Brezhnev era, the leadership did not demand real unity between words and deeds. The individual could easily be a shirker in the workplace and active in politics.

Increasingly, people perceived the public sphere, including the place where they worked, as hostile to their interests, and the expanding sphere of informal activities to redistribute the national wealth was parasitic upon the state sector.

On the one hand, informal and illegal economic activities functioned as oil for the state economy, on the other hand they undermined its functioning. The increasing non-participation of people in the public sphere was a time bomb under the political and economic system. The growing shadow economy was less the forerunner of a modern market economy than a pre-modern economy, based on primary groups and kinship relations.

The period of 'stagnation' began in 1975. The increase in living standards slowed down and, more importantly, most people began to experience deadlock in all spheres of life. All kinds of escapism attained epidemic proportions, and the personality cult surrounding Brezhnev reached its peak. However, Soviet power felt more secure than ever because it had attained parity with the USA and spread its influence all over the world. High energy prices allowed for approximately a decade of relatively high import levels, disguising declining economic performance. While Soviet leaders were more self-confident and arrogant than ever before, Soviet power was undermined from within.

Increasing disfunctionalities, the process of state privatization, the spread of clientele networks and patronage furthered a widening gap between what was considered as the private sphere, the in-group, and those who were not in the in-group. The sphere of public life and the state was increasingly perceived as inimical to their own interests. A moral for the in-group developed that was quite distinct from the moral for the out-group. Certain pre-modern characteristics of Soviet society became more prominent, although the collective memory of its peasant roots faded as the second generation of city dwellers grew up (it was only in the early 1960s that the majority of the Soviet population became town dwellers).

In this period of 'stagnation', the general crisis in society was reflected in the decay and infantilization of the Soviet leadership.

On the micro-level, stagnation was visible in the spread of the 'sovak', the 'model' personality masked by conformism, laziness, inefficiency, hypocrisy and irresponsibility.

Stagnation meant ultra-conservatism. Power in the Soviet Union meant the ability not to listen or to learn. This meant, especially in the

Brezhnev era, a pervasive resistance to change and innovation. All feedback mechanisms were blocked, which resulted in increased inefficiency at all levels. Social indifference spread, and the ruling caste gradually let its developmental façade drop.

Performance of individuals became less rewarded while loyalty gained in importance. This was not only reflected in increased egalitarianism, the wage differences between various professional groupings decreasing, but in the general incentive structure within the economy. Repeatedly the Soviet leadership sought to address the problem of lack of incentive by rewarding enterprises and workers that performed well. As one woman worker said: 'I prefer to do nothing for 200 rubles than to plod for 220 rubles.'[13]

Since the late 1950s, the Soviet people had gradually diverted their interests from the state to their primary groups and to semi-legal and illegal civil society and to illegal activity within the public sector. Gradually people developed a mentality that allowed them to ignore public interests and to absorb themselves in private and illegal activity.

It was only during the early 1980s that Soviet sociologists began to notice that a new class of Soviet workers had emerged with deeply ingrained negative attitudes to work. Tatiana Zaslavskaya was the first to point to the phenomenon, in 1984:[14]

A low level of labor and production discipline, indifferent attitudes toward the work being done, low quality of work, social inertia, low importance of work as a means of self-realization, and a low level of morality are traits common to many workers, which have been shaped during recent five-year plans. It is enough to recall the broad scale of the activities of the so-called 'pilferers', the spread of all sort of 'shady' dealings at the public expense, the development of illicit 'enterprises' and figures-finagling, and the 'worming out' of wages regardless of the result of work.

The party state tolerated increasingly semi-illegal networks that redistributed scarce goods and services because these networks corrected failures of the centrally planned economic system. However, this also led to the feudalization of the political system, the gradual political privatization of the state as well as the extraction of resources from the state sector for non-productive use. The consumer-oriented reprivatization of state resources became a basic feature of the organization of daily life in late socialism, in order to sustain living standards. In such a way a parasitic vicious circle developed. This extraction of resources from the state sector eroded the viability of the economic system.

The relaxation of discipline had gone too far, according to the ruling elite, and the disciplinary campaign that started under Andropov and that lasted until 1986 had some positive impact upon economic performance.

The parasitic activities of the above-mentioned networks became visible and substantially expanded when, under Gorbachev, the scope of activities of the so-called cooperatives broadened. It was not productive private activity that spread but rather parasitic activities that profited from widespread and intensified scarcities.[15] The sudden weakening of coercion under Gorbachev weakened the economy. Under Gorbachev opportunistic and corrupt behaviour became more pronounced and went unpunished. According to Solnick, the unprecedented public failure to enforce ownership rights delegated at each level prompted agents at every level to try to assert their own control rights competitively; this unleashed a run on state assets which brought about the state's collapse from within.[16]

As Srubar noticed, in a society where there are hardly any legal private sources of goods and services, only the link with redistribution networks through the re-routing of resources from the 'state sector' in the network channels can bring substantial private gains. 'Those who are in the center of the distribution system of goods and services, or those who can dispose the freest with employers time, are the winners in this system, independent of their formal qualifications.'[17] Increasingly, parasitic activities were rewarded while productive activities were discouraged.

Perestroika encompassed the introduction of diverse property forms (cooperatives, leaseholds, joint stock companies) up to, but not including, full privatization of state enterprises: the revision of the price structure to reflect costs, and increased autonomy for and democratization within state enterprises. This undermined the 'administrative-command system' inherited from Stalin's era. The reforms vastly reduced the power of the centre. They also caused the disintegration of the distribution system. However, they did not lead to significant changes at the micro-level, other than increased shortages, a growing shadow economy and a legitimacy crisis. All together, the Gorbachev reforms unleashed a Pandora's box that accelerated the decline of Soviet socialism.

Perestroika meant an acceleration of the disintegration of the centrally planned economy. Distribution channels for consumer and producer goods were increasingly blocked. Enterprises increasingly had to rely on informal channels or their own resources, producing more in-house.

The gap between the pretensions of policy-makers and Soviet reality widened with Perestroika.

The centrally planned economy allowed technological innovation inasmuch as it was ordered from above. Technological innovation was conceived as a top-down sequence, from conception at the design table of specialized institutes to implementation on the shop floor. Technological innovation in the developed market economies has increasingly been based on trial and error in the enterprises and as a result of collective learning within and between enterprises. Systems of innovation comprise R&D institutes, universities, enterprises and public administration in a complex interchange of experiences in which a facilitative environment was created. All this was lacking in the former Soviet Union. Creative potential in society was suffocated. The lack of innovative capacity proved to be a crucial weakness in the centrally planned economic system, contributing to its demise. The lack of self-regulating mechanisms that would allow self-corrections in the economic system were largely absent in the Soviet economy. The Soviet economic system missed the adaptive mechanisms crucial for economic development.

Ukraine also suffered from the economic stagnation that engulfed the Soviet Union from the mid-1970s onwards.

Increasing economic difficulties contributed towards a general feeling of deadlock situation but not towards the idea that a market economy should be introduced. Preparedness for reform was minimal, related to the isolation of Ukraine.

According to Khanin's account, Soviet national income grew by 3.2 per cent in 1928–40, by 7.2 per cent in 1950–60, by 4.4 per cent in 1960–65, by 4.1 per cent in 1965–70, and by 3.2 per cent in 1970–75. After 1975, quasi-stagnation settled in, and growth became negative in 1980–82, and after 1987. During 1987–88 the growth rate was –4.6 per cent.[18] The process of catching up with the West came to a halt during the mid-1970s.

This stagnation was reflected in less funds for investments rather than a drop in living standards. Also, return on investments declined. Capital productivity dropped from 2 per cent during 1981–85 to 1.6 per cent during 1986–90 and –5.1 per cent in 1990.[19] Production outlays became even more obsolete. According to Kakwani, the average living standard in Ukraine increased quite significantly up to the late 1980s.[20] This meant that the Soviet leadership deliberately prepared for even less economic growth in the future. There is evidence that by 1988 elements within the ruling elite in Moscow were preparing for the demise of the centrally planned economy and to safeguard its interests.[21]

Thus the legacy of socialism not only constituted for Ukraine a distorted economic structure, over-integration into the former Soviet Union and lack of experience with a market economy and managing a state, but also a legacy of deep-rooted attitudes and social practices. After the collapse of communism there was no *tabula rasa* in terms of social and economic institutions, but an amalgam of economic and social practices that constituted the building blocks of the new economic and social system. It was as if with independence and the demise of the party-state, a world that was hitherto hidden came to the surface.

The centrally planned economy epitomized modernity, the ability of mankind to steer its destiny in a comprehensive way, to steer social, economic and even psychological processes. With the disintegration of 'really existing socialism', the modernist façade of Soviet socialism gradually fell away, revealing a, in many respects, pre-modern world and a fragmented and disorganized society. When the shell of communist institutions burst and socialism collapsed under its own weight, the underworld of socialism, that was part of the system, came to the fore. However, in independent Ukraine, this underworld created its new pretensions. The new ideology came to legitimize a new economy that was even more virtual than the old one (see Chapter 10).

Independence as a result of implosion in Moscow

During the second half of the 1980s a Ukrainian nationalist movement came to the fore that quickly became influential. However, up until 1989, when ultra-conservative party leader Shcherbytsky stepped down, they failed to loosen the grip of the Brezhnevist leadership in Kyiv. In January 1990 almost one million people formed a human chain from Lviv to Kyiv, commemorating the 1918 declaration of independence. In October 1990, a pro-independence demonstration attracted 200 000 people. However, the independence of Ukraine in 1991 came about mainly as a result of external forces that brought about the collapse of the Soviet Union.

The gradual disintegration and destruction of the Soviet system, which accelerated in Perestroika times, was the background to Ukraine's movement towards independence. Few Ukrainians actually desired the creation of their own state, even as late as 1989.[22]

Ninety per cent of the Ukrainian population voted for independence in a referendum held in December 1991. This high percentage was related to fears of a repetition of the reactionary coup of August 1991 in Moscow. Even the large Russian minority was in favour of independence. Many were convinced that Ukraine would gain economically from independence.[23] More importantly, the Ukrainian elite thought its interests were best served with independence.[24] The conditions in which independence was gained can be compared with the unification of Italy and the decolonization of a number of Latin American states. In the latter cases, local elites reacted to profound shifts in the international system to protect their own power and privileges. Thus, the motive force for independence was socio-economic in nature.

The task faced by Ukraine was gigantic. While in 1990, Ukraine controlled only 5 per cent of GDP created on its territory, after independence it had responsibility for the whole economy.[25] Ukraine had to create all the institutions of a normal country and also build a new nation.

In the fragmented Ukrainian society, Ukraine's communist elite succeeded in reinventing itself. It co-opted some representatives of miner's regions, thus satisfying the demands of miners, and nationalists from Western Ukraine. Nationalist rhetoric sought support for Western Ukraine, while rhetoric of social justice opted for support in industrial Eastern Ukraine. Under the guise of this rhetoric the elite began the task of appropriating the resources of the country. Ukraine continued to be dominated by the old Nomenclature, whose main strength lay in the continued weak state and passive polity.[26] As Miller *et al.* (1997) noticed in their focus group discussions in Ukraine and the Czech Republic, there was the perception in Ukraine, unlike in the Czech Republic, that 'the transition was itself the final ceremonial act of the communist regime and its officials'.[27]

When Ukraine gained independence, the new country lacked all the traditional attributes of a nation. There was no single language, no sense of common destiny, no common culture, and no national and deep-rooted institutions. Moreover, the new state emerged in economic turmoil as a result of the dissolution of the Soviet Union. Given this context, it is not surprising that the Ukrainian government saw as its priority to further the nation building process and to safeguard the very existence of Ukraine. Consolidation of the new state meant the creation of a number of institutions, from an army to a well functioning customs service, from a constitution to tax collection apparatus. The Ukrainian elite had to reinvent the state.

Economic policy did not figure high on the agenda. The prevalent idea was to proceed very slowly with economic reforms in order not to upset the social balance. There was also the idea that the maintenance of a bureaucratically controlled economy, with some market elements, could produce a viable economic system. Also, there were no powerful social forces that were interested in market reforms. A social force of its own was the powerful bureaucracy. Both bureaucracy and political elite exhibited a low level of economic competence, due to the fact that there was no experience at all of administrating and governing a country. Also, the only familiar experience was the Soviet one and many of the most competent economists had gone to Moscow.

The emergence of independent Ukraine was received with mixed feelings in the West. The unexpected appearance of a large European country on the map caused a lot of confusion and upset the balance of forces in the eastern half of Europe. The birth of Ukraine was not welcomed by most European nations and initially it operated in a kind of vacuum, not being integrated into European institutions.

The new state seemed very fragile, with 22 per cent Russians and almost half of the population Russian-speaking.[28] There was an East–West divide, the East being industrialized and anti-reform while the more agricultural and nationalist West was more reform-minded. The new state did not have any natural boundaries and the status of the Crimea was contested by Russia. Moreover, there was the problem of nuclear warheads on Ukrainian territory. The environmental threat of Chernobyl constituted an issue of major concern for Western countries.

The state and nation building project was the most important objective of the new Ukrainian elite. The forging of a political community was of the utmost importance. Transformation to a market economy was secondary and largely limited to rhetoric.

Around 1994 the Ukrainian nation went through a crisis, during the presidential elections, when a large part of the population in Eastern Ukraine was disillusioned with the fruits of independence. Just before the presidential elections in 1994, a poll in Eastern and South-Eastern Ukraine showed that if the referendum of 1991 were to be repeated, 47 per cent would vote against independence.[29]

The CIA issued a warning in the same year about the dissolution of Ukraine.[30] The national consensus that led in 1991 to independence was in 1994 in the process of dissolving. However, the emerging conflict showed that the interests of elites in Eastern Ukraine, i.e. the appropriation of state assets, was best guaranteed in the context of a

Ukrainian state. Therefore, the historical compromise of 1991 was finally renewed amongst elites in various parts of the country.[31]

By the late 1990s it appeared that the reasons for the possible disintegration of Ukraine had mostly disappeared. One of the major achievements of Ukrainian governments is that in a relatively short time the Ukrainian state has consolidated, in the sense of establishing all the institutions of statehood and international recognition, that the problem of nuclear weapons has been resolved by removing them from Ukrainian territory, and that most of the areas of conflict with Russia, among others the division of the Black Sea fleet and the Crimea, have been removed.

Nevertheless, the Ukrainian statehood still has a rather fragile base, because (1) the economic base is very weak, (2) the division between East and West Ukraine is still topical because the Ukrainisation campaign has created widespread discontent, (3) the international position of Ukraine is very weak, (4) the new state is weakly linked to the population and (5) a problem of governability has arisen.

Short-term political rationality conflicted with economic rationality and long-term political rationality. The ruling elite rallied around the nation and state building project because it guaranteed the continuation of generalized rent-seeking activity, that could in the long term undermine the viability of the Ukrainian project.

Economic free fall and the slow pace of economic reform

Inconsistent economic policies in the first years after independence rendered the difficult situation disastrous. During 1990–94, according to official figures, industrial production halved. Politicians wanted to give priority to a peaceful institutionalization of the new Ukrainian nation, and this could only be achieved by discarding the conflicts of economic policies in the context of a fragile national alliance between Ukrainian nationalists, turnaround bureaucrats and miners. No consistent economic policy could be formulated and government policy was more a result of the requests of various pressure groups.

The primary objective of subsequent governments was to consolidate Ukrainian statehood. It was also in this context that the maintenance of the social balance, a prime objective of Ukrainian governments, can be seen. In the government's view, 'maintaining the social balance' means easing the pain of transformation for the population. In practice, inequalities and poverty increased more than in any other Eastern European country. Maintaining the social balance meant in practice opting for compromises with the powerful in society. It meant a slow pace of reform to keep vested interests supporting government.

This meant that a comprehensive strategy and a comprehensive concept of control were largely absent. The ruling elite was never a genuine governing class. Traditions of conflict resolution within the elite were absent, as were the informal mechanisms that in other countries led to consensus on major policy issues. The main consensus with respect to domestic policy was conservatism, maintaining the status quo.

The government tried to preserve an industrial structure that could not be preserved. The new Ukrainian administration tried to emulate the institutions of the Soviet Union at a national level, including all facets of state planning, with the addition of some elements of a market economy.

Conclusion

There are many different views on what has happened in Ukraine since independence. One view is that of a country trapped by the difficulties caused by the inheritance of Soviet rule and the impact of the dissolution of the Soviet Union, but on its way, albeit slowly, to the rule of law, parliamentary democracy and a market economy, as envisaged and pursued by its leaders. Here one can take the declarations of government and president at face value, while assuming that there is basically no alternative to a market economy and parliamentary democracy and that transition is a teleological process, inevitably leading to a market economy and democracy.

As is shown in this chapter, the communist party-state produced a society and economy that was a far cry from the envisaged socioeconomic formation. Also, the pretensions of the rulers provided few guidelines for analysing the dynamics of Soviet society and economy. Behind the economy of communist propaganda functioned the real economy, hidden behind the pretensions of the rulers.

Similar caution should be observed when analysing present-day Ukraine. The transition process should be seen as open-ended and declarations of government should not be taken for granted. Behind the rhetoric of politicians, their talk about a market economy, preserving the social balance, democracy and national values, a grab and run process took place in which the ruling elite took hold of the nation's resources. Behind the rhetoric of politicians, a process of redistribution of national resources took place in which the new state was used as a feeding ground by the ruling elite. Liberalization and privatization allowed kleptomanic behaviour to spread, less so a new incentive structure, guided by market forces, that would allow more efficient production.

In order to reconstruct what really happened in the Ukrainian economy, economic change is not only described in terms of macro-economic indicators.

Changes in the Ukrainian polity are described and how questions of power and influence are resolved. The changing role of the state and its bureaucracy examined. Privatization is assessed not only in legal terms, but in terms of social property relations and to what extent it may have affected corporate governance. Governance mechanisms in major economic sectors and in the regions are analysed. Changes at the micro-level are assessed, even at the level of attitudes and social practices. All this provides the elements to describe an economic system that is neither a market economy nor a centrally planned economy, but a new type of socio-economic formation that can be labelled as a virtual economy leading to an economic system that eats its own economic base.

3
Politics, State and Bureaucracy

The Soviet legacy has had a major impact on the economic development of independent Ukraine through its social practices, economic
dislocations and institutional inheritance (Chapter 2). In this chapter,
political and bureaucratic power and its influence on the economic
process is studied. First, the structure of government is described. Then,
the functioning of the Ukrainian bureaucracy is analysed, as well as the
nature of the state, the character of elite networks and interest
representation.

The structure of government

When building up a new state apparatus, the Soviet legacy was important to the extent that it had created a political elite and some embryonic attributes of statehood. However, the administration in Kyiv
never had substantial powers and even in Perestroika times, the
Ukrainian administration had to ask permission to build a pedestrian
crossing in Kyiv. This does not mean that the political experience at
the republican and provincial level was irrelevant. Politics at these
levels was not merely reduced to administrating those territorial enti-
ties on behalf of Moscow. Party committees at the local and regional
level fulfilled important roles as far as the functioning of the centrally
planned economy was concerned. They functioned as a kind of fire
brigade, solving the many problems not foreseen at the national level
(see Chapter 8).

It is on the basis of this bureaucratic apparatus and traditions that
the Ukrainian polity has been based. Surprisingly, the Supreme Rada,
i.e. the parliament, assumed an important role. Unlike the Duma in
Russia, the Supreme Rada has been a powerful player at the national

level. It assumes functions that in other countries are the prerogative of the executive power and here lies a major problem. The new constitution (1996) did not provide for a clear demarcation of competencies between president, parliament and government. Often, confusing situations exist that paralyse the decision-making process. The usual pattern is a battle between president and parliament in which the parliament vetoes draft laws passed by the government and the president vetoes legislation passed by the parliament, while the legislative threatens to impeach the executive.

In Ukraine, the president has important executive powers, although they are not precisely circumscribed. According to the 'interim provisions' of the Constitution of Ukraine, the president was authorized to issue, within a three year period after the adoption of the Constitution, i.e. until July 1999, and on approval of the Cabinet of Ministers, decrees on economic 'matters' which are not regulated by the legislation in force, and with a simultaneous submission of a corresponding draft law to the parliament. Such a decree would come into force unless the parliament rejects the draft law within 30 days of its submission. The decree would be valid until the law, adopted by the parliament on the same matter, came into force. This regulation is ambiguous.

Firstly, subjects on which the president can issue decrees are not defined clearly: different and conflicting notions of the 'economic' concept are possible. Controversy and confusion have been caused while deciding whether or not the matter in question is regulated by the legislation in force.

Secondly, the highest legislative authority is the parliament. This has implications for the enforcement of presidential decisions. In view of a possible revision of the contents of presidential decrees by parliament, made possible by the interim constitutional provisions, state administrative organs are likely to hesitate to enforce or even deny accepting measures stipulated in the decree.

Another problem is that the parliament can pass resolutions that are in the nature of executive institutions. For example, the parliament can decide on additional expenses above those stipulated in the budget. On the other hand, government can issue quasi-legislative decrees.

An additional problem is that the government is nominated by the president and does not usually reflect the composition of parliament.[1]

The continuous battle between parliament and president, in the context of an obscure division of competencies, has paralysed decision-making in Ukraine.[2]

This paralysis at the top allowed the asset stripping behaviour of the elite, especially at the regional level. Government and parliament actively contributed to this predatory behaviour.

The question is to what extent the continuous battle between the president, posing as reform-minded, especially with regard to Western institutions, and the parliament, depicted, especially in the Western press, as obstructing and left wing, should be seen in these terms. The question is whether there is substance behind the rhetoric of the president. Often, the rhetoric itself is contradictory and revealing. There have been instances where, in one speech, the president defends opposing concepts.[3]

Leonid Kuchma was prime minister from October 1992 until September 1993, and then ruled Ukraine as president from July 1994 onwards. Parliament has given Kuchma wide-ranging powers to implement economic reforms. The fact of the matter is that President Kuchma was himself not willing to implement economic reforms.

Legislation proposed by the president provided ample scope for asset stripping and blocking the so-called 'reform process'. Also, there are many corrupt people in the president's entourage.[4]

The stalemate between parliament on the one hand and presidency and government on the other, with its diffuse division of powers, was only a reflection of a deeply entrenched problem with the Ukrainian polity. There is not only a problem over competencies with the parliament, government and presidency. Ministries and governmental and presidential agencies have wide-ranging powers and can issue instructions which are akin to presidential and cabinet decrees. For example, industrial branch ministries can impose taxes on enterprises in their branch. There is a multi-layered policy-making body in which various branches of government and bureaucracy produce a huge amount of legislative and quasi-legislative documents, which are poorly coordinated and often not published. The multitude of laws and decrees is frequently contradictory and can often be interpreted in different ways. And enterprises and citizens are supposed to know the law.

The main features associated with an effective system of state governance are clarity of objectives, freedom to manage by government institutions, accountability, effective assessment of performance and adequate information flows. In Ukraine there are major problems with each of these issues.

Diffusion of authority

According to Sundakov, there are three main factors through which the diffusion of authority weakens the system of governance in Ukraine.[5]

1. The distinction between the political and the civil service aspects of government administration is blurred. The rule-making authority extends to administrative sub-units, and even relatively junior officials assume the essential political role of deciding what objectives should be pursued by government institutions and how resources should be distributed in society. According to Sundakov, the Ukrainian public sector is professionally rather weak because technical staff in the ministries are appointed for their political loyalty rather than their expertise.
2. A high burden of coordination is placed on a relatively weak civil service. The unfulfilled demand for coordination can be seen in the growing number of government institutions designed to play that role. There is an in-built tendency for government institutions to multiply according to mechanisms akin to Soviet times. The presidential administration can be compared with the former apparatus of the Central Committee. However, the coordination remains poor.
3. The diffusion of authority delays the emergence of a stable legislative environment.

Much is regulated by decrees and resolutions rather than by law because the former are more easily passed and prepared. This is according to the Soviet stereotype that good government responds rapidly to even small changes in the economy, rather than one that creates a stable legal environment (Sundakov).

An important institution is the 'apparat' of the cabinet of ministers, which is like a separate ministry that sits above all the 'normal' ministries and below the prime minister. Originally designed as a coordination mechanism, it has become an additional administrative layer that slows administrative processes, makes it more difficult for ministries to do their work, and reduces the accountability of individual ministers.[6]

As in Soviet times, the numerous executive bodies in the public administration are organized along sectoral lines.[7] Few functional ministries exist. The sectoral ministries still try to run 'their' sectors on a day-to-day basis. Although formally these ministries should deal primarily with creating a regulatory framework in their sectors, they are usually still involved in interfering in the production process, although state enterprises have achieved a large degree of autonomy. A further problem is that the ministries are inclined to favour state-owned enterprises over the private enterprises in their sector. The sectoral organization of government furthers lobbying to such an extent that, as Sundakov noticed, the regulators are controlled by the regulated.[8]

The large number of ministries and state committees make the cabinet of ministers' meetings like parliamentary sessions. The mass media are often invited. This means that real decision-making is done in informal groupings. The fact that state institutions are usually dealing with the day-to-day running of their sectors creates a 'fire-fighting' culture, in the cabinet of ministers as well, that distracts attention from strategic issues. There is also a culture of 'pragmatism' in which political decisions are seen in managerial rather than strategic terms (Sundakov).[9]

The process of making and implementing budgets is reminiscent of Soviet practices. During the first round of budget preparation, the ministries are invited to submit estimates of the costs they have incurred. These estimates are usually extrapolations of expenses in the previous year. The sum total of expenses from all ministries far exceeds the expected revenues. Subsequently, during the second round, the ministry of finance imposes arbitrary cuts and then the parliament reviews the budget and proposes minor revisions. The ministries are not given any guidance on how to cut expenditures. Generally, there is no underlying policy relating to budget allocations and the budget process is *de facto* separated from policy-making.

A crucial problem is that the budget is not the final spending arbiter. There are no constitutional obstacles to issuing new laws or decrees mandating new spending without amending the adopted budget. Different agents often mandate increases in expenditure but do not take responsibility for financing them. For example, the central government can set wages for government employees in general, but these are mostly paid at the level of local government, which may then have to run into arrears on its other expenditures to meet these mandated wage levels. For example, the parliament has in many cases ordered the government to make expenditures for specific purposes, other than those foreseen in the budget. In 1998, it ordered government to give additional money to the coal industry following a miner's strike. When, in November 1994, the deputy minister for the economy, Naumenko, said that the IMF agreement included slashing the central budget deficit, the parliament decided two days later to donate US$350 million to industry.[10] As a document from the World Bank and Ministry of Economy put it: 'Budget formulation is an open-ended request process that emphasizes needs over availability, and ultimately ends up being a bargaining process rather than a priority-setting exercise.'[11]

The Ukrainian government decided in its Memorandum of Economic Policy (11 August 1998) to improve fiscal transparency: 'All extra-budgetary funds (except the Pension and Social Insurance Funds) will be included in the budget starting in 1999'. The problem was that extra-budgetary funds were used for subsidizing enterprises. However, in an IMF report about fiscal transparency, dated September 1999, we can read that extra-budgetary funds still do not appear in the state budget. Also some local taxes, such as the local payroll tax, would be eliminated. At least, that was the government's intention. In January 1999 the Cabinet of Ministers ordered a new off-budget fund under the National Agency for Management. This was a double violation of the Memorandum presented to the IMF in August 1998 and agreed under the IMF Extended Fund Facilities measures because there was also a commitment to reduce the number of ministries and agencies.

The Ukrainian government has very little control over the implementation of its decisions. Numerous resolutions are passed, yet very little is done. At the same time, a formidable apparatus of control over the machinery of government has been inherited from Soviet times. The problem is that civil servants are inundated with tasks without being given instructions as to priorities. This means that they are free to choose what they do. Any failure can be explained by the demands of other pressing tasks. This means that almost every civil servant fails to comply with all requests imposed upon them. In practice, nobody can be held accountable.

Improved control over the implementation of policies can only be achieved if there are clear objectives and attainable targets for all public services. A clear system of incentives and sanctions needs to be put in place.

There is also a practice in the civil service of avoiding taking responsibility for their own actions, which weakens the capacity of the government to make and execute effective decisions.[12]

Lack of transparency in the structure and functioning of government seems to be a crucial element in the newly emerged socio-economic formation. It allows a continuation of the traditional rule by uncertainty. Uncertainty is fostered by the jungle of decrees and often contradictory laws that make it almost impossible to act without violating a law. It means that almost everyone might be violating the law and it allows the bureaucracy to act with discretion: anyone can be punished and it is bureaucrats who decide who will be punished. Uncertainty is enhanced by the fact that the state administration promotes misinformation. It is almost impossible to obtain information about laws and regulations from the bureaucracy.

It was because of the inefficiency of the administrative structure, with its overlapping competencies, that the IMF approved the granting of a new extended fund facility in mid-1998, upon an administrative reform. The Ukrainian government had already initiated this process in mid-1997, when the president issued a decree creating the State Commission for Administrative Reform.

In a letter to the IMF the Ukrainian government confirmed the reduction in 'budgetary employees of nearly 300 000 in 1998'.[13] However, the IMF failed to check this and no reductions in the size of ministries could be observed. Later, the prime minister stated in an interview that no reduction in the number of staff had taken place and that no significant change had resulted from the presidential decree on administrative reform.[14]

In some services, employment levels are very high. For example, in Ukraine there is one policeman for every 150 citizens, whereas in the UK there is 1 per 2000 citizens and in the USA 1 per 1200. There are 60 000 tax officials for 600 000 registered enterprises.[15]

On 14 March 1999, President Kuchma signed a decree cutting the number of ministries from 21 to 18, by downgrading three ministries to state committees, abolishing some state committees altogether and downgrading others.[16] However, at the same time new committees were created and in the 13 March 1999 presidential decree on administrative reform there was no mention of cutting personnel.[17] Surprisingly, Prime Minister Pustovoytenko said that the administrative reform was aimed at enhancing the role of the economy's state sector.[18]

An analysis carried out by the Harvard Institute for International Development concluded in May 1999 that the process of administrative reform, initiated in mid-1997, could be characterized as a preliminary stage. As a result of this reform, three ministries and three state committees were replaced by four state committees. However, there is very little legislative and practical distinction between a ministry and a state committee. The main success of the administrative reform was that 'it helped Ukraine 'fulfil' one of the conditions for the resumption of the IMF Extended Fund Facility loan'.[19]

The administrative reform demonstrates how the government maintains its pro-reform image with the IMF by introducing some cosmetic changes, while leaving the basic mechanisms of the present system untouched. This was not at all related to 'obstruction' on the part of parliament. The president several times vetoed a law, approved by parliament, that provided for (1) a relatively small Cabinet of Ministers comprised of political figures who would meet frequently, (2) clearer political direction over the government executive branch by decentralizing legislation preparation and policy formulation responsibilities to ministries, and (3) consolidation of the ministries into broad functional portfolios.

The short-termism of policy-makers is furthered by the fact that they let themselves become snowed under by permanent crisis management at the micro-level. The focus on cash management, i.e. the management of cash flows in order to remain within the budget, is at the expense of strategic planning. Economizing is not a function of strategic policy options.[20]

By mid-2000 it can be said that the executive power is still geared towards administering the economy and managing enterprises, as was the case under the centrally planned economy. Central government is too large and there are too many government agencies.[21] Existing departments are vertically isolated from one another and lack efficient coordination. There are many executive authorities with overlapping responsibilities. Budget spending units lack fiscal discipline.[22]

The state bureaucracy as an independent force

A major challenge for any political leadership is to control and direct the bureaucratic apparatus, a principal prerequisite for governance. In Ukraine, this is a problem because the bureaucratic apparatus has become increasingly autopoietic, i.e. it has pursued its own goals.

The numerous ministries proved to be an important obstacle to reform. Minister Viktor Suslov resigned from the Cabinet in May 1998, after criticizing the anti-reform stance of the many departments of his ministry.[23] Ministries can often effectively block reform measures due to non-transparent legislation.[24]

The present functioning of Ukrainian bureaucracy is not only rooted in the Soviet bureaucracy but also in the Tsarist bureaucracy. Tsarist Russia was always a bureaucratically coordinated economy. In Tsarist Russia, the landlord, the state and the bureaucracy formed a single unity. Communism extended the bureaucratic system over the whole of society and the economy.

In sociological theory, 'bureaucracy is a communication system in which the efficient transmission and processing of information is necessary to effective decision making'.[25] The peculiar characteristic of the Soviet state bureaucracy was that it was highly inefficient and not very transparent. The maintenance and extension of power became the ultimate goal. In economic matters, the job of bureaucrats, in enterprises and in lower echelons of the ministries, was partly to conceal from their superiors real production capacities, in order that production plans were not too ambitious. The centrally planned economic system generated misinformation and the top officials were usually badly informed about the real situation in the enterprises.

Beetham (1987) noticed a principal-agent problem in the Soviet bureaucracy because the agent is motivated to act in areas of discretionary behaviour contrary to the interests of the principal. Principals and agents have asymmetrical information. This was obvious with the statistical offices whose task was to conceal the real situation rather than to reveal it. Generally, this was the case with all those dealing with social and economic problems. This led to a situation in which the leadership lost touch with reality.

Thus, 'rational' Soviet managers engaged in dysfunctional activities, such as concealing enterprise capacity. Due to misinformation at the central level and the impossibility of planning anything, many frictions arose that could only be solved at the local level, usually through informal exchange systems, which increased in importance as the Soviet economy became more complex. However, there were no strong incentives for Soviet bureaucrats in the ministries to create institutions that would allow the managers in the enterprises to operate more efficiently. It would entail a transfer of power, a decentralization of power that was perceived as endangering the position of the state bureaucracy and the party-state.

According to Hirszowicz, communist bureaucracies are sovereign bureaucracies, whereas other bureaucracies exist and operate within larger societal frameworks.[26] Communist bureaucracies function in totally administered societies and became therefore total bureaucracies.

However, as Ledeneva emphasized, there was a degree of freedom, which was predicated upon following the unwritten rules and a subtle understanding of what was possible and what was not, and to what extent one could pursue one's own interests.[27] Basically, the Soviet system combined 'dictatorship of rules and norms' with local discretion. The rules were not primarily codified in law or decrees, but rather institutionalized practice. Ukraine and Russia have always been countries governed by 'mores' rather than 'laws'. The availability of unwritten codes alongside the written ones, and the usual practice for authorities to switch to the written code only 'when necessary' created freedom and flexibility. The bureaucracy itself decided the kind of legal shape it wished to give for its various rulings.[28]

The practice of creating exceptions to general rules was conspicuous. The rigid socialist system could only function with some degree of flexibility. Scope for departing from general rules was given. The 'exception principle' showed a tendency to multiply and opened up a variety of loopholes by which people could push for their interests.[29] Solnick (1998) found that the weak mechanisms for controlling bureaucrats in Soviet organizations allowed them great latitude in their actions. These mechanisms weakened further with the Gorbachev reforms and led to open insubordination by seizing the organizational assets they were supposed to be managing. When the servants of the state stopped obeying orders from above, the state's fate was sealed.[30]

Typical of the Soviet and Tsarist bureaucracy was its control mania. It appears that the ultimate goal was to administer all human activities. This is epitomized by Stalinist totalitarianism. It was in these times that people learned that everything is forbidden, unless it is explicitly allowed.

The personalization of the bureaucracy, or informal connections within formal structures, became a significant factor in keeping the command economy afloat. According to Fleron, great importance was attached to face-to-face relations and interpersonal trust in the Soviet Union.[31] It was this 'rampant particularism' that led Jowitt to characterize communist political systems as neo-traditional. Crozier characterized the Soviet regime as an attempt to integrate primary groups more and more within the sphere of influence of the central power and within the domain of rationality and efficiency.[32]

The characteristics of the Soviet bureaucracy mentioned above explain many of the peculiarities of present-day Ukrainian bureaucracy. The 'exception principle' is still very prominent in Ukrainian bureaucratic practice. Also, the idea is widespread that everything is forbidden unless it is explicitly allowed. It is difficult to know how to behave according to the law because laws and regulations are inconsistent and decrees are often not published. The interpretation of the law is further complicated by the fact that court decisions are not published.

However, with the gaining of independence and the collapse of the party-state and centrally planned economy, the power of the state bureaucracy diminished greatly. In 1992–93 the ministries lost their formal control over the economic activities of enterprises, which were granted full freedom in their economic activities. However, after the fall of Fokin's government (February 1992), the number of ministries began to increase again. From 1992 to 1994, the share of state expenditures in GNP increased considerably and administrative control in economic life increased. Generally, the number of civil servants in local and state administration has increased greatly since independence. Many former party officials changed the labels on their offices and achieved the status of civil servant.[33]

More important than quantitative changes are the changes in the role of civil servants. They began to transform their role, from authorizing and monitoring economic relations in the centrally planned economy to one of providing public services. The latter often occurred, however, in the form of blackmail, offering services in exchange for bribes. Bureaucrats remained so powerful that we can still speak about the Ukrainian polity as a bureaucratic regime, i.e. a system of government that is so completely in the hands of officials that their power jeopardized the liberties of enterprises, other organizations and ordinary citizens. New also is the coexistence of state bureaucracy and commercial structures. Their interface is governed by horizontal contacts that create a niche for 'mutual favours'. Other than in socialist times, the 'mutual favours' have become more profit-oriented and transformed into corruption practices.

What remains is the fact that personal contacts are still crucial in dealing with bureaucrats.

Anyone who has dealt with the state bureaucracy in Ukraine must have observed that a public service ethos is completely lacking. Usually, bureaucrats behave as if their clients are there for their sake and not vice versa. Related to this, there is no tradition of public accountability. There is no due regard to law because the law enforcement agencies are very weak and often closely linked to the state bureaucracy. There is no independent judicial power. There is no incentive for bureaucrats to take the public interest as the focus of their concerns. Rather, they are more concerned with their private or sectional interests.

The Ukrainian state bureaucracy can be seen as an archipelago of domains controlled by bureaucrats who see their domain as a kind of private plot. According to Piirainen:

> In transitional circumstances – that is, as the control mechanisms of communist society are no longer working, and, the new rules of the game are not yet enforced effectively – the patrimonial legacy, the blurred demarcation line between political power and private property, contributes to the merging of economic and political interest, to the emergence of conglomerates of economic and political power whose activity is guided by the unwritten rules based on primary group solidarities and Gemeinschaft ethics rather by the formal prescriptions and abstract solidarities that typically govern public conduct in modern industrial society.[34]

Political parties are mainly organized around personalities rather than around ideologies or political programmes. Because political parties do not represent the interests of specific social groups, the process of interest articulation takes place to a large extent outside the party system, and within the ramified structures of the state. Clans try to control and penetrate the most important links in the state apparatus. This leads to a hidden politicization of administrative decisions, particularly economic ones. Therewith the activities of the bureaucracy become increasingly discretionary and non-transparent.

Since independence, the industrial ministries have increasingly asserted themselves as powerful players.

Bureaucrats at all levels have high discretionary power because their clients, subordinates and superiors do not usually have much leverage to influence their behaviour. Enterprises and citizens dealing with Ukrainian bureaucrats are usually powerless. This situation furthers corruption.

In a certain sense the present transition of Ukraine can be described as a transition from bureaucratic socialism to parasitic economic structures contained in a semi-feudal bureaucratic context.

The state bureaucracy and corruption

An incompetent legislature is to a large extent to be blamed for highly inefficient bureaucratic rules. For example, a government decree issued in May 1998 foresaw that enterprises were to pay advance value added tax on the 15th and 25th of the month under review and on the 5th of the following month, equalling one-third of the total incurred in the preceding month's tax declaration. By the 20th of the following month the difference between the sums of the actual VAT paid each 10 days was to be established.[35] With such rules it is obvious why legally operating enterprises pay so much for administration and book-keeping, and why so many enterprises operate in the shadow economy.

There are 26 state institutions that are authorized to perform inspections of any business and fine entrepreneurs for any infringement of the agency's rules. However, the rules are not published and frequently the inspectors will not even tell the business owner which violations are being cited.

The head of the State Committee for Entrepreneurship Development, Alexandra Kuzel, said in September 1998, '... domestic producers have no other way out but to go to the shadow economy, just they cannot stand all those numerous inspections held throughout their enterprises'.

Monomakh company director general Volodymyr Barabash said, 'Moreover, all of these inspections are rather expensive, because unless you pay somebody off with a bribe, they come back again and again to repeatedly inspect the same products'.[36]

Increased corruption is a problem in all transition countries. Transition worsens corruption because traditional rules weaken before new legal constraints become effective, and because the state is redistributing large-scale wealth. Moreover, uncertain rules give officials exceptional powers and opportunities to seek bribes.

According to a survey carried out in 1996, 45 per cent of Ukrainians interviewed said that the behaviour of officials had become worse compared to communist times, while only 8 per cent said it was better. Corresponding figures for the Czech Republic were 31 per cent (worse) and 23 per cent (better).[37] In Ukraine, the most frequent explanation for the worse behaviour of officials was that they were no longer afraid.

Politicians and bureaucrats try to acquire as many control rights over the operations of the enterprise sector as possible. Such control rights are often exercised through administrative controls and regulations, which lead to corruption.[38]

Corruption is recognized by the Ukrainian government as a major problem and since 1992 more than 20 laws have been enacted to fight corruption. President Kuchma admitted in 1998 that abuse of power, bribery and extortion by bureaucrats were the main obstacles to economic development in Ukraine.[39]

Despite this, no one is actually fighting corruption, according to Inna Pidluska, from the Ukrainian Center for Independent Research. One of the reasons, she says, is the totalitarian attitude of the state towards business – the taxation system has not been reformed, nor has the criminal code. She noted that there is still a law on the books making 'speculation' illegal. Speculation is defined as reselling something to gain profit. According to Pidluska, the average entrepreneur spends 55 days registering his or her business and it is not unusual for it to take 90 days.[40] Hryhory Omelchenko, member of the parliamentary Organized Crime and Corruption Committee, complained about the inactivity of the president with respect to allegations of corruption:

No matter how many documents we submit showing malfeasance by high officials, we remain, alas, like an advertising agency. Those deserving to be dismissed from their posts on the basis of such evidence for abuse of power by presidential decree – here I have in mind a number of ministers and people from the presidential entourage – were in fact promoted by the President to a higher post or transferred horizontally, or even honored with various presidential decorations.[41]

The office of the president and government organized numerous sell-offs of state property in which members of government and presidential staff profited greatly. The dealings with gas companies are widely published. A telling example is the selling off of the Black Sea fleet. Although parliament prohibited privatization of the fleet, with an estimated value of US$1 billion, approximately 100 ships have been sold or leased.

A comparative analysis of corruption practices in the Czech Republic, Slovakia, Bulgaria and Ukraine, showed that Ukraine clearly distinguishes itself from the other three countries in terms of tolerant attitudes towards corruption.[42]

The US News and World Report (22 December 1997) wrote that, 'numerous bureaucrats may need to sign off on just one issue in a complicated business-permit process. Functionaries cook up procedural obstacles that are removed only after entrepreneurs pay ad hoc 'fees'. Some businessmen spend a month on applications only to be told that they used wrong-colored ink. Jacob Yampel, a native of Brooklyn, N.Y., describes a health inspector's call on his pasta factory in Ukraine. 'You are guilty' the inspector told him. 'But of what and for how much I'll decide in a few minutes.' Deputy Prime Minister Victor Penzik, before resigning in frustration, conceded corruption's grip: 'They try to set up a business in Ukraine and you can be certain of failing unless you pay bribes every step of the way'.

The Wall Street Journal reported (23 April 1997) on bureaucratic interference in the economy. From the 34 US companies registered with the commercial section of the American Embassy, 24 had asked for help after encountering serious difficulties with the Ukrainian authorities.[43]

According to Freedom House, many services in Ukraine are subject to bribery, including university entrance, hospital admission, telephone installation, licences for operating businesses, and processing of official documents. Bribes are taken by the traffic police, by passport and visa registration offices to speed up the procedure, and by law-enforcement officers to evade or ease punishment.

In her study of 'blat', Ledeneva suggested that the transition from communism had two effects upon the use of contacts and bribery in the countries of the former Soviet Union. First, the predominant use of 'blat' shifted from the everyday life of normal citizens to the networks of former Nomenklatura, now turning themselves into quasi-criminal businessmen. Second, in the everyday life of citizens, crude monetary bribes increasingly supplemented or even replaced the subtle and sometimes civilizing use of contacts.[44] It is estimated that more than 60 per cent of the income of high officials originates from bribes.[45]

The European Bank, Transparency International, the Economist Intelligence Unit, DRI/McGraw Hill Global Risk Service and the World Bank all estimate that corruption levels in the former Soviet Union are amongst the highest of any region in the world. Corruption scores for the Central European and Baltic countries are substantially lower.[46] In the World Corruption Index 1998, Ukraine occupies position 70 out of a list of 85 countries.[47] The survey in the 1997 Global Competitiveness Report published a bureaucratic discretion index. Ukraine was ranked 2 (next to worst) on a 6-point evaluation scale of regulatory discretion, roughly equal to Russia. The Czech Republic, Poland and Hungary ranked between 3 and 4, while Chile rated 5.[48] According to a 1997 survey, corruption in Ukraine was the leading cause cited for negative economic conditions.[49]

Although the level of corruption is higher in the former Soviet Union than in other regions, the predictability and credibility of such transactions are also higher.[50] The pattern of corruption is in stark contrast to the predictability and credibility of government policies in the region. In a survey of entrepreneurs the questions were asked, 'Do you regularly have to cope with unexpected changes in rules, laws or policies which materially affect your business' and 'Do you expect the government to stick to announced major policies', and predictability was rated lower than in any other region.[51] High uncertainty with respect to government policy and close personal networks between firm managers and individual government officials fuels corruption. Generally, government policy instability and corruption are closely related.

From a developmental to a predatory state

Karl Polyani argued that for capitalist economies the 'road to the free market was opened and kept open by an enormous increase in continuous, centrally organized and controlled interventionism'.[52] Weber noticed that 'capitalism and bureaucracy have found each other and belong intimately together'.[53] Comparative analysis of the conditions under which states in newly industrialized countries create innovative conditions for private enterprises shows that the role of the state is crucial in economic development. According to Evans the important question is what kind of state intervention is necessary.[54] Social and economic development occurs if state structures fit into the social environment. Predatory states like Zaire miss the bureaucratic institutions that can resist capture by rent-seeking actors. According to Evans, developmental states show that state institutions must be embedded in a dense network of ties that bind them to societal allies with transformational goals. However, in order to further development, the state and its bureaucracy should have a certain level of autonomy. 'Autonomy complements embeddedness, protecting the state from piecemeal capture, which would destroy the cohesiveness of the state itself and eventually undermines the coherence of its social interlocutors.'[55] According to Evans, it is the delicate blend of autonomy and embeddedness that makes the difference. Evans also argues that political elites should share a common sense of purpose and direction, an esprit de corps.

Looking at Ukraine from the above perspective, it seems that some crucial ingredients for a developmental state are missing. Politicians and top executives do not share a sense of common purpose and direction. Usually, their first loyalty is towards their clan and the private interests of this clan. The bureaucratic domain they are occupying they consider as their private lot and connected enterprises can freely feed from state resources. A sense of public accountability is missing. Clientelistic networks dominate the state apparatus that has become predatory with respect to society at large. Thus, the state hardly enjoys autonomy with respect to private business networks of ruling clans. In a certain sense, the state is privatized by influential financial-economic groupings and bureaucrats. Also, professionalism within the bureaucracy is very low because meritocratic recruitment principles are hardly applied. In many respects, Ukrainian bureaucracy is reminiscent of the bureaucracies of the Ottoman and Byzantine empires.

Under conditions of transition to a market economy, the state has to fulfil a very complicated role. State power, which was overwhelming and suffocating in socialist times, has to be decentralized. The function of the state should change from that of a command role in all spheres of life to that of facilitator. During this process, transition goals have to be clearly set and the state has an important role in monitoring this transformation, formulating new rules of the game and seeking the enforcement of new rules.

The World Bank recently began to emphasize the role of the state in the developing world and in transition countries. It said in its World Development Report 1997 that for human welfare to be advanced, the state's capability, defined as the ability to undertake and promote collective actions efficiently, must be increased.[56] The World Bank pleaded to reinvigorate public institutions by designing effective rules and constraints, to check arbitrary state actions and combat entrenched corruption. Also, the state should match its role to its capability. Where state capability is weak, how the state intervenes – and where – should be carefully assessed. According to the World Development Report 1997, without an effective state, sustainable development, both economic and social, is impossible.[57]

Western 'transitologists' often assume that the state is a relatively autonomous social power that can impose transition to a market economy in the context of impartial rules and the juridicial transformation of the property forms. However, the state is rather used as a tool by ruling clans to promote their interests, that is selling off state property. Ironically, the Marxian concept of the state as an instrument for the ruling class seems adequate in Ukraine. As argued earlier, it is not only the ruling elite but also the state bureaucracy that instrumentalizes the state for its own private purposes. No polity has been created that is a reflection of society and that could adapt political structures to changing social needs, creating preconditions for evolutionary institutional change. The continuing deep divide between the state and society can be considered as one of the major causes of failed modernization attempts.

The question is whether there has been any progress in the building and transformation of the state. An overall judgement is complicated and the picture looks mixed. Of course, a nation-state with all its attributes has been built up almost from scratch and the Ukrainian state is more viable now than many could have expected in the early 1990s. This is a major accomplishment, at first sight, if only looking at formal institutions. If looking at substance, a parasitic state has emerged. Forces have grown that undermine the rule of law, like the shadow economy and criminal structures. Although the legal framework has definitively improved, the situation with respect to the rule of law, or rather the absence of it, has not improved.[58] There is little progress towards a well functioning market economy and parasitic structures suffocate productive economic activity. By mid-2000, the elite was still mainly interested in rent seeking and elaborating structures that allow them to continue doing so.

A state has been created that seems to be self-destructive as it undermines its infrastructure and cripples its own instruments of governance. The state is dominated by a ruling class that is short-sightedly only interested in plundering the state. The social base of this state has weakened and become dependent on Western economic and political support to sustain itself. The state allows the massive exodus of human, material and financial resources out of production into exchange.[59] It allows the collapse of the scientific and industrial infrastructure. According to what happened to the economy, the Ukrainian state is a de-developmental state.[60]

In Ukraine, economic and political power gravitates towards those at the head of the state apparatus. Although there are some oligarchs, they are less powerful than their Russian counterparts as the money economy and merchant capital is less developed in Ukraine. This is also related to the fact that the sell-off of state property is less advanced in the Ukraine and its mineral resource base is rather poor.

The Ukrainian state can be characterized as patrimonialist. The Ukrainian state arose out of the patrimonial tradition of the Russian and Soviet states. The Tsar 'owned' the nation and its resources and its citizens were assigned duties but had no rights. In the Soviet state, the party leadership 'owned' the country. The Ukrainian state is also reminiscent of underdeveloped economies where the appropriation of surplus is severely constrained by the low level of cash transactions, where there is an absence of a well paid, professional public service that gives rise to a state 'pathologically swollen by nepotism and terminally infected by graft'.[61]

Table 3.1 Government expenditure as a percentage of GDP, 1992–99

Year	1992	1993	1994	1995	1996	1997	1998	1999
Government expenditure (% GDP)	45.0	46.5	59.7	48.0	43.2	49.6	41.7	38.1

Source: Ukrainian Economic Trends, December 1999.

Obviously, the Ukrainian state is not a state in the traditional meaning of the word. It is a disintegrating state, despite the appearance of it being built up from scratch. Society and economy have increasingly become ungovernable.

The weight of the state in the economy is still very important. Even taking into account the growing role of the shadow, non-registered part, of the economy, which now comprises more than half of estimated GDP, government expenditures are considerable, compared to countries at a similar level of development (Table 3.1).

Not only is the persistent high share of government expenditures as share of GDP remarkable, but also the high fluctuations. More important, but not reflected in these figures, is the pervasive state control over the economic process. A defining characteristic of the Ukrainian state is the continued depth and breadth of power exercised by the state over every aspect of society and economy, being immune from public scrutiny.

There seems to be a close cooperation between the political class and the criminal world. This cooperation had already emerged in Soviet times and was most visible in the centre, Moscow, as well as some Central Asian and Kaukasus republics. There is evidence that as early as 1988, members of the Soviet leadership had anticipated the break-up of the Soviet Union and created an underground economy in order to safeguard their economic interests after an eventual break-up.[62] Since 1987/88 cooperation between the political class and organized crime included coordinated operations chiefly designed to protect economic activity conducted on the orders or in the interests of ruling elites. Here, private security guards played an important role. Knabe (1998a) argues that instability and confusion in 1989–91 may have been deliberately created in order to divert public attention from the really important processes going on, particularly regarding the transfer of property. A system-Mafia came into being.

This system-Mafia was most pronounced in Moscow, but less visible in Ukraine. However, in 1996, according to a report written for President Kuchma, organized crime had increasingly imposed its rule and begun to pose a threat to the stability of the state (see also Chapter 10, page 179).[63]

Rather than a catalyst for social and economic development, the state and its bureaucracy constitutes the most formidable obstacle to any social and economic progress. The question is what strategy should be used to overcome this obstacle and to what extent is it possible to change the nature of state and bureaucracy.

There is ample experience in the developing world of attempts to transform the state and public administration. Four to five decades of post-colonial 'development administration' have provided a variety of instruments for transforming public administration.[64] Common to most approaches is the view that the bureaucracy is a key instrument of development. Only with the 'structural adjustment' approach, furthered by the IMF and the World Bank since the early 1980s, has the bureaucracy been seen as an obstacle rather than an instrument for development. This view was based on the failure of attempts to transform Third World bureaucracies. It appeared that few political leaders in the Third World were willing to overhaul the bureaucracy: 'Having failed to turn the bureaucracy on its head, or to bypass, decentralize or reorientate it, the new answer was (with structural adjustment programs) to privatize it, or at least part of it'.[65]

International financial institutions often had the leverage to force governments to downsize bureaucracies. According to Hirschmann the structural adjustment programmes led, however, to uncertain and very fragmented bureaucracies, to 'a depleted and demoralized civil service'.

Another approach is that of 'governance'. It is an attempt 'to make the bureaucracy accountable, transparent, and even responsive to the public; but the objective is not to achieve this outcome by supply (that is it does not expect the state and the bureaucracy to become accountable of its own account), but by demand (that is, civil society builds the capacity and skills to press government to be accountable for its actions'.[66]

Third World experience shows that there are no unequivocal successful receipts for reforming public administration. The situation in Ukraine is more complicated given the much more important role of the state in public life, compared to typical Third World countries. While many Third World countries have over-large states, which means employing too many civil servants, they are not over-powerful, that is they do not have too many powers of regulation and control. However, the Ukrainian state is also over-powerful. Downsizing the civil service, coupled with administrative reform, based on transparency and avoiding overlapping competencies, should be a focus of any reform programme. However, it seems that an efficient and accountable public service is only feasible in conjunction with a developed civil society, with its multiplicity of governance mechanisms.

In the developed market economies, governance structures beyond state and market became increasingly important, especially since the changeover to a knowledge-based economy. Messner (1997) concludes that the most effective societies in economic, social and ecological terms are not unleashed market economies, but active and continuously learning societies that solve their problems on the basis of a complex organizational and governance pluralism.[67] Governance refers to some forms of administrative or regulatory capacities. Agencies, which either are not part of any government (non-governmental organizations), or are transnational in character, contribute to governance.[68] Modern, post-industrial societies became increasingly differentiated at the institutional level. A multiplicity of new patterns of organization and governance has emerged alongside hierarchical governance of society by the state. A new socio–technological–organizational paradigm appears to be gaining ground. Messner highlights especially the meso-level as the domain in which new governance structures emerge. Countries at a lower development level in particular have problems in developing governance structures at the meso-level.

In Ukraine, actors at all levels are geared solely to lobbyist orientations and are unable to develop any common problem-solving orientations. Generally, Ukraine fails with respect to meeting the institutional–organizational demands of modern society.

The lack of historical experience with methods of compromising, conflict management and network structures tends to result in endless disagreements. Also, a lack of due process of law is hampering the formation of 'generalized trust' between actors, one of the important conditions for the development of network governance. According to Messner, international competitiveness, owing to the increasing significance of industrial clusters, regional economic zones and network structures between firms and their environment based on collective efficiency, results from specific patterns of social organization and governance. Social governance capacity is a condition for economic efficiency and development. However, the blocked Ukrainian society is characterized by a lack of governance capacity.

The character of elite networks

The previous chapter described how, since the reign of Brezhnev, patronage-clientele networks operating on the borders of illegality have gained in prominence.

Under communism, elite networks gradually acquired qualities reminiscent of European feudalism.[69] Loyalty towards the local chief was primordial, less so competence. Secrecy was paramount. Instructions were usually given orally, not in written form so as to avoid problems with accountability. Informal dealings were crucial to the functioning of the economy and gradually became more important. There was no rule of law. Exertion of power was absolutist and arbitrary, on all levels. Wheeling and dealing became crucial for survival in all spheres of life. In this political tradition the Ukrainian polity emerged.

The falling away of the party state did not unleash market forces, but rather paved the way for the Nomenklatura networks to appropriate the state for their private purposes. It was a transition from 'plan' to 'clan', rather than from 'plan' to 'market'.[70]

Elites operate primarily in the sphere of the state and its administration because Ukraine remains largely a bureaucratically controlled economy. The state and its administration set the parameters in which the elite operates. As the rules of the polity are not clear and as there is not a strong countervailing power, patronage-clientele networks spread.[71]

Political patronage can be defined as an informal network of personal, political relationships, which are at the same time both asymmetrical and interdependent.[72] Also, the relationship has to be tested over time. It encompasses the mutual exchange of political goods. Political patronage can be found in all societies. It allows politicians to govern more effectively. Typical of the Soviet Union was that political patronage developed into a crucial mechanism for elite mobility, hardly being checked by other mechanisms, such as open selection procedures on the basis of meritocratic criteria. Therefore, political loyalty to the party and the patron became of utmost importance.[73] Formal decision-making procedures increasingly became a façade to mask the decision-making by a set of coteries.[74]

When Ukraine became independent, loyalty of the elite to the state was promoted by the fact that the state was the most lucrative feeding ground and it gave elites the opportunity for career advancement and self-enrichment. As Garnett suggested, the pursuit of self-interest may have proven to be the most patent source of state building and nation building in Ukraine.[75] At the same time, elite parasitism was an obstacle to social change. Motyl suggests that elite parasitism may transform Ukraine into an Eastern European version of former Zaire. In Pokhalo's view, 'The Ukrainian paradigm of state building today is but the manifestation of creating... a state for its own sake, outside society and above it'.[76]

Elite networks in Ukraine are characterized by secrecy and distrust towards those not belonging to the inner circle of the clique. Important lobbies are grouped around specific industries and related banks and, above all, based in specific regions. For example, President Kuchma, who came from Dnipropetrovsk, promoted many friends from his town to influential positions in Kyiv. It has been estimated that up to 200 Dnipropetrovsk clan members were appointed to top executive positions in Kuchma's government and administration.[77] Clan leader Lazarenko, then the Dnipropetrovsk province governor, was initially appointed deputy prime minister in charge of energy. Other clan members were given almost all the ministerial portfolios involving industry. They included Valery Pustovoytenko, who became prime minister in 1998. In May 1996 Lazarenko became prime minister. He gave the clan's major company, United Energy Systems, half the wholesale natural gas market, so helping it become the richest private company in Ukraine.

The main competitors for natural gas profits came from the Donetsk clan, which was organized around parliament member Volodomyr Shcherban. That clan was swept aside with the assassination of another member of the Donetsk clan, Yevhen Shcherban.

President Kuchma dismissed Lazarenko in mid-1997 without ever explaining why. Perhaps Lazarenko's seizure of the gas supplies at the expense of other clans became an embarrassment to Kuchma. The Dnipropetrovsk clan split in two and open warfare ensued. Both clans used the media. The Kuchma clan used the judiciary power to fight its opponents. Newspapers from opposing clans were regularly closed. Companies linked with opposing clans were fined.

The lobbies linked to the gas companies belong to the most powerful in Kyiv, although Ukraine only produces 20 per cent of the gas it consumes. Trading of gas is one of the most lucrative activities in Ukraine. Particularly profitable are licences that allow companies to buy gas in Russia and sell it on the Ukrainian market. In November 1998 seven deputies from the ruling People's Democratic Party (PDP) quit the PDP faction in parliament, and since then the gas lobby has been outside government.[78]

Unlike Russia, oligarchs have come less to the fore in Ukraine, partly related to the less advanced state of privatization. Five oligarchs control the bulk of the mass media and all support President Kuchma.[79]

President Kuchma has fostered various corrupt clans in order to play them off against each other and thereby stay in control. According to the Kyiv Post he has done so by maintaining and even adding to Ukraine's maze of arbitrary rules and corrupt officials 'which deters most investment but is a gold mine for the brokers who can guarantee safe passage through'.[80]

Power was mainly focused on redistributing the economic wealth of the nation, less on creating new wealth. As the most influential lobbies represented value-subtracting industries and declining regions, they succeeded in squeezing substantial sums from the national budget. However, the nature of the redistribution process changed, from direct subsidies from the budget to hidden subsidies in the form of tax exemptions, non-payment of the energy bill, etc. (see Chapter 4).

On the micro-level, redistribution mechanisms caused an enormous income divide, a rapid impoverishment of the overwhelming majority of the population and a fabulous enrichment of the ruling elite (see Chapter 9).

The new economic elite was mainly interested in short-term gains. The short-term interests of the main lobbies also dominated the policy agenda. Generally, one can see in the transition process that groups who gain substantial rents in the early phase of transition, based on distortions of the inherited economic structure, have a stake in maintaining a partial reform equilibrium that generates high private gains but at considerable social costs. The peculiarity of Ukraine is that, unlike countries such as Hungary, the Czech Republic and Poland, this partial reform equilibrium seems rather structural and stuck in the very early phase of the 'reform process'. It seems that in Ukraine the ruling elite has an interest in keeping the economy in limbo between a centrally planned and a market economy in order to continue its rent-seeking behaviour.

In Ukraine, the new economic and political elite emerged out of the old Nomenklatura. Whereas in countries like Poland, the elite became more diversified and the first post-socialist governments hardly counted ex-communists, in Ukraine the old elite retained its power. It is telling that the first president of independent Ukraine, Kravtchuk, was responsible for ideological affairs in Kyiv under the old communist regime.

Democracy, interest representation and political parties

Many Western observers are studying the political process with a focus on political parties and the formal aspects of the electoral and political system. However, political parties fulfil a marginal role in Ukrainian politics. Political parties are grouped around personalities rather than ideologies and party programmes. Political parties function in Ukraine as vehicles for self-interested individuals.

The main party is the Party of Power, an informal label for a centre–left–liberal bloc that Kuchma used as a vehicle for his advent to power. Its main political party is the People's Democratic Party, which has its roots in the Democratic Platform of the Communist Party of Ukraine.[81] This party represents mainly the interests of the 'red directors', the directors of state-owned enterprises, with their main base in Eastern Ukraine. The Party of Power were turn-around communist bosses that have always controlled the state apparatus, the media and the economy.

If studying interest representation on the political level, rather than political parties, it is more fruitful to study the functioning of various interest groups. The problem with the existing political system is the inability of finding a way of developing and implementing policies for the whole country without being completely swamped and dominated by these interest groups.[82] State policies reflect the balance of power between various lobbies at a specific stage rather than a specific strategy of government. It is remarkable that industrial lobbies have increased their influence since the demise of the Soviet Union. This is partly related to the fact that the old industrial planning apparatus was recreated at the level of the Ukrainian state.

The government does not want transparency, as is demonstrated by its bullying of the critical press. The judiciary is consistently used by the Presidency to discipline the press. The Council of Europe and the European Union have severely criticized Ukraine for its bullying of the press and political interference with the judiciary.

The executive power has many ways of influencing the media. Laws are so complex and contradictory that the government finds it easy to discover alleged fraud and impose sanctions against undesirable publications. There is hardly room for impartial and objective journalism. Most of the media are at the mercy of the authorities. An important leverage of state authorities is the fact that most of the print media use state-owned publishing houses. Broadcasters use state-owned frequencies and broadcasting time. Also, most kiosks that distribute newspapers are state-owned. Overt censorship is substituted by economic levers of influence.[83]

Lack of transparency is reflected in the secrecy surrounding the state and its activities. Lack of transparency is at the core of the socio-economic formation in Ukraine, and it provides a legitimization of the lack of accountability at all levels. It provides a legitimization of cross-subsidization of economic sectors, and enables the perpetuation of belief systems that sustain the socio-economic formation.

Douglas North observed that for inefficient economies 'the increasing returns characteristic of an initial set of institutions that provide disincentives to productive activity will create organizations and interest groups with a stake in the existing constraints'.[84] This is exactly what has happened in Ukraine.

Conclusion

The Ukrainian polity emerged organically out of the Soviet polity and is characterized by lack of transparency, an absence of a clear division of power, a predatory state and a parasitic bureaucracy that exhibits a control mania. The Ukrainian economy is still to a large extent bureaucratically coordinated. The discretionary power of the bureaucracy and the lack of countervailing power has led to growing corruption and a criminalized state in which productive activity is paralysed. A predatory state is a crucial element in the newly emerged socio-economic formation that leads to an economic system that devours its own economic base. The new ruling and governing elite developed out of the old Nomenklatura and uses the state as a feeding ground. It still has, predominantly, a short time perspective.

Reform of the state apparatus faces numerous obstacles. A developed civil society appears to be a precondition for an effective state.

4
Economic Reform

In this chapter economic reform will be analysed, focusing not so much on government rhetoric but rather on concrete government policies and policy implementation with respect to price liberalization, financial infrastructure, privatization and conditions for the development of small- and medium-sized enterprises, de-monopolization and tax reforms. The liberalization of foreign trade, another major area of reform, will be dealt with in Chapter 7. This chapter will focus on economic reform and institutional change.

1991–94: muddling through

Usually, there is a gap between government rhetoric, concrete policy measures and the way in which they are implemented. The peculiarity of Ukraine is that this gap is very wide. Also, rhetoric is contradictory and differs according to the audiences addressed. One of the problems is that policy-makers have to manoeuvre between the Chylla of public opinion, which has been against market-oriented reform throughout the 1990s, and the Charibdis of the international financial organizations that press for market-oriented reform.

Therefore, there is a problem with taking government rhetoric as a point of departure when analysing the transformation of the Ukrainian economy during the 1990s. When doing so, it is easy to assume that the government and the president want market reform, while the parliament and conservative ministries are obstructing the reform process. Rather, all major players in the Ukrainian polity use a language that has many interpretations. The term 'reform' is usually used by government to denote the policy aim of improving the present system, rather than market-oriented reform.[1]

International institutions assisting 'transition economies' promote the idea that these economies go through a transition from a centrally planned to a market economy, conceived as a linear path. They use various yardsticks to measure progress on this path. However, the notion of transition to a market economy is misleading, as a new type of socio-economic formation is consolidating in Ukraine that is neither centrally planned nor market.

Up until President Kuchma came to power in late 1994, no economic reform programme had been implemented. The Kravchuk administration tried to preserve a bureaucratically controlled, state dominated economy, while introducing some market elements. Gradualism in economic policy was chosen as it was thought that radical economic measures would upset the social balance and endanger the nation building process, which was a priority. The state hardly withdrew from the economy. Rather, the government reacted to increased economic difficulties with intensified controls.[2]

Many laws were passed between late 1991 and mid-1994. However, they were not coherent and often contradictory. They only evoked the appearance of resolute action. Apart from chaos and rapid economic decline, the period 1991–94 was characterized by a rapid accumulation of fabulous richness by the ruling elite. According to the Ukrainian Information Service (1994:14):

> A lot of decisions in the field of monetary and import–export policy were adopted with the results considered beforehand. They were intended to enrich certain persons and coteries...The aggravation of the situation may be beneficial for some deputies, state and local administrators. It is a great chance for them to establish themselves in a good way. Ultimately, it's a harmful and suicidal policy but they won't let the chance of a lifetime slip.[3]

High tax rates have contributed to the rapid growth of the shadow economy, which reached approximately half of estimated national income in 1994. Real purchasing power of the Ukrainian population declined by 74 per cent between December 1991 and November 1994.[4]

The basic traits of the present-day Ukrainian economy were established in the period 1991–94.

Price liberalization

Price liberalization was seen as a cornerstone of reform. Initially, inflation was spurred by Russian economic policy, because up to February 1992 Ukraine still used the Russian rouble as currency and did not have its own schedule of liberalizing prices. Russia's unilateral price deregulation in 1991 also caused inflation in Ukraine. Since early 1992 prices have gradually been liberalized.[5] In addition to formal price controls, enterprises faced informal pressures from various levels of government to keep prices at 'reasonable' levels. However, throughout 1992, enterprises manufacturing non-food consumer goods were in effect free to set prices without direct government interference. Administered prices (i.e. prices directly fixed by the government) applied to goods and services accounting for about 12 per cent of the retail and 17 per cent of the wholesale turnover. The remaining 57 per cent of wholesale and 67 per cent of retail turnover consisted of goods and services with regulated prices.[6] Regulated prices, while not fixed by central authorities, are directly influenced by the government.

Initially, consumer goods whose prices remained under state control were energy, housing, transportation and basic food items. The fact that they were controlled did not mean they did not increase. Government controlled prices were allowed to skyrocket following price liberalization in January 1992, which freed the prices other than those of monopolistic producers.[7] While annual inflation in 1990 was only 4.2 per cent, it reached 1000 per cent during the first four months of 1992. As a result of this hyperinflation, approximately 40 per cent of the population came to live below the official poverty line. The advent of Kuchma as prime minister (October 1992) and the fact that parliament gave him rule-by-decree authority, failed to control inflation and when he resigned as prime minister, in September 1993, the economy was in a much worse state. From January 1992 until mid-1994, prices increased by a factor of 5816.

In October 1994, most direct price controls were eliminated. The only goods and services that remained subject to price controls were bread, utilities, public transport and rents.[8] Since 1993, administered prices have been raised periodically with the aim of moving towards cost-recovery prices for these products.

Since 1994 inflation has fallen: consumer prices increased by 891 per cent in 1994, 377 per cent in 1995, 80.2 per cent in 1996, 15.9 per cent in 1997 and 10.6 per cent in 1998.

The driving force behind Ukraine's hyperinflation was the price increases of goods and services that have remained under government control. Subsequent governments (up to late 1995) did not take any action geared to price stabilization.[9] Deregulating state controlled prices without proper preparation initiated the inflationary spiral: monopolies, budget deficits, uncontrolled money supplies and irrational credit policies contributed to the inflationary spiral.[10]

It is noticeable that during the period 1991–95, controls were mounting in many areas, but not in the field of price policy.

During the 1990s, the distorted price structure that existed in the early part of the decade and that hardly reflected the cost structure was replaced by a pricing mechanism that better reflects the real cost structure of products. However, there are still important products whose prices are regulated and a category of products, primarily in the sphere of basic foodstuffs and public utilities, whose prices are often far below production costs. Taking privileges into account, in 1998 only 30 per cent of the cost of gas was covered.[11] Monetary transparency in the economy at large has not increased to the same extent as costs are reflected in price structures, given the fact that budget constraints of enterprises have not hardened to the same extent, related to hidden subsidies and bad debt chains. Also, enterprises often do not know what the real cost price of their products is, due to the lack of monetary transparency, and therefore often price their products too low.

A less studied impact of hyperinflation is that on the distribution of the national wealth. For example, if the state decides to increase electricity tariffs, enterprises decide to compensate for increased energy costs by charging higher prices to their consumers. In turn, wage earners who see their purchasing power decrease, ask for wage increases. This in turn leads to further price increases. In this spiral the weakest lose out. This was also the case in Ukraine, where wage earners and people with savings lost. Speculators, anticipating price rises, earned a lot. It was during the time of hyperinflation that many personal fortunes were made. According to V. Yeremenko of the Institute of World Economy and International Relations in Kyiv, price liberalization with its concomitant hyperinflation, was a well thought confiscation.[12]

This redistribution of national resources as a result of hyperinflation, is not primarily related to price liberalization as such, but to the specific mismanaged mode of price liberalization as occurred in Ukraine.

Monetary stabilization under President Kuchma?

In July 1994 President Kuchma and his government proposed an economic programme based on IMF recommendations that was approved in November 1994. However, in April 1995 there was a sudden shift in the government's position, with Kuchma insisting that, 'rapid market transformation of the economy must address the social needs of the population and provide a strong safety net'.[13] It meant a return to the Kravchuk economic strategy: gradualism, characterized by a large role of the state.

Many institutions from the Soviet era remained in place, such as the many industrial ministries. Privatization proceeded very slowly. The Ukrainian elite thought that the private sector could not fill the gap created by dismantling the structures of a centrally planned economy. Reform efforts focused upon monetary stabilization.

In September 1996, the new currency, the hryvna, was introduced, replacing the provisional currency, the karbovanets. The hryvna was kept stable until September 1998. Inflation was relatively low and the exchange rate with the dollar was fixed. Whereas the hryvna/dollar exchange rate was 1.85 at the end of 1996, it was 2.01 during the first half of 1998. With respect to the ECU, the value of the hryvna increased during this period.

Budget deficits ranged between 7 and 11 per cent of GDP during the 1991–94 period. According to the IMF, real budget deficits may have ranged between 25 and 30 per cent of GDP. These deficits were financed by printing money and contributed to hyperinflation. From 1994 onwards budgetary discipline gradually improved: budget deficits were 6.5 per cent of GNP in 1995, 5 per cent in 1996, 6.5 per cent in 1997 and 2 per cent in 1998. However, many off-budget payments were not included in these official budget deficits. These official deficits are not large compared to the deficits of many developed market economies. The deficits were financed by borrowing, mainly from Western institutions, but from 1997 onwards they were increasingly financed by short-term treasury bills against very high interest rates. Many of these bills were sold to foreign investors.

According to Western advisers, Ukraine should first 'invest' in the building of its market infrastructure, the basis of which is the stabilization of prices and the exchange rate. This would allow Ukraine to subsequently restructure the economy. This would lay the foundations for economic growth. The assumption was that a current account deficit may develop if foreign direct investment was attracted, so financing productive investment and substituting for insufficient domestic savings in the early stages of transition.

The problem with Ukraine was that this scenario did not materialize. The situation of monetary stabilization was not used to restructure the economy and privatize enterprises. No economic environment conducive to investments was created. Therefore the debts accumulated by Ukraine functioned as a time bomb under the financial system. Foreign loans were used to finance the budget deficit and not used for productive purposes. By the end of 1997, the domestic debt of the Ministry of Finance amounted to approximately 8 billion hryvnas, or 8 per cent of GDP. The foreign debt amounted to approximately US$10 billion (20 per cent of GDP), while the debt issued by local governments, which is implicitly guaranteed by the central government, was 5 per cent of GDP.[14] This amounted, with on average 18 per cent interest on most loans, to 33 per cent of GDP at the end of 1997, rising to 35 per cent by mid-1998. An adverse cumulative process came into being in which more debt created more budget expenditure and so more deficits and more debts. Some Western European countries have an indebtedness of 60 per cent but pay an interest rate of 5 per cent per year. This means that they are burdened with only 3 per cent of their GDP. In terms of interest payments, these countries have less debt than Ukraine. Therefore, given Ukraine's debt service burden, it can be considered as over-indebted.[15]

Ukraine has to pay its debtors US$3 billion in 2000, which amounts to approximately 20 per cent of expected export earnings in 1999.

All this means that the macro-economic stabilization achieved since mid-1996, and interrupted by a devaluation of the hryvna in dollar terms of 100 per cent in the half-year since September 1998, has had a rather fragile basis. Monetary stability was not brought about by a healthy economy and balanced state budget, but by selling bonds at unrealistic interest rates to optimistic investors who assumed the fundamentals would improve in time to catch up with mounting interest rates. This kind of financial stabilization can be compared with an aspirin for a deadly ill patient.

In 1998 the hryvna was put under heavy pressure, especially when the Russian financial crisis erupted (August 1998). Ukraine spent about US$1.5 billion during March–August 1998 to defend the exchange rate. But after reserves dropped below US$1 billion (about three weeks of imports), Ukraine allowed the currency to adjust (1 September 1998). The banking system lost almost US$1 billion dollars in capital, falling from US$2.2 billion in early 1998 to US$1.2 billion at the end of 1998.[16]

With the Russian financial crisis (August–September 1998) it became apparent how vulnerable the financial situation in Ukraine was. It was somewhat better compared to Russia because the financial system in Ukraine was in such an embryonic stage that it could do less harm than in Russia. Also, foreign debts were less of a problem in Ukraine than in Russia (see Chapter 7, page 123).

But, as in Russia, the government was financing budget deficits by issuing bonds with very high interest rates to mainly Ukrainian banks. Real yields on domestic debts exceeded 60 per cent. Therefore, despite the cautious financial policy since August 1998, the financial situation has remained very fragile. Since September 1998, the government has tried to keep the hryvna fixed within a band with respect to the dollar, between 3.5 and 4.5 hryvna. However, since June 1999, this band has been exceeded.

Many expected that the devaluation of the hryvna, combined with low inflation, would give a boost to Ukrainian exports. Ukrainian Economic Trends argued in November 1998 that, with an exchange rate of 3.5 hryvnas for one dollar, the hryvna was undervalued. It was argued that with such an exchange rate, Ukrainian GDP per capita was US$660, at a similar level to Zimbabwe, Congo, Sri Lanka, Cameroon and Egypt. 'Anyone who has visited these countries may understand that the resources of Ukraine are a bit higher.' The rate of 3.50 hryvnas per dollar 'ensures a sufficient competitiveness of Ukrainian products abroad, more than the exchange rate has ever permitted'.[17]

However, the opposite happened: exports during the first half of 1999 were 25 per cent down compared to the first half of 1998. This was related, among other factors, to the collapse of Russian markets and the fact that Ukrainian exporters are heavily reliant on imports, which increased in price in hryvna terms.

After the financial crisis of 1998, currency regulations were tightened. All transactions had to go through the Kyiv exchange, which implied a ban on direct inter-bank transactions. A list of 'critical' imports was decreed and foreign currency was provided in principle only to corresponding importers. The exporters were required to surrender 50 per cent of their currency earnings and the rate for cash in exchange points has been regulated and only a narrow margin around the official rate was allowed.[18]

The creation of a financial infrastructure

1992 and 1993 were the fat years for the banks. However, by the end of 1995, 70 per cent of the entire share capital had been eaten away by inflation. Since 1995 the licensing system has been tightened and during 1996 the National Bank of Ukraine put 45 banks into various categories of restricted licence, rehabilitation, closure or liquidation. The number of banks fell to 180 by the end of 1997.

In early 1999, the five largest banks held approximately 60 per cent of all loans extended to the economy, and the next 10 banks held an additional 20 per cent of this loan total. Approximately two-thirds of banks are single branch banks that operate only in the provinces within which they are registered.

Altogether, one-third of loans are non-performing. The smaller banks were more successful because they were less exposed to bad loans. Total assets of the banking sector amounted to US$11.6 billion on 1 January 1998.[19] Deposits totalled US$4 billion by the end of 1998.

The banking system is very underdeveloped in Ukraine. Before the Russian financial crisis (August 1998), the capitalization of all Ukrainian banks amounted to only one-third of that of the largest Czech bank and equal to that of a small Western bank.[20] By October 1998, only 2 per cent of Ukrainian banks had more than 10 million Ecu in their statutory funds. The number of banks with less than 2 million Ecu amounted to two-thirds of all banks.[21]

There is only a small amount of cash in the economy, amounting to 13.6 per cent of GDP, which is one of the lowest percentages in Europe.[22] In 1998, 42 per cent of trade by industrial enterprises was barter trade, furthered by the so-called Kartoteka 2 rule which implies that tax authorities have the power to freeze and confiscate the bank accounts of any enterprise that owes taxes to the state.

From 1996 onwards the banks shifted activity from lending to servicing state securities. Lending to enterprises was mainly done by small banks and company banks. Banks were also widely used for money laundering. Enterprises rarely use banks for paying their personnel and try to avoid banks for inter-enterprise transfers. Very few citizens have bank accounts.

Until 1996, the parliament could order banks to provide soft credits, guaranteed by government, to designated enterprises. Since 1996, the use of banks for political purposes has diminished, although the state has continued to organize state-guaranteed loans to the agricultural sector and the coal industry. A large portion of this money has never been paid back, which caused big problems for Bank Ukraina. Ukrainian banks mainly lend to government (8.1 billion hryvnas in 1997), to state-owned enterprises (5.5 billion hryvnas) and only to a minor extent to the private sector (2.3 billion hryvnas).

Banks rarely lend to enterprises on commercial terms because, generally, the chances are minimal that loans will be repaid. This is also related to government policy that forces enterprises to pay taxes first, then to pay wages, then to pay urgent needs, and only last, to pay back bank loans.[22]

Banks on the other hand have invested heavily in their own sector, constructing large buildings. Although banking is one of the few profitable activities in Ukraine, the banking sector is very fragile. A Standard's and Poor report (July 1998) stated that the risks within the Ukrainian banking system are among the highest of all the transitional economies of Central and Eastern Europe, and that Ukraine even lags behind Russia and Kazachstan's fragile banking system in terms of developing regulatory supervision.[23]

In 1992 the National Bank of Ukraine became the country's central bank and has since enjoyed formal independence. The National Bank played a major role in keeping the hryvna stable and inflation low. The government largely respected the independence of the central bank. This helped the Ukraine to limit the damage caused by the Russian financial crisis. However, the banking system was extremely fragile and there was almost no supervision from the side of the Central Bank. One of the most important conditions of the IMF during 1998/99 was the reform of the banking system. Among other measures, international accounting standards were introduced in banks, bank supervision was strengthened and diagnostic analyses for large banks were completed.[24] The National Bank of Ukraine has implemented the development of a new bank accounting concept compatible with international accounting standards. Also, capital regulations and risk regulations (e.g. maximum exposure to single borrower and to aggregate large credit exposure) have been introduced, compatible with the norms of the Bank of International Settlements. Guidelines have been established for more effective on-site and off-site inspection. Since 1 January 1998, the minimum level of bank capital is 1 million Ecu. Since July 1997, foreign banks have been allowed to transact business in hryvnas. There is a limit of 15 per cent on foreign owned capital as part of total banking system statutory capital.

The essence of banking is savings intermediation and payments services. Ukrainian banks perform some payment services at the retail level, especially by the Savings Bank. The Savings Bank has 60 000 employees. The average deposit per employee is 25 000 hryvnas. With an average wage of 2000 hryvnas, the Savings Bank needs an interest rate margin of 8 per cent just to pay for labour costs.[25] This shows the underdevelopment of financial services.

Inter-enterprise debts constitute an informal substitute for the credit functions banks normally fulfil in other countries. These debts totalled more than 100 per cent of GDP in 1998, of which three-quarters remain overdue.

The capital market in Ukraine is even more underdeveloped than the banking sector and barely plays any role in economic development.

The state as redistributor

From the point of view of international financial organizations, a major step in the direction of a market economy is the withdrawal of the state from the sphere of production as far as it goes beyond the sphere of regulation and facilitation. To this end the state should stop redistributing funds from the value-producing to the value-subtracting industries.

Although government funds available for redistribution have continuously decreased since the early 1990s, it seems that regional authorities and large state-owned enterprises continue to focus their energy on lobbying the state for additional resources rather than on restructuring and enhancing their own development potential.

Despite a deep economic crisis since independence, the government continued to squander government resources instead of targeting them on priority areas. Also, government policies still appear to be more the outcome of the work of powerful lobbies, mostly from sectors of the past, than the result of a clear strategy.

Spending on 'the national economy', a euphemism for mostly open subsidies, decreased from 24 per cent of GDP in 1992 to 15 per cent of GDP in 1994, a cut of 70 per cent in real terms.[26] State-guaranteed credits to state enterprises were eliminated in 1996. By 1997 direct industrial support was down to 3.2 per cent of GDP.[27] This is high compared to other transition countries. On average these countries spent 1.84 per cent of GDP on direct subsidies in 1997.[28] In Central European countries it was much lower during the early phase of transition: 3.0 per cent in Poland (1992), 2.9 per cent in Hungary (1993) and 4.4 per cent in the Czech Republic (1993).[29]

However, if looking at other forms of state support, it appears that direct subsidies are much higher. On the basis of government data, the level of subsidization was 5.67 per cent of GDP in 1997.[30] If all implicit subsidies are taken into account, that means tax deferment, privileges, soft-rate bank loans to enterprises and state purchases of goods at prices higher than market prices or purchases of illiquid goods, total subsidies amounted to 19.22 per cent of GDP in 1996, 20.73 per cent in 1997 and 19.37 per cent in 1998.[31] Not taken into account is subsidization through non-payment of deliveries by state-owned enterprises.

An important subsidized sector is agriculture. On average, 2.7 billion hryvnas has been spent each year in the agricultural sector in the form of state-guaranteed loans. On average, 1.4 billion hryvnas has been repaid. According to the Ukrainian Auditing Chamber, the non-returned amount was 'hanging' on the accounts of the intermediaries, leaving the budget and the agrarians with huge debts.[32]

The large financial flows redistributed by the state point to enormous government interference in the economic process.

Privatization

Privatization of state-owned enterprises is seen as a crucial dimension of the transition process. Privatization is an extremely complex and non-transparent process, with respect to procedure and outcome. Western advisors promoted privatization in Ukraine on the assumption that private owners of enterprises would be more responsible with respect to resource allocation and would promote efficiency and profitability. It is doubtful what the motives behind privatization were for Ukrainian policy-makers.[33] With respect to privatization there are two aspects: (1) the legal change in ownership of state enterprises, and (2) the question of effective ownership rights.

Large-scale privatization officially began in 1992, mainly via non-competitive methods, including management/employee buy-outs and leasing to employees, but progress was very slow.[34] In 1991, Ukraine had an estimated 18 000 state-owned medium-sized and large enterprises and an estimated 45 000 state-owned small-scale enterprises. At the end of 1994, approximately 3000 medium-sized and large enterprises and 7000 small enterprises had been privatized. By mid-1999 the privatization of small firms was almost complete. The status of these privatized enterprises is difficult to determine. Some were corporatized enterprises still in government hands, others were of indeterminate mixed ownership. Often, it was spontaneous privatization in which employees and/or management gained strong *de facto* control over enterprises, mostly through lease agreements.

Up to late 1994, 'privatization' of Ukrainian industry had been very limited and was confined to 'spontaneous' privatization, whereby the Nomenklatura was involved in the widespread appropriation of state assets.

In July 1994, mass privatization was suspended altogether by the Ukrainian parliament. Following this suspension, a presidential decree of November 1994 introduced a new voucher-based mass privatization programme. The process of direct privatization was strengthened through a centralization of power in the State Property Fund. The privatization accelerated, albeit still at a rather slow pace. By mid-1997, 86 per cent of Ukraine's citizens had received their vouchers under the mass privatization programme and over 45 per cent had invested them in exchange for shares in joint-stock companies that were included in monthly auctions.

By April 1997, over 9600 of the 18 000 existing medium-sized and large enterprises had been privatized, of which it is estimated some 6300 had been completely privatized (with more than 70 per cent of shares sold to private owners). In addition, 38 600 of 45 000 small enterprises owned by the state had also been privatized. By early 1999, the overwhelming majority of the 277 largest enterprises, with assets exceeding 170 million hryvnas, had not been fully privatized, about half having a minority private participation. Many of the enterprises registered as private enterprises, only had a minority stake of the enterprise privatized.[35]

Two important areas were excluded from privatization: the energy complex and many enterprises in the 'strategic' military-industrial complex. It is not clear what the rationale was in deciding which enterprises were strategic. 6110 enterprises were considered as strategic.[36] The non-privatized firms were firms with strong links to the Community of Independent States, firms that were the least profitable, like coal mining, and the most profitable firms, like natural monopolies and other protected sectors such as alcoholic drinks. In 1998, of Ukraine's ten most profitable firms, nine were state-owned, while the tenth, Ukrnaft, had only 39 per cent of shares in private hands.[37]

For the newly created private investment funds, the privatization of medium and large enterprises through auctions was an efficient way of accumulating capital quickly. For this, the funds used mainly external resources, i.e. privatization vouchers entrusted to them by individuals.[38]

The mass privatization was rather complex and non-transparent. Kaufmann, of the World Bank, has argued that this was because it gave the bureaucracy more opportunities for rent-seeking at every stage.[39]

As far as government was willing to proceed with privatization, parliament acted as a brake.[40] Once the obstacle of parliament had been removed, numerous problems appeared in the process of implementation. The result is that by early 2000 many state-owned enterprises could not be privatized.

Estimates of the share of the private sector vary widely. According to the European Bank for Reconstruction and Development, the private sector accounted for 55 per cent of estimated GDP in 1998 (Poland 65 per cent, Russia 70 per cent). According to official Ukrainian figures, in 1994 74 per cent of Ukrainian enterprises belonged to the non-governmental sector. According to the Statistical Yearbook 1997, 22.9 per cent of employees work in private enterprises, 37.9 per cent in the state sector, and 39.2 per cent in collective enterprises.[41] If limiting ourselves to industry, it appears that the share of private enterprises in total industrial output was only 0.1 per cent in 1997, the share of collective enterprises 65.2 per cent and the share of state enterprises 34.7 per cent. In terms of industrial employment, the figures are respectively 1 per cent, 65.4 per cent and 33.6 per cent (1997).[42]

According to official figures, 80 per cent of enterprise turnover in the province of Donetsk comes from non-state enterprises. However, according to a survey in the province, 72 per cent of those with a permanent job work in state-owned enterprises.[43]

Estimates of privatization may differ according to the eventual inclusion of the shadow economy. Also, it is not very clear what the notion of private or privatized enterprises means. Many consider enterprises in which the state still keeps a majority share to be privatized.

The above figures show how blurred the divide is between private and public. An example is the privatized Ferroalloy enterprise in Zaporizhzhya. Although the state has a minority share in the enterprise and handed over management rights for a very small sum to the Ukrainian Credit Bank, it continued to have a blocking vote in the shareholders' meeting.[44]

More important than the question of formal ownership is that of *de facto* control over enterprises. The main concern for enterprise managers is not formal ownership but control combined with opportunities to squeeze the state.

Irrespective of formal ownership changes, spontaneous privatization took place which means the *de facto* appropriation of state assets. The first form of spontaneous privatization is that of leasehold or joint stock companies.

A second form of spontaneous privatization develops out of the formation of cooperative and small leasehold enterprises as subsidiaries of state enterprises. Most of these enterprises are very small. Moreover, the vast majority remain subordinate to the state enterprises on which they rely for supplies, labour, financial resources and political protection.

Another form of spontaneous privatization is through the 'siphoning off' of profits from state enterprises through private commercial and financial intermediates.

Insider privatization has been widespread, with management of enterprises privatized them without competition and at a very low cost which comprised only a fraction of the real market value.

It is telling that President Kuchma's own party, the People's Democratic Party, asked Kuchma 'to substitute the practice of privatizing property through distributing state corporate rights to 'clan business structures'.'[45]

Characteristic of the Ukrainian-style voucher privatization is that it has created ownership diffusion, which makes control over enterprise activity more complicated.[46] Often, it means that there are no effective owners.

Privatization in agriculture mainly meant the issuing of land shares to employees of collective farms, without any impact on the way they are managed. The number of private farmers increased to 35 900 farmers in 1997 and has stabilized since then, accounting for about 2 per cent of agricultural land (see Chapter 5, page 93).

The emergence of private small and medium-sized enterprises

Many so-called cooperatives were established during Perestroika times, and in 1991 the Soviet Union legalized the establishment of private enterprises.[47] In 1991, 19 600 small enterprises, mostly private, existed in Ukraine.[48] Shortly after independence, many new small private enterprises emerged.

In mid-1998 there were some 93 000 small businesses in the Ukraine, accounting for over 9 per cent of its GDP and 10 per cent of the working population.[49] However, at the end of 1995, there were already 91 000 small enterprises.[50] This means that there has been hardly any growth in the number of small and medium-sized enterprises since the mid-1990s.

Small and medium-sized enterprises mostly engage in service and trade activities. Only 14 per cent of small and medium-sized enterprises are active in industry, and 10 per cent in construction.[51] Whereas small private industrial enterprises accounted in 1991 for 21 per cent of small-scale industrial production, this figure was only 20 per cent in 1996 and 15 per cent in 1997. The share of collective firms in the output of small-scale industrial production increased between 1991 and 1997 from 44 to 79 per cent.[52] The share of small-scale industrial enterprises in total industrial output was only 0.8 per cent in 1991 and 4.7 per cent in 1997.[53]

Often, small private companies were established by managers as a means of squeezing the state-owned enterprises where they work. A large number of small private enterprises emerged as a result of the privatization of small enterprises, mainly during the first half of the 1990s. These are mostly shops and restaurants. More than three-quarters of small and medium-sized companies work in the shadow economy and do not pay taxes.

Obstacles faced by small and medium-sized enterprises differ significantly according to the type of enterprise. For example, the problems faced by a small enterprise that grew out of a large mother company are quite different from those faced by a small greenfield enterprise.

Generally, small enterprises are at a disadvantage *vis-à-vis* big enterprises that are supported by the state. Also, large enterprises often do not allow small enterprises to supply goods. Foreign markets are more difficult for small enterprises to serve than large enterprises.

The state administration makes the life of small enterprises extremely difficult. Harassment from local authorities is a big problem. Without bribing local administration officials it is practically impossible to survive. The former Ukrainian vice-minister of economy, Viktor Pyznyk, estimated that in order to start up a small business in Ukraine, you need to hand out nearly US$2000 in bribes.[54] A survey found that it costs businesses nearly US$900 in bribes for a telephone installation and nearly US$300 for an import licence. Managers spend over a third of their time dealing with rules and regulations.[55]

A survey in December 1997 found that, although the legislation specifies that the process of registration of an enterprise should only take five days, respondents reported the process taking an average of 35 days. Licencing requirements for trade in consumer goods were similar. To obtain a single licence, the respondents on average had to visit 2.6 ministries. Moreover, about one-third reported that they hold licences that are not valid for the entire country. The cost of obtaining licences was greater for small than for large companies. Inspections by various authorities were frequent. Because many state agencies are partially self-financing, it is not surprising that violations were found and fines were levied in almost one-third of the visits by the fire and the tax authorities.[56] This all means that entry costs are rather high.

Comparing complaints from new private enterprises in the Ukraine with those in Russia shows that Ukrainian enterprises face even more impediments than in Russia.[57] In particular, Ukrainian enterprises rate the following impediments as significantly higher: import and export restrictions, taxes, the remaining price interventions, and slow privatization. Harassment at the local level and foreign exchange restrictions are regarded as similarly constraining in both countries, while inflation and legal instability are considered a somewhat more serious issue by Russian enterprises. The surveys also provide evidence that new private firms face more daunting regulatory, tax and local administrative impediments than older firms. Also, firms have to make unofficial payments. These payments are widespread and sizable per licence as per tax, health or fire inspector visit.[58]

A survey of Vinogradskaia (1999) showed the following factors hindering the development of small business: inadequate legislation, high taxation, no state credits or state support, book-keeping, information deficiency and a deficient consulting environment, absence of investment incentives and the fact that the population is psychologically not ready for small and medium-sized enterprises.[59] Surprisingly, corruption and the Mafia are not mentioned as inhibiting factors.

It also appears that the time costs of regulatory constraints, measured as the average percentage of senior management time spent with government regulations/officials is excessive in Ukraine. According to a comparative survey, in Ukraine managers spend on average 37 per cent of their time (April 1996) and 30 per cent (February 1995) of their time respectively on these matters, while it was approximately 15 per cent in Lithuania and Brazil and 13 per cent in Pakistan.[60] A 1997 survey by the International Centre for Policy Studies found that in Kyiv, managers of private enterprises meet with tax, customs, licencing and other officials on 103 days of the year. A survey by the State Committee on Entrepreneurship Development and the International Centre for Policy Studies of market vendors suggested that officials inspected them 25 times a month.[61]

While extra-legal payments per firm per year were US$3340 for state firms, they were US$21 900 for lease/collective/privatized firms and

US$26 400 for new private firms. The average bribes paid per firm's employee was US$21 for the first category of firms, US$29 for the second and US$400 for the third (1996).[62]

Small and medium-sized enterprises in particular are vulnerable to Mafia influence. Nevertheless, the majority of small and medium-sized firms do not see organized crime as a major problem. They can deal better with organized crime than with local authorities.[63]

In many cases small and medium-sized enterprises have difficulties finding accommodation. Another problem is that of licences. Special certificates or diplomas are needed for many licences. For example, you need a diploma to set up as a barber.

Lack of know-how is a specific problem for small and medium-sized enterprises, as is the lack of skilled personnel. The personnel policy of most small enterprises is to employ close friends and family. This poses problems with respect to qualifications.

The final problem is that of obtaining credit. It is almost impossible for small and medium-sized enterprises to obtain loans.

Demonopolizing the economy

A precondition for an efficient market economy is a demonopolized economy. However, a government survey conducted in 1994, comprising 15 000 individual goods, revealed that a large number of markets were characterized by a high degree of business concentration. In more than half of the cases markets were found to be dominated by single enterprises, and in some 17 per cent of the examined markets there was only one supplier.[64] In the early 1990s, 1500 enterprises had a production monopoly.[65] A survey analysing the market in steel pipes over the period 1990–97 revealed that overall, monopolistic tendencies strengthened and the number of absolute monopolies increased.[66] An IMF survey found that in the period January 1996 to January 1998, the percentage of monopolists increased in machine building and the military-industrial complex (from 10.7 to 15.1 per cent) and in heavy industry (from 23.6 to 24.2 per cent). Significant reductions were observed in the energy sector (from 34.5 to 23.2 per cent) and in chemicals and pharmaceuticals (from 36.1 to 9.8 per cent).

The existence of monopolies and vertically integrated firms is seriously impeding market-oriented reforms. This is recognized by the government.

Tax reforms

Tax reforms in 1992 and 1993 resulted in a heavy tax burden, especially for non-state enterprises. Taxes of up to 90 per cent on profit discouraged production, caused massive tax evasion, and pushed many new businesses into the shadow economy. More than half of the economy is in the shadow sector and therefore does not pay taxes. On top of that, farms only pay land tax and many ailing state-owned enterprises receive tax exemptions. Enterprises are faced with more than 100 taxes and contributions. Since 1997, Ukraine's tax system has been based on a combination of value added tax (VAT), profit tax and wage taxes. This structure is roughly comparable to those used in Western European countries. Unlike Western Europe, where VAT revenues account for 5–8 per cent of state revenues, in Ukraine VAT provides 25 per cent of tax revenues (1999). This is because VAT is difficult to evade while other taxes are evaded efficiently and almost legally. The problem with the tax system is the numerous exemptions and amendments that reduce transparency and increase the difficulty of administration.

Peculiar to Ukraine is the fact that tax authorities get special bonuses for the collection of fines and penalties.

The structure of tax rates does not favour the efficient use of available resources. For example, the taxes on labour, which is abundant, are high, while those on energy, which is scarce, are low.

Tax compliance has been made difficult by the large number of taxes to be paid and constant changes in amounts and calculations, as well as by the heavy tax burden. The effective tax burden is exacerbated by the burden of tax administration. According to the World Economic Forum 1997, the tax rate burden of Ukraine was rated 1.58 on a scale ranging from 1 (worst) to 7 (best). Ukraine appeared to have the highest burden, Russia scored 1.8, Brazil 2.2, Hungary 2.3 and the Czech Republic 3.6.[67] A survey found that the average business faced seven annual tax inspections. Small businesses endure an average of 78 inspections a year, requiring 68 written responses, consuming two days of a manager's time per week and requiring a cash outlay of US$2100 a year.[68] The average inspection lasted more than 10 days and required more than 80 per cent of enterprises to provide the inspectors with office space, telephones, computers and other equipment.

Small and medium-sized enterprises suffer more from the tax burden because they have less resources to lobby for tax exemptions.

The shadow economy

Related to taxation policies is the rapid growth of the shadow economy, one of the most pronounced changes in the Ukrainian economy. While the estimated size of the shadow economy was approximately 12–20 per cent of registered GDP in 1991, by the late 1990s it was larger than registered GDP, according to most observers.[69] Some observers estimate that approximately 60 per cent of economic activity in Ukraine takes place in the shadow economy.[70] Enterprises in construction, agriculture and trade are most able to move their activities in the shadow sector. Enterprises try many ways of avoiding high taxation. Moving in the shadow economy is a preferred method.

At first sight the taxation rate in Ukraine is not very high, and is lower than in many Western European countries. However, businesses operating in Ukraine are allowed few deductions. In effect the overall tax bill is comparable to a 70 per cent rate in the West.

It appears that the costs of being formal are excessively high for enterprises in Ukraine and the benefits doubtful. The high costs and minor benefits of participating in the formal economy have created an enormous shadow economy.[71]

Although the government says it wishes to destroy the shadow economy and to exert maximum pressure upon enterprises to pay taxes, the state bureaucracy appears not to be very interested in combating the shadow economy because they profit from the bribes. So there is a peculiar symbiosis between the state and the shadow economy.

According to a report written for President Kuchma in 1996, the shadow sector is 'a parallel illegal power that grows and begins to duplicate the most important functions of the state'.[72] Indeed, part of the shadow sector has its own order, imposed by criminal groupings. Enterprises active in this sector have to pay for 'protection'. Many enterprises prefer this kind of 'protection' over the lack of protection offered by the state. However, the Mafia can never be a real alternative to the economic environment the state can create.

Also, the huge size of the shadow economy prevents the Ukrainian government from pursuing any economic policy and makes the economy largely ungovernable. Moreover, the large shadow sector makes the tax burden of the registered sector of the economy even higher.

Some say that the shadow sector keeps the economy afloat and keeps living standards to a minimum. On the other hand it hampers the investment process and has very negative consequences for business ethics. It drains the strength of the economy.

Technological innovations have allowed the shadow sector to circumvent the state more efficiently. In the shadow sector, the dollar is the preferred currency. As it is risky to have large amounts of dollars in cash, recently more enterprises have shifted to Internet banking, using accounts in tax havens. When the shadow entrepreneur needs cash, he uses his visa card.[73]

It is important to distinguish three types of activities within the shadow economy:[74]

1. Those enterprises that only want to hide for tax inspection;
2. Those enterprises that conduct criminal activities;
3. The informal economy that is difficult to tax and to register. It consists mostly of the marginal subsistence activities of very small enterprises.

The overwhelming part of the shadow economy consists of category 1 and an adequate government policy could lead to an incorporation of this vast segment into the officially registered economy.

It is in the realm of shadow economy that capital flight takes place. During 1995–99 approximately US$15 billion were illegally transferred abroad.

The role of international financial organizations

Since Ukraine embarked upon its first comprehensive economic reform programme, in the autumn of 1994, international organizations have played a prominent role in Kyiv, exhibited by Ukraine's dependence on financial support from the IMF, the World Bank and other international financial institutions.[75]

When communism collapsed in Central and Eastern Europe, the IMF began to take the lead in Western policy formulation towards the countries in transition. The Washington Consensus was the starting point for policy advice to the transition countries. Originally the Consensus was a response to Latin America's structural crisis in the 1980s, a kind of policy advice agreed in Washington between important organizations such as the IMF, the World Bank and the US Treasury. The Consensus can be summarized as follows: 'liberalize and privatize as quick and as much as possible, and be tough in fiscal and monetary matters'. The assumption was that the transition economies were simply affected by financial disequilibria similar to the Latin American economies. IMF policy was also based on demand rather than supply management. The assumption was that once financial stabilization has been achieved and low inflation attained, growth would take place. It was the Washington Consensus that dictated the IMF approach towards Ukraine until 1998.

In the least developed transition economies, in particular in the former Soviet Union, it appeared that the policy based on the Washington Consensus did not have the desired effects. Some even say that liberalization and privatization fostered a rent-seeking state and a privatization of the state rather than the privatization of state-owned enterprises. The newly emerged banking sector spurred a wave of soft credit rather than fulfilling the role of disciplining enterprises while imposing hard budget constraints. Also, low inflation levels did not lead to economic growth. C. Gaddy and B. Ickes suggested that international institutions like the IMF contributed, in the case of Russia, to the emergence of a Virtual Economy, rather than a market economy.[76]

It led the international donor organizations to rethink, in 1997 and 1998, the relationship between state and market and that of governance mechanisms in the economy. The IMF started to address structural problems of the economy.[77] In Ukraine, the IMF recommendations were extended to include, for example, reform of the state administration. IMF decisions were crucial for Ukraine's economic survival. IMF credits could unlock or block credit streams to this credit-starved country.

If we look at the rhetoric of the Ukrainian government, it seems that the IMF is successfully pushing Ukraine in the direction of market-oriented reform. Financial support is dependent on new steps in the direction of a market economy. It seems that many steps have been made towards a market economy, but that many other steps have neutralized this 'progress'. Many observers see the Ukrainian government signing on major reform programmes with the IMF and World Bank only to grab the initial tranches of low-interest loans while leaving the reform programmes to die in their infancy.

Financial stability was only attained at the surface, as became apparent shortly after the Russian financial crisis in August 1998.

However, it seems that this borrowing without reform has become more difficult. The Memorandum of Economic Policies, as presented by the Ukrainian government to the IMF on 11 August 1998, is much more detailed and contains many more benchmarks than the reform programme approved by the IMF in 1994. Nevertheless, when the IMF approved an Extended Fund Facility in March 1999, not all of the 80 conditions posed in mid-1998 were fulfilled. Ukraine could not even comply with the key condition of administrative reform. The IMF accepted some cosmetic changes (see Chapter 3, page 29). Although conditionality had become more detailed, the IMF apparently does not take these conditions seriously. Within the IMF there is also a problem of accountability. The officials who negotiate with Ukraine and draw up conditions do not decide about assistance. Decisions are made at a higher level, apparently without giving due account to conditionality. Another problem with the IMF is the frequent changes of personnel dealing with Ukraine. A further problem with conditionality is that conditions change over time. In 1998/99 administrative reform and reform of the banking system were deemed important. However, many important fields were overlooked. It is exactly those fields not covered by conditionality in which step backwards have been made.

It can also happen that the Ukrainian government issues decrees to please IMF delegations just before important decisions are made, only to annul these decrees shortly afterwards.

It seems that IMF conditionality is also encouraging the Ukrainian government in its short-termism by emphasizing the cash management aspects of policy-making, focusing upon monitoring expenditure and revenue levels. The IMF focused upon short-term financial performance criteria. Also, the IMF has supported the government in its efforts to finance its spending through short-term debt markets. It kept the time horizon of policy-makers fixed on the debt roll-over date.[78]

The main concern of the IMF is financial stability in Ukraine. However, the question is whether the relative monetary stability Ukraine has enjoyed since 1996 has a sound basis, given the unfavourable structure of its debts, payment arrears and fragile banking system.

Hitherto, the IMF looked primarily at government initiatives, less so to the implementation of government decisions. According to Gregory Jedrzejczak, representative of the World Bank in Ukraine, 'no reforms stipulated by co-operation programs with international financial institutions have been carried out in Ukraine'.[79]

The point is that IMF policy towards Ukraine is not only motivated by furthering economic reforms, but also by furthering political stability in a region ravaged by political turmoil. Thus, the granting of new tranches from the side of the IMF is a balancing act in which multiple motives play a role. Generally, it was not considered in the Western interest to leave Ukraine alone and to push Ukraine towards Russia.[80]

However, on 1 October 1999, the IMF refused Ukraine a new instalment of a loan, due to non-compliance with IMF conditions. The situation changed with the re-election of President Kuchma in November 1999 and the appointment of Viktor Yushchenko as prime minister. Yushchenko is a former head of the Central Bank and known in the West as a reformer. Also, a pro-reform majority was formed in parliament after President Kuchma announced a referendum that proposed to dissolve parliament. A window of opportunity appeared to open. However, the first steps of the new government did not indicate a radical break with the past. The IMF made it clear that it wanted to end the practice of loans in return for promise of reform. Relations with the IMF reached a new low with the revelation in the Financial Times of abuse of IMF funds by the Central Bank in 1997 and 1998. There were even allegations of speculative dealings with money transferred by the Central Bank to a Swiss bank by individuals in President Kuchma's entourage. These allegations led the IMF to postpone the release of loans in the framework of an Extended Fund Facility. This restricted the manoeuvring space of government, which has not received any IMF loans since late September 1999, while faced with the inability to service its debt.

In most Central European countries the ruling elite opted for market-oriented reform not because their material interests dictated them to do so, because at the onset of reform policies, they were not yet owners of productive capacities. They saw, however, that the centrally planned economy has led to a deadlock and that only the allocation of resources by the market could bring economic efficiency and therewith a viable socio-economic system. At the onset of reform, a constituency for reform had to be created. In the Ukraine the situation differed as the deadlock situation of socialism was and still is not obvious for the ruling elite. This lack of awareness is partly related to the fact that, other than for example in Poland, a revolutionary elite, arising out of the political opposition under socialism, was absent in the Ukraine.

Verbally, the Ukrainian government says to opt for market economy. This is under pressure from international financial institutions and donors. However, looking in more detail at government policies and in particular at the implementation of government decisions, the kind of reform the Ukrainian government has in mind is an improvement of the present system, rather than market-oriented reforms as outlined in the memoranda written for the IMF and other donor organizations.

Conclusion

Although the legal infrastructure for a market economy has certainly improved since the early 1990s, many obstacles to economic development remain in place because laws are often contradictory and not properly implemented. There are so many legal loopholes that generally, if one sticks to one law, one will violate another. This gives the state bureaucracy high discretionary power, fostering corruption. Generally, steps forward in some fields were neutralized by steps backward in other fields. Instead of furthering the market, government policies furthered a new socio-economic system, characterized by a set of parasitic mechanisms, preventing productive activities from unfolding.

Professor Duchêne from the World Bank noted in mid-1998 that the Ukraine:

> ... did not undertake the reforms, which were devised at the end of 1996. It should be clear that the slowness of the privatization process, the many declarations about the need to attract foreign direct investment (but without any concrete implementation), the support which is granted to obsolete and loss making enterprises and industries at the expenses of taxes taken from modern, profitable business, the pervasive bureaucracy and the bribery which goes with it, the innumerable hindrances which confront small private entrepreneurs, the high level of taxation and the artificial monopolies which are created for favoured firms cannot be considered 'market reforms'.[81]

An increase in the number of privatized enterprises, the liberalization of prices and trade and low rates of inflation do not automatically result in a change to the incentive structure of enterprises. Economic change cannot be measured with the strait-jacket of the above-mentioned indicators. Institutional change in Ukraine worked partly against the marketization of the economy. A telling example is the change in the taxation system.

For a better understanding of economic processes in Ukraine it is crucial to see exactly what happened in the sphere of production, at the macro and the micro-level.

5
Structural Change in the Economy I: Sectoral Analysis

In this chapter transformations in the sphere of production are examined from a macro and sectoral perspective. The dynamics of industrial decline and restructuring will be analysed as well as changes in major economic sectors.

Deindustrialization

The Soviet economic system caused enormous dislocations. Entire branches of industries were developed that became value-subtracting. Many products were produced that nobody needed. A huge military industrial complex emerged for which there was less need in the new circumstances after the Cold War. A lot of high value added production took place for which there are no markets in a situation of free competition. Also, branches that were tightly integrated into the Soviet industrial complex had no chances of survival when disconnected from this system after the independence of Ukraine. On the other hand, the service sector was hardly developed.

Many expected that, with the gradual development of a market economy, the value-subtracting industries would suffer most while the traditionally underdeveloped consumer goods industry would develop better if freed from the constraints of a centrally planned economy.

In fact, the opposite happened. The value-subtracting ferrous and non-ferrous metallurgy and energy sectors enhanced their share in industrial production and increased enormously their share in exports. The coal mining industry is still absorbing huge amounts of subsidies while the sector has hardly been restructured. On the other hand, the consumer goods industry completely collapsed, not being able to compete with foreign products and faced with an enormous decline in demand.

The share of power utilities in total industrial output increased between 1990 and 1999 from 7.3 per cent to 16.2 per cent, that of oil and gas from 9.5 to 10.2 per cent, that of coal from 7.0 to 11.6 per cent and that of steel from 14.4 to 26.0 per cent. All these branches together increased their share in total industrial output from 39 per cent in 1990 to 64 per cent in 1999. On the other hand, the machine-building industry's share dropped from 29.8 per cent to 8.3 per cent and that of food from 14.0 to 13.3 per cent.[1] Light industry collapsed, with output declining between 1990 and 1999 by 85–95 per cent. In the same period industrial output as a whole declined by 63.9 per cent.[2]

The increase of base industries in total industrial production is only partly related to the fact that these industries can less easily divert activities to the shadow sector.

An increased importance of resource rich sectors can be observed. The same trend can be observed in Russia. But unlike Russia, Ukraine does not have a rich resource base and is a net energy importer.

The employment structure changed less dramatically than output structure, due to the inclination of many enterprises to hoard labour. Nevertheless, remarkable changes occurred: from 1990 to 1997 the share of industry dropped from 30.7 per cent to 24.7 per cent, but that of agriculture increased from 19.6 per cent to 24.7 per cent, although the share of agriculture in GDP decreased substantially.[3] The share of construction and transport declined (from 9.4 to 6.4 and from 7.1 to 6.4 per cent, respectively) and the share of the health sector and state apparatus increased (from 5.9 to 7.4 and from 1.6 to 3.5 per cent, respectively). The financial services sector appeared with 1.0 per cent. Other sectors remained relatively stable.

Instead of changing its employment structure in the direction of most developed market economies, employment structures began to resemble the less developed economies. According to official figures, in terms of employment, the service sector did not develop dynamically. If the shadow sector is included, the picture changes and a larger share of the population is active in trade, visible in the phenomenal growth of the bazaar.

Thus, the structure of the economy changed, but not in the direction many expected in the early 1990s and not as the outcome of deliberate government policies, but rather as the result of differential decline.

Table 5.1   GDP and industrial output, 1992–99

	1992	1993	1994	1995	1996	1997	1998	1999
GDP (market prices)	–16.6	–14.2	–23.0	–11.8	–8.0	–3.2	–1.7	–0.4
Gross industrial output	–6.4	–7.6	–27.7	–17.4	–2.7	–1.8	–1.5	+3.4

Source: Ministry of Economy, Ministry of Statistics, Ukrainian Economic Trends, World Bank, Statistical Yearbook Ukraine 1997.

Between 1991 and 1999, gross national product (purchasing power) fell by approximately 60 per cent (Table 5.1). On the basis of data from the Ministry of Economy, the Ukrainian–European Policy and Legal Advice Center calculated that the index of real industrial production in 1999 (1990 = 100) was 26.1 per cent.[4]

Many argue that real decline in GDP and industrial production is lower, given the increasing share of non-registered economic activities. In 1998, the shadow economy was larger than the officially registered economy. Moreover, the argument is that with the changeover to a market economy enterprises produce goods that people really want, unlike in socialist times.

However, this argument is doubtful as the share of value-subtracting activities in total production increased, given the surge in the share of heavy metallurgy and the energy complex (coal industry) in total output. If we take into account real value added of enterprises, the overall production picture is even gloomier. Also, one should take into account that part of value added that appears in the books of enterprises is virtual, i.e. never realized, related to overstated prices for products sold. This part amounted, according to Ihor Zhyliaev, to 8.1 per cent of GDP in 1997 and almost 10 per cent in 1998.[5]

Many suggest taking electricity consumption as a yardstick to measure real GDP growth. In countries with a small shadow economy and high elasticity in demand for electricity, electricity consumption and production closely correlate with change in GDP. In Ukraine, reported decline in GDP is more than twice the decline in electricity consumption.[6] However, it should be taken into account that there is no high elasticity in demand as there is in most enterprises, no incentives to curb electricity consumption once production is falling. Budget constraints with respect to energy use are still very soft, because electricity providers do not cut off non-payers.

Table 5.2 GDP structure, 1990–98 (per cent)

Indices	1990	1993	1998
Final household consumption	54.8	44.0	67.8
Final consumption of non-commercial organizations	2.3	4.0	3.2
Final state sector consumption	16.5	16.0	23.6
Gross accumulation of fixed assets	23.0	24.3	19.3
Change in inventories	3.4	11.8	1.4
Acquisition less disposals	1.0	0.2	
Net export	–1.0	–0.3	–2.9

Source: Ukrainian Economic Trends, June 1998, p. 87; IMF (1999), p. 76.

Investments as a share of GNP have dropped from 23 per cent in 1990 to 19.3 per cent of GNP in 1998 (Table 5.2). The total value of investments dropped from 55.4 billion hryvnas in 1990 to 11.5 billion hryvnas in 1998 (constant prices). From 1991 onwards, capital investment declined faster than gross industrial output and GDP. However, investment ratios in the second half of the 1990s were on a par with most medium income countries. The problem is not so much that investment levels declined but that investments have been channelled towards the value-subtracting industries.[7] In 1997, 37 per cent of investments in manufacturing went to heavy industry and 29 per cent to fuels and power generation. Less than 2 per cent went to light industry.[8]

During 1993–94 a large share of available capital went into the accumulation of inventories that could not be sold, raising the annual growth of inventories to more than 10 per cent of GDP and significantly lowering the share of fixed capital in total investment.

Declining investment ratios and misallocation of investment funds are reflected in the state of industrial enterprises across Ukraine. Industrial districts have been transformed into rustbelts.

Machine building and the military-industrial complex

In 1991, 700 enterprises belonged to the military-industrial complex, whose 1.3 million employees mainly produced for the military market. Another 1100 enterprises, with 1.4 million employees, were indirectly linked to the military-industrial complex.[9] Ukraine used to produce 20–25 per cent of Soviet tanks, 20 per cent of warships and between

60 and 80 per cent of military electronics.[10] Planes and missiles were also made. Military exports, especially to countries like Iran, Pakistan and India, have become an important source of income for Ukraine.

The enterprises that belonged to the military-industrial complex traditionally were better managed and had more resources than other enterprises. This heritage of the Soviet past is still visible. These enterprises are the only ones capable of attaining world market level.

However, it is exactly these strategic enterprises where restructuring is blocked by government interference. Nowadays, hardly any military hardware is produced by military enterprises and most of it is exported. In 1996, the share of civil production in the sector reached 96 per cent.[11]

Machine building, which was the main strength of Ukrainian industry on independence in 1991, has been one of the hardest hit sectors. The share of machine building in total industrial output increased from 30 per cent in 1990 to 38 per cent in 1993, but then fell to less than 7 per cent during the first quarter of 1999. It meant a 90 per cent decline in real output during 1993–99.[12] The reason for this sharp decline was the non-competitiveness of its products on international markets, the loss of markets in the former Soviet Union and the disruption of supply chains as a result of the demise of the Soviet Union and the sharp decline in domestic demand as a result of the economic crisis.

Heavy metallurgy

Ukraine is the world's fifth largest producer of iron ore and the world's second largest producer of magnesium. Its most important natural resource is the coal basin in Donbas. These natural resources make Ukraine a natural producer of steel and iron. In 1989 Ukraine was the highest per capita steel producer in the world, with 1060 kg. The USA produced only 382 kg per capita.

Production volumes of heavy metallurgy have declined sharply since independence, albeit by less than the industrial average (Table 5.3).[13]

The relatively good performance of the Ukrainian heavy metallurgy sector is related to its export performance. By 1998, 70 per cent of Ukrainian steel production was exported. Also, heavy metallurgy has been supported by the state through direct and indirect subsidies. By mid-2000, the state had a majority share in almost all Ukrainian steel mills.

Table 5.3 Production volumes of heavy metallurgy, 1990–98 (000 tonnes)

	1990	1995	1996	1997	1998
Iron ore	104.0		50.4	60.9	53.5
Cokes	34.5	15.8	18.0		
Cast iron	45.0	17.9	20.5	20.6	20.1
Steel	50.0	210.0	24.0	25.6	24.1
Steel tubes	6.5	1.5	2.7	1.8	
Rolled iron	38.0	16.5	17.5	19.5	17.9

Source: Ekonomika Ukraini, June 1998, p. 25; Statistical Yearbook 1997,
p. 8; Zerkalo Nedeli, 10 April 1999, p. 8.

Production costs in this sector have increased due to the fact that
production volume has declined sharply.[14] In some cases, (official) production costs exceeded world market price levels. For example, in the
production of ferromanganese, domestic prices were more than
20 per cent higher than world market prices in 1997 and with exports
there were losses of more than 7 per cent.[15]

Fifty-five per cent of Ukraine's steel production is from open-hearth
furnaces, which is the most primitive and energy-intensive technology. 45.5 per cent of output is produced by oxygen converters and
1.5 per cent by electric arc furnaces. By comparison, in the USA
57.4 per cent of output is from oxygen converters and 42.6 per cent
from electric arc furnaces.[16] Continuous casting accounts for only
12 per cent of output in Ukraine while in the USA it is 93.3 per cent.
In Ukraine, energy consumption in ferrous metallurgy is 30 per cent
higher than in Japan.[17] Labour productivity is also very low in
Ukraine: in the Ukrainian heavy metallurgy sector labour productivity in tonnes per man year is 43, in Germany 350, Japan 556, Brazil
263, South Korea 549 and France 476.[18]

Ukrainian officials acknowledge that their unit costs of steel and cast
iron production are higher than the world average.[19] Many products
have no international certification and are sold at a discount.

Ukrainian ministry officials said in 1998 that the steel industry had
an annual investment shortfall of US$300–400 million.[20] According to
Levine and Bond (1998), restructuring of Ukraine's ferrous metallurgy
sector would require US$2–2.5 billion annually. Enterprises have only
US$300–400 million yearly for investment.[21] Ukrainian domestic
demand has plunged and producers have increasingly depended on

new export markets, with a significant proportion of exports destined for South East Asia.

Since the Asian crisis began, these markets have largely disappeared. Metal exports to the Community of Independent States have also plummeted.[22] Ukrainian steel producers have tried to divert steel exports to OECD markets and Latin America. However, import duties there are higher than in South East Asia.[23] Anti-dumping measures against Ukrainian steel have recently increased. During 1997/98 there were more than 300 dumping accusations.

The prospects for steel production are gloomy given rising energy prices, high energy intensiveness of production and declining prospects on world markets since the Asian crisis. Foreign courts, dealing with anti-dumping procedures, calculate that the price of Ukrainian steel should be about US$350 per tonne, while according to Ukrainian officials, the real price for steel is US$230 per tonne.[24]

Ferrous metallurgy accounted for a third of Ukraine's export earnings during 1996 and a quarter of its export earnings during 1997 and 1998. The OECD suggests that Ukraine's non-market pricing has helped force down world market prices and has allowed for Ukrainian export growth, despite highly inefficient production relative to OECD countries.[25] According to a report commissioned by the EU's TACIS programme, 'the reliance of steel enterprises on exports of low-grade metal to shrinking foreign markets is about to cost them dearly'.[26] Depressed overseas demand, anti-dumping legislation in Europe and the USA, a flat domestic market and meddling by the government now threaten to decimate the Ukrainian mills' impressive revenues, the study argues.

Although iron ore, coal and coke are abundant in Eastern Ukraine, these raw materials are of relatively low purity. As a result, Ukrainian steel plants that buy them are internationally competitive only in low-grade steel. But with Asian demand for low-grade steel falling and domestic energy prices rising, Ukrainian manufacturers must improve the quality of their output, according to the TACIS report. Alternative high-grade steel products such as railroad rails or construction girders are well within the technical capabilities of Ukrainian industry. The quality raw materials needed to make them are also available from Russian coal mines or Brazilian coke plants, at prices comparable to the less pure Ukrainian inputs.

However, 11 of Ukraine's 12 steel mills still have the state as a majority shareholder, which means that they buy raw materials from state-owned coke, iron ore and coal mining enterprises. In case of difficulties, they can rely on state support. This was the case in 1998 with the large steel mill in Kirovograd, which received tax exemptions from the government in order to continue production.

There has been virtually no innovation in the Ukrainian steel mills and they have not adjusted to the demands of their clients. For example, Ukrainian shipyards produce very little, partly due to the fact that domestic steel producers cannot provide steel of the required quality.

One of the recommendations of the TACIS report was to cut the workforce of the steel mills by some 30 per cent, which would leave an estimated 200 000 out of work.

One of the authors of the report, Pierre Vernet, recommended more direct links between Ukrainian steel makers and their European customers:

> Ukrainian factories can produce today a higher value added product like railroad rails fully compatible for sale in the West. But you have to get rid of the middleman. End products require a direct link with the customer. If you have it, they are far more profitable than lower-grade products.[27]

The energy sector

In socialist times, Ukraine was known as an energy-rich republic, because it had huge reserves of energy resources, especially coal. Sixty per cent of coal reserves in the former Soviet Union, i.e. 45 billion tonnes, were in the Donbas region. Now, under market economy conditions, Ukraine has become a country poor in energy resources. This change is related to the fact that under market conditions, the majority of reserves cannot be mined cost-effectively.

Ukraine covers only 42 per cent of its energy needs (1998). In 1998, 38 per cent of all imports consisted of natural gas and oil. In order to reduce the dependency on energy imports, the Ukrainian government decided in the early 1990s to produce more coal and nuclear energy.[28] The government considers the energy sector as strategic, hence a sector that should be controlled by the state. Only energy trading is open to private competition. Here, huge profits have been made from the differences between prices of imported energy, domestic prices and world market prices.

Surprisingly, not much attention has been paid to exploiting the reserves of gas and oil in Ukraine. Potential Western investors, interested in exploiting gas reserves, withdrew due to the poor investment climate.[29] According to British Petroleum, gas extraction could be increased to 40 billion m³ per year, from the 18 billion m³ in 1998.[30] Domestic gas consumption in 1998 was approximately 70 billion m³. Energy savings and 15 billion m³ gas in profits from gas transit could eventually close the gap and eliminate gas imports.[31]

Little has been done hitherto to reduce the energy intensity of production. International comparison of GNP per kg oil equivalent (US dollars) shows that in 1996 Ukraine produced only 0.5 dollars per kg/oil equivalent, while it was 3.0 dollars for South Korea, 2.3 dollars for Malaysia, 5.0 dollars for Argentina and 4.4 dollars for Brazil.[32] With a more efficient use of electricity, 20–25 per cent could be saved on the electricity bill, according to the Energy Center of the European Union, 40 per cent according to the Energy Research Institute of the Ukrainian Academy of Sciences.[33] Yet energy intensity of industrial production has increased during the 1990s, because generally, the decline in power consumption has been less than the general decline in industrial production.

In 1994, electric power use per unit GDP was 4–4.5 times higher in Ukraine than in Western Europe. This ratio was 2.5–3 times that in the 1980s. According to O. Khraban, of the Danish energy technology firm Danfoss, 'the potential market for energy saving technology is huge, but the real market is much smaller, mostly because there is little awareness of the problem'.[34] There is also the misconception that energy saving technology is expensive.

Most households cannot save on energy because many apartments lack thermostats.

Coal output in the Ukraine, most of which is mined in South-Eastern Ukraine, declined from 216 million tonnes in 1975, to 189 million tonnes in 1985, 165 million tonnes in 1990, 84 million tonnes in 1995 and 59 million tonnes in 1998.[35] Since Ukraine's independence in 1991, coal production has declined by more than half while employment has dropped by more than one-third. While the coal industry employed 650 000 in 1995, the start of restructuring, there were only 412 000 employees in January 2000.

The loss-making coal mining sector is still, for the most part, not privatized, and receives large direct and indirect subsidies.[36] Coal mines are being kept afloat that produce coal at one and a half times the world market price while conditions for coal mining are deteriorating, given the prospect of even more expensive coal in the future.

The easily available coal has been extracted so that what remains lies in thin and sloping seams, often more than 1200 metres deep, and with each passing year the average depth of the coal face increases by

10–15 metres. The quality of the coal is declining. Mining technology is very primitive: 75 per cent of all jobs in the mines are done manually (from the mid-1970s onwards investments in coal mining were channelled to regions other than South-Eastern Ukraine).[37] One-third of the mines are more than 50 years old, and some date back to the 19th century. Many key pieces of equipment, including one-third of the ropes hauling the mine elevators, are well beyond their service life.[38]

Miners have found themselves in a downward spiral of declining rates of productivity and investment, leading to their work becoming more hazardous. In 1998 every thousand tonnes of coal cost the lives of four miners.[39]

Table 5.4 shows that the UK produces 57.9 per cent of the coal produced in the Ukraine with only 3.8 per cent of the number of miners. Labour productivity of miners in the USA is 58.7 times higher than that of Ukrainian miners. Here we do not take into account the fact that, on average, Ukrainian coal contains 4000–5000 kcal/kg, while internationally, 7000 kcal/kg is usual.[41]

On average, production costs of coal in Ukraine are US$50 per tonne compared with a world price of US$35 a tonne, requiring government subsidies of 1.85 billion hryvnas in 1997.[42] In 1997 each tonne of coal was subsidized by approximately US$28.[43] According to the minister for the coal industry, Mr Tulub, coal enterprises owe 8.5 billion hryvnas to creditors and 63 per cent of mines are operating at extreme losses.[44]

Still, Ukrainian decision-makers think that investments can solve the problems of the coal mining industry rather than changing the *modus operandi* of coal mines. Well functioning mines are still punished by siphoning off profits while badly performing mines are rewarded with subsidies.

Table 5.4   Comparison of mining sectors in four countries, 1997

	Total number of miners	Production (million tonnes)	Total number of deaths
Ukraine	450 000	76	290[40]
Poland	243 000	201	27
USA	99 600	989	30
UK	17 200	44	4

Source: EIU Country Report Ukraine, 3rd quarter 1998.

A large amount of (expensive) coal is consumed by electricity power stations. Here the economic situation is disastrous because many clients, including industrial clients, do not pay, or have large payment arrears. In Ukraine as a whole, only 7 per cent of delivered electricity is paid for in cash, while half is paid in barter, and the rest is not paid for at all.[45] Electricity tariffs are still below cost price. On top of that, government has denominated 645 000 energy consumers as privileged energy payers. The government does not compensate the energy enterprises for these discounts.[46] As a result, electricity power stations do not pay for a large part of their coal supplies. Also, large state enterprises, like coke and steel enterprises, consume a lot of coal that is only partially paid for.

As far as coal is paid, payments are usually in kind. At the end of 1998, 60 per cent of coal was paid for in barter, down from 77.5 per cent in early 1997.[47] In January/February 1999, just 20 per cent of coal sold to consumers was paid for using cash. This contributes to wage arrears. Also, barter trade increases transaction costs enormously. An important loophole is the middlemen selling coal. Despite great personnel resources from the central budget, private middlemen selling coal keep one-third of the proceeds from coal sales, according to federal tax police.[48]

Most of the money allocated for the managing of mine closures, in agreement with and co-financed by the World Bank, has not been used for this but for other purposes.[49] This is partly related to the fact that the World Bank failed to prescribe in detail how much money should be spent on the closure of each mine.

The coal sector is part of a sector of the economy that is closely intertwined, comprising, among others, steel enterprises, coke factories and electricity producers, which is still state dominated and state planned, without any monetary transparency. In this sector, the main aim is output maximization and preservation of employment, at any cost.

Instead of fostering reforms and providing competitive coal mines with new business opportunities, the government, under pressure from the Coal Ministry, institutionalized central planning for coal production, trade and prices. Cross-subsidies between efficient and inefficient mines are maintained. The ministry fixes the output for each mine as well as the price of coal. Mines can freely sell only the coal produced beyond the plan. Coal imports, too, were controlled by the state coal trading agency until 1995. In 1996, an average US$2 import duty per tonne was imposed. The government plan for the coal industry requires it to increase production to 130 million tonnes by the year 2010. In January

1999, the government issued a new plan for the coal industry, introducing new procedures for support. Not only will the volume of coal produced be taken into account when deciding subsidies, but also the quality of the coal. 'The indicators of coal quality will be established by the Coal Industry Ministry, and will be revised each year.'[50] This contradicts the memorandum on economic policy presented by the government to the IMF on 11 August 1998, in which it is stated that between 1998 and 2001 at least 20 mines will be closed each year. This memorandum suggests that a marketization of the coal industry will take place.[51]

Ukrainian gas consumption was 80 billion m^3 in 1997; 18 billion m^3 was domestically produced.[52] In 1999 Ukraine received from Russia 62 billion m^3 of gas; 15 billion m^3 of this was delivered as payments for transit of Russian gas. These payments are not used to carry out necessary repairs on the gas pipeline infrastructure, which is in a dire state, but to cover losses for unpaid domestic gas deliveries. In its Memorandum of Economic Policies to the IMF (11 August 1998) the Ukrainian government promised many measures to rationalize the gas market: among others, measures would be taken to accelerate gas meter installation for the budgetary organizations (with the aim of completing the process by November 1998), to install heat meters for these organizations and to raise the bill collection ratio for budgetary organizations to 100 per cent and for households to 80 per cent. Gas providers would be allowed to enforce payment discipline. Electricity prices should be cost covering.

However, by late 1999 not much progress had been made. A government draft law to increase tariffs for gas and electricity by 25–30 per cent was rejected by parliament in early 1999. A large proportion of customers still kept their discounts. According to the Ukrainian government, consumers have paid only US$817 million of the US$1.8 billion of gas consumed in Ukraine in 1998. By far the worst offenders are the municipalities, which paid for only 48 per cent of the gas consumed. Industry paid for 61 per cent of gas consumed and households for 67 per cent.[53] Still, the Ukrainian government continues to use the energy sector as a substitute for the social safety net and as an instrument for industrial and agricultural policy.

In early 1998, the gas price was US$83 for industrial consumers and US$66 for budgetary organizations and households. Von Hirschhausen calculated that under competitive conditions the price could be 40 per cent lower. One cost factor is the salaries of workers in the Ukrainian gas sector, where employment is 20 to 30 times higher than in comparable market economies.[54]

In 1998 and 1999, Ukraine siphoned off gas destined for Western Europe and Turkey, without asking Russia for permission. Ukraine is herewith undermining one of its major assets.[55] There have been problems about the price Russia charges for gas deliveries. Ukraine pays higher gas prices than other customers in Western Europe. On the other hand, Ukraine charged high tariffs for Russian gas transfers and Russia has been lenient about Ukraine's gas payment arrears.

Given the chains of bad debts and discounts it is no surprise that almost all energy producers are loss-making and for a long time have not made any investments. Eighty per cent of all Ukrainian thermal electricity stations have exceeded their life times, according to recent investigations.[56]

However, the gas distributors are some of the richest and most powerful companies in Ukraine. The Ukrainian government has given monopoly rights, on a regional basis, to gas distributors. They supply gas to, among others, exporters who pay for part of the gas in barter. Gas distributors then export the steel, aluminium and chemicals obtained for a profit, without paying taxes. Part of the profit is kept in foreign bank accounts. In 1996, when he was prime minister, Pavel Lazarenko gave United Energy Systems monopoly rights and a five year tax break. He had control over this company and was able to drain their profits. United Energy Systems made more than US$1 billion profit in 1996 but paid only 22 000 hryvnas in taxes. The system of regionally based gas monopoly rights that Prime Minister Lazarenko created is still in place and protected by President Kuchma. Kuchma vetoed a law that would give rights to the accounting chamber to inspect budget revenues, so protecting the gas traders who drain the Ukrainian economy, giving nothing in return but allowing these traders to transfer huge sums on foreign bank accounts.[57]

By mid-1999, the gas market was dominated by 10 private firms who accounted for 80 per cent of gas turnover. All these private firms depended heavily on government protection.[58]

Gas and oil traders can get rich despite the fact that the government forces them to supply fuel to non-payers. The point is that these so-called non-payers are paying under the table, often in the form of goods. In such a way, supplying gas without payment becomes quite an attractive business for all parties involved.

About half of Ukraine's electricity is provided by nuclear power stations. As with all power stations, they are faced with non-payment of their energy bills. This has resulted, among others, in non-payment of wages, lack of investment funds and even non-payment for fuels supplied from Russia.

The agro-industrial complex

Ukrainian agriculture suffered in Soviet times. Forced collectivization and fear created a workforce unable to show any initiative. Alcoholism was rampant in the countryside. Production was extremely wasteful – between 20 and 30 per cent of Soviet agricultural production was lost in the food production chain.[59] In Soviet times the maximization of production in a short time was the main goal, while the long-term maintenance of soils was neglected. As a result, 33 per cent of the soil in Ukraine was washed away, including 44 per cent of the most productive and extensive steppe soils.[60] According to the World Bank, this slow deterioration of soils requires the additional use of fertilizers. However, even where additional fertilizers are used, productivity of soils will decline.[61]

When Ukraine gained independence in 1991, Ukrainian nationalists saw agriculture as one of the biggest assets of their new country. They referred above all to the very fertile soils.[62] However, at the end of the 1990s Ukrainian agriculture was in a disastrous state. Annual grain harvests were only half of those before independence and the production of other crops had also declined sharply. Agricultural production was worth US$44.1 million in 1990; by 1999 it was only worth US$16.3 million. The agricultural sector has become even more backward technologically and yields are far below those in Western European countries.[63] The food processing industry is in deep crisis and many food products are imported (see Chapter 7, page 118).

Agriculture is still extremely important to the Ukrainian economy. Twenty-one per cent of the Ukrainian labour force works in agriculture.[64] Both in 1990 and in 1997 5.0 million people were employed in agriculture.[65] However, the share of agriculture in GDP declined from 24.5 per cent in 1990 to 11.9 per cent in 1998. This points to a very sharp drop in labour productivity.

Land reform began in January 1992 with the attempt to transform the agro-food sector, based on market principles and private ownership. Since then, little progress has been made in this direction although the organizationally monolithic sector, with about 10 000 kolkhozes and sovchozes, has been transformed into a mixture of Collective Agricultural Enterprises, private farms and state farms.

Denationalization of agricultural enterprises is almost complete. Almost 6 million Ukrainian citizens have received certificates of the right to a land parcel. Moreover, more than 9 million citizens have received land plots, usually used as kitchen gardens. However, land is not yet really owned as no land market exists and land cannot be mortgaged.

Land reform has not resulted in a reform of large agrarian enterprises. Part of the reform was the issuing of shares to agricultural employees. However, the beneficiaries of the land-sharing process appear to be uninformed about the rights attached to their land shares. In 1995, only 8 per cent of respondents with shares thought that they were allowed to sell land shares, only 22 per cent thought that land shares could be leased out, and only 26 per cent thought that shares could be received in the form of a plot of land when an individual exits the farm enterprise with the aim of establishing a private farm. However, all these options were perfectly legal at the time the survey took place.[66] The problem is that the farm managers, who usually rule as feudal lords, are the main source of information about land reform.

Most farm employees prefer to stay in collective farms. Their basic attitude is risk aversion. Almost half of respondents in a survey carried out in 1995 were opposed in principle to the right to exit with land and asset shares, although this right is protected by existing legislation.[67] About one-quarter of respondents supported the right of exit, but mostly with qualifying conditions. This shows the deeply conservative attitude of employees of Ukrainian Collective Agricultural Enterprises. Envy towards private farmers is common.[68]

The dairy sector

The situation in the dairy sector is typical of the general situation in the agro-industrial complex. Consumption of dairy products in 1997 was 215 kg per capita, while in 1990 it was 373 kg per capita.[69] The number of cows has almost halved and milk production per cow has declined sharply. Privatization of dairy plants and Collective Agricultural Enterprises could not prevent the decline in dairy production.

The problem is that, despite privatization, the whole dairy sector is still state-controlled and this very fact prevents restructuring. Provincial authorities continue to monitor herd sizes in Collective Agricultural Enterprises. They force these enterprises to sell milk to them through designated processing plants against low, artificially set, prices. Provincial authorities monitor the transport of agricultural products and prevent such products from crossing provincial borders. All this is done illegally. Monetary transactions between enterprises should be through bank accounts. However, state authorities police bank accounts and have the right to automatically deduct tax arrears from the bank accounts of Collective Agricultural Enterprises. Dairy plants often pay farmers in goods, usually in butter. However, it would be more efficient and cheaper for the farms to keep the milk and produce the butter themselves. This means that there is no incentive to deliver to processing plants.

Provincial authorities are still deeply involved in the supply of goods to Collective Agricultural Enterprises and the marketing of their products. This gives them additional leverage.

Dairy processing plants are compelled, illegally, to sell dairy products to state institutions. Payments are usually late or not made at all. The breaking of contracts by state institutions is the norm rather than the exception. There is no way of enforcing contracts. Although dairy processors are privatized, the provincial authorities usually appoint managers and interfere in management, as was the case in Soviet times.

Most dairy plants are loss-making but continue to operate without restructuring, and without laying off redundant personnel. Provincial authorities have a strong interest in maintaining this situation because tax collection is based on the volume of wage payments and the revenues of dairy plants.

The national and provincial authorities keep the prices of dairy products low in order to protect consumers. In such a way the old Soviet policy of protecting urban dwellers and putting pressure on the countryside is continued. This is done despite the fact that with present policies the dairy sector is vanishing because there are no incentives to produce. Today, the mere survival of the dairy sector is at stake.

Old inefficient production methods are still maintained on the Collective Agricultural Enterprises. For example, cows are milked three times a day because there are three shifts of workers and it is stipulated that each shift should milk. However, daily yields scarcely justify one milking a day.[70] With three milkings a day, overall milk production is reduced significantly.

Farmers have little incentive to work because they are usually not paid. As a result, farmers squeeze the collective farms in every possible way.

Increasingly, farmers are being pushed into the shadow economy. The number of cows they care for is gradually on the increase, while the number of cows owned by the Collective Agricultural Enterprises, for which they work, is decreasing.[71] However, many supplies for the private plots of farmers continue to be delivered by the Collective Agricultural Enterprises. Private cows are grazing on collective pastures and farmers are paid in products that are much lower priced than procurement prices.[72]

Eighty-six per cent of milk produced on household plots is consumed on the farms, and the rest is sold on the bazaar. Farmers mainly process their raw milk into cream, kefir and yoghurt. This shadow market is rapidly expanding but cannot replace the dairy processing plants.

Collective Agricultural Enterprises get very low prices for their products. In 1998, milk delivered to the local milk factory was valued at 25 kopeks/litre while the price on the market was 50 kopeks.[73] On the other hand, prices of farm inputs, such as machinery, fertilizers and detergents, have risen sharply.

The dairy industry employs 40 000 people, i.e. 40 per cent of those employed in the food industry in 1998. In 1997, the dairy sector represented 3.7 per cent of Ukraine's GDP and 23 per cent of the food industry. Dairy farming employed 450 000 people or 28 per cent of the Ukrainian farm labour force.[74]

The whole sector is now in danger of collapse. Repeated attempts at centralized control have failed to stop the decline. However, there are signs that the market may function. There are an increasing number of private traders that buy up milk in cash, and let it process by dairy plants and subsequently market it. Little is known about these traders as they can only operate with the approval of local authorities and this is likely to involve bribes.[75]

Grain production

Grain production is hampered by monopolistic structures. The state-owned Khlib Ukrayiny still controls the grain market. Grain elevators, solely owned by the state, can charge 50 per cent of the value of the grain stored.[76] Grain prices in Ukraine are much lower than world market prices. The difference, when exporting grain, goes to Khlib Ukrayiny and the pockets of corrupt officials.[77] In 1996, the state paid the farmers US$85 per tonne when the world market price was US$200 per tonne.[78]

According to Striewe and Cramon-Taubadel (1999), grain producers get only 43 per cent of the price paid by the consumer, while the corresponding figure for Germany is 72 per cent. In Ukraine, prices for many marketing services are determined by enterprises with monopoly powers. Also, losses are enormous. During storage, 13 per cent is lost in Ukraine, while this figure is only 3 per cent in Germany. During handling at sea ports, 10 per cent is lost in Ukraine, only 6 per cent in Germany. The trade margin in Ukraine is 10–15 per cent, in Germany 5 per cent.[79] Traders in Ukraine take 20–25 per cent of the grain price, while internationally approximately 5 per cent is usual.

Radio Free Europe calculated that in recent years Ukrainian grain farmers have been deprived of more than US$1.2 billion a year that could otherwise have been invested in badly needed tractors, seed, fertilizers, fuel and long-term infrastructure projects.[80]

Bureaucratic interference in grain production deters Collective Agricultural Enterprises to produce. Grain harvests show a continuous declining trend. The grain harvest in 1999 was 24.4 million tonnes, a 35.5 per cent decline compared to 1997. The average grain crop during 1986–90 was 47.4 million tonnes a year.

Government agricultural policies are aimed at the continuation of bureaucratic control rather than the introduction of a market economy. The state monopolizes trade in a number of staple crops, such as grain and sugar beet. The sale of land is still illegal, blocking credits to farmers.

Government policies with respect to agriculture are reminiscent in many ways of socialist times. The government plans farm inputs and decides where farm products should go. For example, the Cabinet of Ministers decided in December 1998 that 2 million tonnes of domestically produced petroleum products and 500 000 tonnes of mineral fertilizers would be supplied to the agricultural sector.[81] Also, 650 John Deere tractors were bought for loans against government guarantees. However, they stood idle because the Ministry for Industrial Policy failed to organize the production of ploughs compatible with the American tractors. With government subsidies and on government order, the Slavutych and Lan factory will produce 500 combines. According to a government resolution, the factory should turn out 2000 annually.[82]

The 'privatization' of state farms has not broken up the large inefficient collectives left over from the Soviet era. It simply meant changing door signs. In most cases, the renamed 'joint stock collectives' are managed by the same inefficient directors who were appointed by provincial authorities in the 1970s and 1980s.[83] In most cases, the managers of Collective Agricultural Enterprises maintain an allegiance to one of the regional clans – networks of state officials, province administrators and powerful local businessmen, who rule Ukraine's 24 provinces, although formally, managers are elected by the workers' collective.

Approximately one-quarter of employees in Collective Agricultural Enterprises are craftsmen. They are still employed even though the work could be done more effectively and cheaper by outside contractors.[84]

Farm workers have a certificate that gives them the rights to a tract of land and a share of collective profits. However, with continued reported losses for Collective Agricultural Enterprises and many workers not having received their pay for months, they can forget about a share in any profits.

Agricultural workers also have a right to vote for their managers. However, the workers' voting rights are made irrelevant by the fact that provincial authorities can sack collective managers on a whim. In practice, those who have been fired are the managers who refuse to fall into line with the demands of regional clan leaders. As a result, Ukraine's state farming has been transformed into a patchwork of private semi-feudal estates.

As key players in the agricultural sector are only interested in short-term profits and squeezing the farm sector, restructuring and hardly needed investments may not be expected in the near future. These key players see the Collective Agricultural Enterprises as a source of trans-fers: to the state, to the household plot, and to whomever has access to cash payments, primarily the middlemen, who trade agricultural prod-ucts, and the food processing industry. Ninety-seven per cent of the Collective Agricultural Enterprises are – on paper – bankrupt and dependent on their debtors. They survive without any surplus available for investment. They do not have the money to repair agricultural machinery. As a result 40 per cent of farm equipment is standing idle.[85]

The state, local and provincial authorities have an interest in keeping Collective Agricultural Enterprises indebted, as it gives them a pretext for continued control. Indebtedness is furthered by charging Collective Agricultural Enterprises too much for inputs and too little for output. Government at all levels can control the bank accounts of Collective Agricultural Enterprises.[86] All this is driving Collective Agricultural Enterprises underground and into barter trade. According to Baker:

> The prevalence of barter allows those with access to money the access to the Collective Agricultural Enterprises' profits.... It is likely that collusion amongst government agencies, local government and priva-

tized processors of agricultural products provide sufficient personal gain to encourage local governments to resist farm restructuring.[87]

It is estimated that barter trade costs farmers 15–20 per cent more than if they had cash.[88]

It is through government policy of imposed suppliers and imposed customers with imposed unfavorable pricing that Collective Agricultural Enterprises are indebted and becoming dependent on government 'support'. It is in this context that the government claim should be seen as the agricultural sector being indebted. According to the minister for agriculture, agricultural support will amount to at least 7 billion hryvnas for 1999.[89] As argued above, the farmers are squeezed rather than subsidized. This is in sharp contrast to OECD countries, where on average 38 per cent of the value of gross farm receipts is subsidized (the figure for the European Union is 45 per cent).[90] In Soviet times farmers got indirect support in the form of low prices for agricultural inputs. Since independence prices of agricultural inputs have increased sharply. The agricultural terms of trade were 22 in 1997 if taking the index for 1990 as 100.[91]

Exports of agricultural products have dropped sharply since independence. This is mainly due to the disappearance of markets within the former Soviet Union where most Ukrainian agricultural exports previously went. Whereas the share of food and agricultural products in total exports was 18–19 per cent during the 1980s, in 1994 it was 10 per cent, in 1997 12.7 per cent and in 1998 10 per cent.[92] Declining exports are related to producer prices which are too low and the monopolistic trade structure.

The number of private farmers increased from 14 681 in 1992 to 35 927 in 1997 and then decreased to 35 884 in 1999.[93] The total land area of private farms increased from 292 300 ha in 1992 to 1 162 300 ha in 1999.[94] In 1996, it accounted for 2 per cent of agricultural land.[95] It should be taken into account that private farmers have the smallest share of private land.[96] Part of their land is leased from the state.

Private farmers face prohibitive interest rates for loans that are invariably short-term, even though private farmers pay back credits taken from the government while Collective Agricultural Enterprises rarely do. Nevertheless, land productivity decreased less on private farms (by 30 per cent) than on Collective Agricultural Enterprises (by 53 per cent during 1991–96).[97]

According to private farmers surveyed in 1995, the minimum requirements to start a private farm typically include 50–100 ha of land

and a capital of US$25 000–100 000.[98] This says more about their beliefs than about the actual costs involved. Farmers cannot imagine a farm without a tractor and other machinery.

The family entitlement includes a household plot (0.5 ha) and 2 or 3 land shares (10–15 ha). This means that prospective private farmers need to acquire land from additional sources, although there is no land market. With annual family incomes of US$1000 and asset shares valued at about US$700 per adult person, a capital base of even US$25 000 for a new farm is inconceivable.[99]

In a survey carried out in 1995, over 80 per cent of private farmers, who had previously worked in the local collective farm, reported that they did not receive their share of land or assets on exit from the collective.[100] One reason cited for the non-allocation of land share is the price of land demarcation schemes. The 5000–6000 hryvnas required for this purpose is usually not available.[101]

Despite all the obstacles, private farmers are doing relatively well. In a survey conducted in early 1996 among private farmers, family welfare was rated as satisfactory or good by 65 per cent of the respondents. Among farm employees, however, 75 per cent of the respondents considered their living standard to be unsatisfactory.

To summarize, Ukrainian agriculture suffers from mismanagement, low productivity, lack of inputs (including fertilizers, machinery and fuel), absence of appropriate trading structures, lack of economic understanding and knowledge, obsolete equipment, and high production costs.

According to a World Bank Report, 'The famous black earth, considered to be the most fertile soil in the world, turned out to be of little value as long as seaming and harvesting techniques were outdated, many soils eroded, and specific returns only about one sixth of international standards'.[102]

Further reductions in agricultural production can be foreseen as a result of the withdrawal of Western suppliers of fertilizers and herbicides, on which Ukraine is heavily dependent, related to unpaid bills by Collective Agricultural Enterprises.

Many assume that the household plots, both of members of Collective Agricultural Enterprises and citizens whose main occupation lies outside agriculture, provide an alternative to collective agriculture. However, it can be argued that it is rather part of this system of collective agriculture and complementary to it. Household plots can only attain high productivity with the resources provided by the large farms. Large collective farms produce staple crops, such as grain and sugar beet, while household plots produce labour-intensive, high value added crops. Nowadays, the private plots are not expanding further because plot owners lack both the access to potentially profitable markets for their products and the means of buying the inputs to grow them.

According to Van Atta, the real reason behind the policy of the Ukrainian government to monopolize inputs and product markets in agriculture is to use state power to capture rents for the state and for themselves.[103] Monopolies are used to extract profits from the exports of ever smaller volumes of staple crops.

In this respect, the state, together with the intermediary structures and directors of Collective Agricultural Enterprises, have an interest in preserving the semi-feudal structures in the countryside, in which the farmers are tied to the collective farms, as there is no alternative employment, without regular pay.

A survey of discussions with villagers, conducted in 1998, revealed a high level of impotence and despair expressed by participants in focus group discussions. Their inability to resolve the 'big issues' such as the tax policies and price disparities which deprive them of income is exacerbated by the widely held belief that all problems can only be resolved by someone higher up.[104]

Current trends in Ukrainian agriculture point to a return to subsistence farming. Household plots produce an increasingly larger share of total agricultural production; 28.5 per cent of urban households have plots of land, compared to 98.9 per cent of rural households. The rural family has on average a plot of 0.53 ha, while the urban family has on

Table 5.5   Agricultural production in Ukraine, 1990–98

Year	Total production (US$ million)	Share of private sector (%)	Share of animal production (%)
1990	44 133	16.5	31.1
1991	35 903	20.5	35.2
1992	34 175	25.7	32.2
1993	35 427	27.0	27.6
1994	29 339	30.0	31.9
1995	28 727	32.2	28.9
1996	21 283	49.2	35.3
1997	19 335	45.0	34.3
1998	17 343	49.3	36.2

Source: Ukrainian Economic Trends, March 1999, p. 8.

Table 5.6   Household plots as a percentage of total Ukrainian production volume for selected agricultural commodities, 1980–97

	1980	1985	1990	1995	1997
Potatoes	75	67	71	96	97
Vegetables	27	25	27	73	82
Meat	34	33	29	52	65
Milk	27	26	24	45	61
Eggs	41	37	38	56	63

Source: Van Atta (1998), Table 25.

average a plot of 0.13 ha. In January 1998, about 20 million Ukrainians had a plot of land. 11.9 per cent of arable land was in private hands, and 1.8 per cent of total arable land was cultivated by private farms.[105] Urban families secured the bulk of their consumption of potatoes from their private plots, half of vegetables and fruits, more than a quarter of eggs, roughly one-sixth of meat and one-eight of milk.[106]

The country is literally surviving on small private vegetable gardens.[107] Half of the country's food is produced by private citizens.[108] Private land plots occupied 11.6 per cent of arable land in 1998, but produced 82 per cent of vegetables, 97 per cent of potatoes, 70 per cent of fruits and 65 per cent of meat (Tables 5.5 and 5.6).

The disintegration of public services

In modern economies, the state takes care of a large number of public services: education, scientific infrastructure, health services, transport and communication infrastructure, etc. The maintenance and development of these services is not only crucial for the reproduction of society but for the economy as well.

The rapid deterioration of its public service network has been one of the most important structural changes in the Ukrainian economy during the 1990s. The negative impact of this deterioration upon economic development is already being felt but there will also be major consequences in the medium and long term.

With respect to spending money in the public sector, inefficiencies are again conspicuous. The crisis in the health sector is not only related to declining spending in absolute terms, but also to the absence of restructuring. At first sight, the statistics for Ukraine look very good: per trained assistant (nurses, laboratory technicians, medical assistants, etc.) there are 95 patients in Ukraine, whereas the equivalent figures for the UK and USA are 715 and 435 patients, respectively. There are 12 hospital beds for every 1000 Ukrainians, whereas international best practice is about 2 beds per 1000 people. Ukraine has 4.5 doctors per 1000 people, compared to 2.0 in Germany, 1.6 in Sweden and 1.3 in Poland.[109] Despite these statistics, the health of the population is deteriorating, as is the situation in hospitals. If patients are hospitalized, they have to bring bandages, medicines, food and linen for themselves. Despite the large number of medical personnel, medical care is at a very low level and deteriorating; this is reflected in health statistics. Despite worsening circumstances, huge resources are wasted due to numerous inefficiencies. One of the inefficiencies is the lack of energy efficiency, leading to energy bills that consume 20–30 per cent of hospital budgets.

Education is also faced with the inefficient use of resources. It is telling that the cost per child in kindergarten is higher than in vocational and higher education. Again, there is low energy efficiency in schools. Instead of focusing on primary and secondary education, the policy remained at transferring high per capita sums in vocational, preschool and higher education.[110] The pupil to teacher ratio of 13.5 is still substantially below the OECD average of 17. Moreover, the 0.5 ratio of teaching personnel to non-teachers is far below international standards.[111] Salaries of teachers and lecturers are not enough to survive, if they are paid at all. They have to resort to additional sources of income.

Most housing in Ukraine is public property. Because no repairs have been carried out for many years, the housing stock in Ukraine is decaying rapidly. What will be the economic cost of rebuilding Ukrainian towns?

Public transport companies do not get any compensation for the 60 per cent of all passengers who are entitled to free transport.[111] This has contributed to the lack of investment funds. As a result, transport equipment has diminished and deteriorated.

Expenses for public investment fell from 4.6 per cent of GDP in 1994 to 0.27 per cent in 1997.[112] In 1998 this item disappeared from the budget altogether.[113] Generally, in the process of reducing expenses for public investments, this is happening without underlying policy objectives. For example, instead of focusing on priority investment projects, all projects are cut, resulting in a high number of unfinished investment projects.

The extended public services network that developed in Soviet times and which used to be very cheap or free of charge, is in the process of disintegration. This especially affects poorer people, i.e. the majority of the population. The extended public service sector can be seen as the accumulated wealth of several generations that constitutes an infrastructure for the creation of wealth for future generations. This has been broken down in a historically very short period.

When calculating the extent of the economic crisis in Ukraine, economists and politicians mostly look at the development of the purchasing power of people's salaries, which has declined dramatically in Ukraine, to industrial decline or decline of Gross National Product. They usually do not consider the above described disintegration of the extended network of public services from which all Ukrainians used to profit.

Human capital is considered to be one of the major assets of the Ukrainian economy. But how to further this capital as the educational system is broken down? What will be the economic costs of a dilapidated health sector? The weak transport and communication infrastructure is already one of the major factors cited by foreign investors as an obstacle to investment. How long will trains, trams and buses run without any significant investment? What will happen if people can no longer afford to go from their suburbs to the factories because there is no reliable and cheap transport? What will happen if the energy distribution network breaks down?

Conclusion

The economic structure of Ukraine was fundamentally transformed during the 1990s, mainly as a result of differential production decline and not the outcome of deliberate government policies. The share of high value added activities in total production declined while value-subtracting industries, such as steel and coal, increased their share of total production.

The high value added enterprises that performed the best in Soviet times, those belonging to the Military Industrial Complex, are prevented from restructuring and are in most cases designated as strategic enterprises, not subject to privatization.

Heavy metallurgy did relatively well during the 1990s and enhanced its share of total industrial production, as a result of increased exports. However, most of the production is value-subtracting and exports loss making. The energy sector also did relatively well, considerably enhancing its share of output. This is partly related to the inelasticity in demand. The coal sector is, as a whole, loss-making, while nuclear power stations lack the money for even the most urgent maintenance works.

The agro-industrial sector, in principle one of the most promising sectors, is strangled by a semi-feudal production organization. Agricultural production is shifting from pseudo-modern to pre-modern production methods.

Public services have been one of the main victims of 'transition'. As in other sectors, there has been no strategic adjustment in public services.

6
Structural Change in the Economy II: The Micro-level

Restructuring at the enterprise level

In contradistinction with most large enterprises in the developed market economies (Japan is a case apart), enterprises in Ukraine fulfil functions that elsewhere are fulfilled by municipalities. This means that they manage the whole infrastructure of the part of town that they own. For example, Zaporozhstal, the main steel producer in Zaporizhzhya, an industrial centre in Eastern Ukraine, has a network of health care facilities, educational establishments, guest houses, kindergartens, apartments, cultural facilities, sport clubs and holiday centres. Zaporozhstal also has two kolchozes, mainly, but not totally, producing for its employees. It even has a meat factory within the steel factory. Often, these secondary services are more important for the employees than the salary.

The factory can often negotiate in the provision of scarce goods, and also has shops that are open to the general public. For example, Zaporozhstal provides about 15 per cent of all goods traded in retail trade in Zaporizhzhya. Moreover there are additional products, that often have nothing to do with the main product and which are sold to the wider public. Under party leader Gorbachev the production of supplementary consumer goods was stimulated, because these goods were scarce. When, in Perestroika times, distribution systems began to disintegrate, enterprises tried to create autarchic production and distribution networks on a local and regional basis. It was, more or less, a reconstruction of a system of planning from below. Also, for many enterprises, the above mentioned sideline production became more important as the demand for mainline products declined sharply.

All this means that Zaporozhstal has many more employees than a comparable enterprise in the West that produces the same amount of mainstream products. The lower labour productivity of the Zaporozhstal workers should also be taken into account when explaining the high level of employment.

Of course, in the new economic conditions, the above described organizational structure of large enterprises is an obstacle to privatization and restructuring, although there is a trend of economizing on the social activities. However, there is no organizational restructuring of the sideline activities. Sometimes, they are made independent. There is a strong resistance to specialize and to outsource. In the new situation one can see non-specialization as a form of insurance against the uncertainties and costs of transactions.

The Ukrainian government has made a decision to transfer the social sphere of enterprises to the local administration.

The social sphere has become an increasing burden. Also, a greater number of non-employees have made greater use of these services, such as housing, often without payment.

Hindrances to restructuring also have deeper, socio-political roots. The enterprise's organization is done along hierarchical lines, with the enterprise director acting like a patriarch (the 'red director'). Semifeudal relations can be found that revert to pre-revolutionary Russia and Ukraine. It is also in this context that dismissal of personnel is quite difficult for a lot of enterprises.

The above description of Zaporozhstal, a typical Ukrainian state-owned enterprise, demonstrates the deficiencies of a typical mainstream economic analysis of Ukrainian enterprises and the need for a comprehensive socio-economic approach to the restructuring of big enterprises.

Ukrainian state-owned enterprises still exhibit many characteristics of Soviet enterprises. The Soviet enterprise historically performed a number of key functions that in capitalist societies, the market, municipal governments, trade unions, voluntary societies and other civil social institutions have typically fulfilled. The Soviet factory served as the 'melting pot' and community organizer for the largely peasant workforce. The Soviet factory encompassed a system of paternalism in which the workers were completely dependent on the enterprise management. However, due to structural labour shortage, workers also had leverage. Nowadays, the balance of power has shifted to management because there is a surplus of labour.

The Soviet enterprise was almost as different from the capitalist enterprise as was a feudal estate from a capitalist farm. Like the feudal estate, the Soviet enterprise was not simply an economic institution but the primary unit of Soviet society, and the ultimate base of social and political power.[1] The task of the enterprise administration was not to secure the expanded reproduction of capital, but the expanded reproduction of the labour collective. Clarke pointed to weaknesses of many Western analyses:

> ...they are based on the argument that the economic irrationality of managerial behavior can be understood as a rational response to an irrational system. While such analyses provide useful insights, the narrowly economistic conception of rationality that they deploy limits their ability to understand the dynamics of the system in change, for it implies that the liberation of management from political constraint would immediately lead to the spontaneous emergence of capitalist rationality as the enterprise sheds all the impediments of Soviet life.[2]

An important feature of Ukrainian enterprises, both state and private, is that they do not fire employees in cases of declining production, but put them on unpaid leave or simply not pay them while letting them work. They do this for several reasons:[3]

1. Employers avoid paying severance pay. Under the Ukrainian Employment Law, employers must pay three months of severance pay to any workers released by them for economic or organizational reasons. 'Administrative leave' also pushes workers to leave voluntarily, so that no severance pay is required.
2. The system of 'unpaid leave' allows employers to pay remaining employees more, while avoiding the rise of the nominal average wage. With a rise of the average wage, taxation rate on wage taxes becomes higher. With 'unpaid leave' wage tax penalties are avoided.
3. From the viewpoint of the worker, it is preferable to be on unpaid leave than to become unemployed because there is still a possibility of re-employment and access to some enterprise benefits, such as health care and housing, is maintained.

As far as state-owned enterprises have been privatized, this has had little effect on enterprise governance, as numerous studies show.[4] Pryor and Blackman (1998) did not find in their enterprise surveys any difference between public and private firms as far as enterprise behaviour was concerned. They explain this by the fact that ownership in privatized firms may be too diffuse to allow new owners to push for changes in firm operations. Moreover, both public and privatized firms face an extensive system of governmental regulations and licensing, which appear to interfere with the ability of enterprises of any ownership to recognize and use the signals that the market provides.[5] Another survey of 150 enterprises in 1997 did not find any difference between enterprise performance of private and state-owned enterprises, but did find some quatitative restructuring in cases of insider ownership, notably with respect to products and inputs.[6] The bulk (85 per cent) of the shares were given to incumbent managers and workers through preferred share allocations during the closed subscription phase.[6] As a result, relatively little has changed in the operation of most privatized enterprises. There was no impetus for enterprise management to change their behaviour.

Although former state-owned enterprises are faced with gradual hardening of budget controls, these are often too soft to lead to bankruptcies. This is not only related to the fact that enterprises are protected by hidden subsidies in the form of cheap loans, tax exemptions and payment arrears with their suppliers, but also to the fact that internal adjustment takes place by non-payment of workers.

Adjustment also took place by smaller inventories. Investments were postponed by lack of funds. Pressure of government to pay taxes and government interference in the finances of the enterprise, for instance by taking hold of bank accounts, led enterprises to resort to barter trade, which has become increasingly important.

Although accounting practices have been improved since the abolition of the centrally planned economy, by the late 1990s accounting practices were still rather primitive and lacked transparency. For most large enterprises it is not clear what the actual cost structure is and what the profit margin is. Taxation practices of government strengthen the aversion towards transparency in matters of accountancy.

Marketing problems and attitudes towards marketing led to many difficulties. Roughly 53 per cent of firms surveyed by Pryor and Blackman (autumn 1996) lacked separate marketing departments. If there was a marketing department, the average number of workers was 5.6. This is low given the fact that the average surveyed firm had 707 employees. Often, the marketing department functioned as a Soviet-type sales department.

Pryor and Blackman found that the average length of employment of top managers was 9.5 years. Many top managers were leftovers from

the Soviet period. Many complained that the government was not supplying them with the necessary credits.

New products constituted on average approximately one-quarter of
sales. However, only one-fifth of the firms had instituted new incentive
schemes and considerably less than that had reorganized their labour
force.[7]

Often, privatization of state-owned enterprises just meant painting
the signboard of a firm in a different colour. The relationship with the
state, suppliers and customers hardly changed as did the social networks in which the old managers operated. Usually, after privatization,
the asset stripping behaviour of managers did not stop. Also, the rent-
seeking behaviour of the state with respect to privatized firms hardly
changed.[8] Property rights are still not well defined and private firms are
at the mercy of a predatory bureaucracy.

A survey in Donetsk (Lyakh and Pankow, 1998) characterized the
way of thinking of enterprise managers as 'the syndrome of being cap-
tivated by the past'. They think that difficulties faced by their enterprises are connected with causes that lie beyond their influence and
control. 'Results of the incoherence and contradictions in managerial
reasoning are reflected in equally incoherent organizational and institutional solutions.' Instead of simplification of organizational structures, they were made more complex. The researchers observed features
of 'market-oriented thinking' with interviewed managers. These features were, however, not reflected in their behaviour. The actions of
managers often contradicted their claimed adherence to market principles. The authors write about the 'declared domination (and even the
declaimed one) of economic rationality over the realised one' (Lyakh
and Pankow, 1998, p. 79). Directors of Donetsk enterprises treat the
problems associated with the dissolution of markets in the former
Soviet Union as temporary. It is a kind of 'non-returned love'. Market
strategies are adaptive rather than inventive. They are a passive answer
to the threats coming from the market.

Enterprises often maintain numerous assets that have nothing to do
with the core activity of the firm, like collective farms. Although property assets, especially the social ones, are a great burden for the enterprise, the directors cannot refrain expressing their delight about their
size. The directors in Donetsk present their firm as a kind of cultural,
educational and recreational institution, while the production functions are pushed into the background. 'It is difficult for the directors to
get rid of these material evidence of their past power and influence. It
is equally difficult for them to give up their illusions among which the

hope for the come back of old good times of mass production' (Lyakh and Pankow, 1998, p. 80). Only in some cases surveyed enterprises in Donetsk sold above mentioned properties. In rich enterprises there was a tendency to increase the amount of property. It is the reflection of an 'imperialist complex'. The few relatively well-to-do firms also increased employment although neither production level nor sales volume justified this. This was partly related to pressure from local authorities.

Bankruptcy laws in Ukraine are weak. The Law on Bankruptcy was adopted in May 1992. There has been little enforcement so far, mainly because of the cost and complexity of procedures.[9] During the second half of 1996 the National Bank of Ukraine approved regulations that gave commercial banks the power to seize hard currency assets from debtors if they do not settle their debts (in domestic currency) within a specific time. However, inter-enterprise arrears have continued to grow. The shortage of liquidity in the economy is also reflected in the growth of payment arrears to power utilities and in the growth of wage arrears in the economy, estimated at 6.5 billion hryvnas at the end of 1999.[10]

A detailed study of arrears in Ukraine was undertaken on behalf of the National Bank of Ukraine in 1998. The study revealed the high degree of circularity of arrears in Ukraine, which accounts for well over 80 per cent of total arrears. Thus a very large part of gross arrears moves along a chain of enterprises (where enterprise A owes enterprise B, which owes enterprise C, which owes A) without revealing important net debtors financed by net creditors.[11] More than a quarter of all invoices are not settled with domestic money and enter an informal chain of clearing. It is likely that inter-enterprise arrears play the role of a trade credit which, however, is never settled and accumulates ad infinitum, without hindering the transactions of enterprises.

Apart from inter-enterprise arrears, enterprises can use direct state subsidies and delayed tax payments to avoid liquidation.

It appears that macroeconomic stabilization and formal privatization in Ukraine have not led to substantial structural reform and more efficient production, which was the intended outcome of privatization and macro-economic stabilization. Privatization has not led to the imposition of capital constraints. The law of value did not come into operation.

There has been no clear commitment on the part of government that market economy principles should guide the restructuring process. Also, after the advent of President Kuchma to power in 1994, state investment programmes continued to be defined for many sectors.[12] Examples are the automobile industry, copper and nickel mining, packaging, steel, non-ferrous metallurgy, plane and ship building and the agro-industrial complex. Hirschhausen showed that state planning is present almost everywhere in industry, reason enough for him to depict the current transition as one from non-monetary socialism to a monetary planned economy.[13]

The fact that enterprises usually did not restructure according to economic principles does not mean that there was no change at all. Internal organisation of production has indeed radically changed in almost all enterprises: the product mix, production techniques (usually from mass production to individual production), upstream and downstream relations with suppliers and clients and the number of personnel. Also, from 1997 onwards, the fall in industrial employment was steeper than the decline in industrial output, pointing to a more efficient use of labour resources.

What usually did not happen was the reorganization of production according to efficiency criteria.

In the sphere of state-owned companies and sectors, government actually hampered restructuring taking place, under the guise of state restructuring. State-owned enterprises found themselves actually without a real owner. They did not get any guidance from their branch ministry. On the other hand, they did not have any financial freedom. In most cases, corporatization of state-owned enterprises, i.e. being financially independent and having their own book-keeping, did not take place. Strategic state-owned enterprises were not allowed to downscale or to outsource.

The case of Avtozaz

Avtozaz was founded in 1961 in order to produce cheap cars for the whole of the Soviet Union and was a monopolist in this category. Other car factories, like the Lada factory in Togliatti, received priority treatment. With the independence of Ukraine in 1991, Avtozaz, located in Zaporizhzhya, became the only manufacturer of cars in Ukraine. Up to 1991 annual growth was in the range of 14–15 per cent and the capacity in 1993 was 300 000 cars a year.

In 1992 the Ukrainian government was still ambitious and optimistic and saw a brilliant future for the national car industry. A national car manufacturing plan was presented. A lot of money was channelled to Avtozaz and in 1992 a new assembly line was installed with Western machinery. However, in 1996 only 7000 cars were produced. From early December 1996 until May 1998 production was suspended. The 20 000 personnel were sent home on unpaid leave.

Table 6.1 Car production by Avtozaz, 1991–96

Year	1991	1992	1993	1994	1995	1996
Number of cars produced	156 000	13 5000	140 000	94 000	57 000	7000

Source: Business Central Europe, March 1991.

Decline of production was delayed until relatively late, in 1993, due to the fact that many people were on waiting lists for cars and there was still a shortage of cars. In August 1993 there were plans to expand production of cars up to 550 000 by the year 2000.

At the same time the import of cars has increased tremendously. In 1994, Ukraine imported 160 000 cars, and during the first nine months of 1995 200 000 cars were imported. Import tax was only paid on 15 per cent of these cars. From 1 January 1996 import tariffs for cars from outside the former Soviet Union were raised sharply, in order to protect Avtozaz.

The enterprise leadership blamed external factors for the decline. They mentioned high taxes as a reason. However, government and parliament repeatedly helped Avtozaz. For example, the parliament decided in November 1995 that Avtozaz did not have to pay any taxes for 1994. In May 1996, import duties for products destined for Avtozaz were slashed.

Apart from high taxes, supplies from Russia have been mentioned as a major problem. Eighty per cent of car parts, in value terms, came from Russia. Many of these parts were too expensive and could be obtained cheaper in Central and Western Europe. Often Avtozaz stuck to Russian suppliers because they accepted Avtozaz cars in return for payment. Another problem was that some Russian suppliers came to see Avtozaz as a competitor and stopped deliveries.

The gradual deterioration of supplies, that had already started during the Perestroika years, negatively affected the quality of the cars produced by Avtozaz, because the substitute supplies, or spare parts, were often of worse quality. In particular the quality of the engine delivered by the factory in Melitopol (Zaporizhzhya province) deteriorated.

Supplies gradually became more expensive. In early 1993, production costs for a car were US$3000. Later that year production costs increased to US$3700, while in August 1996 costs amounted to US$4800.

A factor in rising costs was the very high material and energy intensity of production. Because costs of energy and raw materials increased after independence, this was reflected in production costs.

The developing financial crisis at Avtozaz made the factory a bad client for its suppliers. Often supplies were not paid for and suppliers began to ask for payment in advance. Whereas in Soviet times there was never any disruption in production due to non-delivery of supplies, since independence this has occurred more frequently.

People in the street, the potential consumers, complained about the poor quality of the Tavria, the car produced by Avtozaz. The Tavria is notorious for continuously breaking down. It is much cheaper to buy a second-hand Western car than to buy a Tavria.

The basic problem at Avtozaz – the way in which production is organized – has never been mentioned in the Ukrainian press. An example is quality control. Although a quality control system existed on paper, it did not function in practice. For example, car parts were often unavailable. In Western car factories, production would stop immediately. Not in Zaporizhzhya. There production continued and workers were asked to write down what elements of the car were missing. However, workers often forgot to do this. The result was that cars were delivered with elements missing, often quite essential ones. A worker in Avtozaz told how he was asked to drive an approved car to the parking area in order to be shipped. After having switched the engine on, he found that the steering wheel was not fixed and came off in his hand.

In Zaporizhzhya it was often young girls, 18 to 20 years old, that worked on the assembly line. They were not strong enough to perform some of the tasks, resulting in poor performance. Employees told how, usually, other employees exhibited a lack of responsibility. They were not at all interested in good performance. The only thing that counted was quantity, not quality.

A big problem in the factory was alcoholism. According to estimates from several informers within the factory, most male workers were drinking in the workplace. Obviously this has a very negative impact upon work performance. A journalist from the Wall Street Journal hinted at low labour intensity when writing in 1989 that 'for every worker on the line, there are several who sit on a wooden bench nearby, watching, chatting and smoking cigarettes'. All this means that the facade of modern production hid fairly primitive production methods.

It is remarkable that, since 1993, when the production decline at Avtozaz began, there was no organizational restructuring. No personnel were dismissed, and the total workforce at the end of 1995 was 28 855, significantly more than in 1990, producing 60 000 cars. By comparison, the Nissan car factory in Sunderland, UK, produced 21 800 cars with 3500 workers in 1992.[15] In 1998 the output in

Sunderland was 105 cars per employee, the highest in Europe.[16] No organizational changes have been introduced in Avtozaz in order to enhance the quality of production.

Up to early 1996, there was a big problem with spare parts disappearing on the black market. Only since then, when production of cars was stopped, everything is being done, according to the enterprise director, to satisfy the demand for spare parts.

Before 1996, the marketing of cars in the former Soviet Union was done informally and, less important, through car centres (25 in Ukraine and 68 in Russia), while nowadays every buyer has the same rights and the same price.

In mid-1996, after the former director had been dismissed and the factory had already been idle for half a year, the enterprise leadership started by separating the cultural sphere, the hospital and agricultural sector (4 kolchozes) from the car factory and making the technical service independent. The salary of factory workers halved.

The enterprise management of Avtozaz claims that relatively modern equipment, bought in Japan and Western Europe, is now in place. The Ukrainian press claim that Avtozaz is a very modern factory. However, Coopers and Lybrand found the technological level of equipment to be mediocre in 1993. They concluded that in the long run the factory had no future. Investment funds have been channelled to a new assembly line with Western equipment that was installed in 1992. The rest of the factory is completely outdated. Even the new production line is not modern and is handled manually.

The prospects for Avtozaz seemed to change dramatically in 1997 when a joint venture with Daewoo was founded. The history of this joint venture is described in Chapter 7.

Conclusion

The restructuring of state-owned and privatized enterprises has been hindered by a number of factors. Firstly, there is the peculiar function and organization of enterprises that retained many aspects of typically Soviet enterprises. Also, the absence of economic rationality in enterprise management, flaws in the taxation system, over-regulation by the state and cross-subsidization prevented profound restructuring from taking place.

Although changes have occurred in the production organization of most enterprises this did not happen according to efficiency criteria.

7
Opening Towards the World Economy?

In this chapter Ukraine's introduction into the world economy is analysed. Trade policy, direction and composition of foreign trade, international industrial cooperation, import competition and debt management are analysed.

Trade war with the countries of the former Soviet Union

Ukraine traditionally looked to Moscow, the centre of colonial power, while it was cut off from the rest of the world, for the larger part of its territory and for most of its history.

During Perestroika, many in Moscow and other major Russian centres became better informed about developments in the wider world and many got the opportunity to travel. However, up to September 1989, with the stepping down of ultra-conservative party leader Shcherbytsky, Ukraine remained shielded from Glasnost, and to a certain extent also from Perestroika. Ukraine experienced mainly the negative side of the Gorbachev reforms.

When Ukraine opened up after independence in 1991, it had to develop an institutional framework for guiding international economic relations from scratch.

After Ukrainian independence, trade with the other states of the former Soviet Union was severely disrupted because all these states changed over to denomination in convertible currencies and world market prices (Figure 7.1). All ex-Soviet republics preferred to buy high quality goods on the world market rather than using scarce convertible currencies for buying low quality goods in the other republics of the former Soviet Union. Ukrainian imports from the former Soviet Union

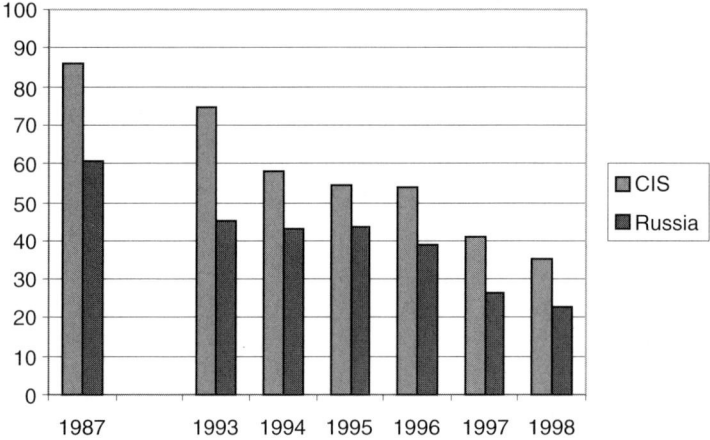

Figure 7.1 Shares of Russia and CIS in Ukrainian exports in value terms, 1987–98 (per cent)

declined, in value terms, by 34 per cent in 1992 compared to 1991, while exports to the region declined by 27 per cent.[1] In 1992, it also became apparent to what extent Ukrainian trade with Russia and Turkmenistan, which accounted for the bulk of trade with the former Soviet Union, was subsidized, first of all by delivering fuels at far below the world market price (15 per cent of the world market price).[2] According to the International Monetary Fund, Ukraine received 22 per cent of its GDP in 1992 in subsidized Russian credits.[3] This ran counter to popular beliefs that Ukraine was subsidizing the rest of the former Soviet Union (see also Chapter 2). In 1992 the balance of trade with the former Soviet Union was minus 126 million karbovanets, while the balance with the rest of the world was plus 223 million karbovanets.[4]

During 1991–94 the terms of trade of Ukraine deteriorated by 70 per cent, mainly due to rising prices of energy imports and lower receipts for Ukrainian exports. The extent of this deterioration is highlighted by the terms of trade deterioration of Western energy importers during the oil crisis: Germany's terms of trade deteriorated by 12 per cent during 1972–74 and by 13 per cent during 1978–80.[5]

According to Gregory and Stuart, the estimated initial impact of the terms-of-trade change on GDP was –2.6 per cent (for inter-republican trade –6.4 per cent and for extra-republican trade +3.8 per cent).[6]

Numerous barriers to trade with the countries of the former Soviet Union have gradually appeared, despite commitments to break down trade barriers. On the part of the Ukrainian government there was, in the period immediately after independence, a deliberate policy to discourage trade with the former Soviet Union.

The key principles of national protectionism were proclaimed by President Kravchuk at a closed session of parliament on 24 March 1992. New measures included a hard currency-only trade regime with the former Soviet republics, a tariff on imports from them, the introduction of VAT on exports to them and customs posts were established at all borders, especially with Russia.

In 1993, a free trade zone was announced within the Community of Independent States. However, since then, trade barriers have mounted. At the end of 1996 President Kuchma spoke about economic warfare after Russia announced the levying of a 20 per cent tax on imports from Ukraine. Ukraine subsequently did the same with respect to imports from Russia. As a result of a visit by President Yeltsin to Kyiv, in November 1997, it was announced that from 1 February 1998 onwards, VAT on imports from Russia would be abolished, if Russia would do the same for Ukrainian goods. However, from late 1998 onwards there were reports that Russia had not implemented the free trade agreement.

Table 7.1   Foreign trade, exports, imports of goods and services and overall balance, 1992–98 (US$ billion, current prices)

	1992	1994	1995	1996	1997	1998	1999
Total							
Total exports	12.1	16.6	17.1	20.3	20.4	17.6	15.7
Total imports	11.1	18.0	18.3	21.5	21.9	18.8	13.9
Overall balance	1.0	−1.4	−1.2	−1.1	−1.5	−1.2	−1.8
Former Soviet Union							
Total exports	8.9	9.4	9.5	12.3	10.3	7.7	6.0
Total imports	10.2	11.9	11.6	13.5	12.8	10.2	7.9
Overall balance	−1.3	−2.5	−2.4	−1.2	−2.5	−2.4	−1.9
Rest of the world							
Total exports	3.2	7.2	7.6	8.0	10.1	9.9	9.6
Total imports	0.9	6.1	6.6	7.9	9.1	8.7	6.0
Overall balance	2.2	1.1	0.9	0.1	1.0	1.2	3.6

Source: Ukrainian Economic Trends, December 1999, for 1992; Shen (1996) p. 139; figures for 1999 estimated based on first nine months of the year.

A recurrent theme in Russian–Ukrainian relations was the repayment of the mounting debts Ukraine had with Russia. The Ukrainian debt to Russian Gazprom amounted to US$2.2 billion in February 2000, while the total trade debt with Russia was US$3.58 billion in February 2000.[7] Russian oil and gas supplies to Ukraine have been cut several times, in an attempt to force Ukraine to pay debt arrears.

As a result of the financial crisis in Russia in August 1998, trade turnover with Russia fell by 22.5 per cent in 1998. There was a further substantial decline in 1999 (Table 7.1).

Mismanaged opening up

The opening up to the world market can be divided into two phases. The period 1991–94 was characterized by very slow liberalization, and in 1993/94 a Soviet-style foreign trade system with export quotas and licences was introduced. In February 1993 the decision was taken that 50 per cent of foreign currency earnings should be converted into local currency against the unfavourable official rate.[8] The result was that many enterprises started to accumulate foreign currencies in foreign bank accounts, and more than half of export earnings went unreported. A high official said, 'There are between 6 to 8 billion dollars in the country. But there are between 15 to 18 billion dollars abroad in foreign banks. Nobody keeps hard currency here in local banks'.[9] In January 1994 about 90 per cent of exports were administered by quotas and licences.[10] Export taxes ranged from 20 to 75 per cent, with most exportable products subject to rates between 35 and 50 per cent.[11] Private exporters reported that they spent half of their time chasing licences.[12] On the one hand enterprises gained the right to conduct foreign trade themselves, on the other hand numerous obstacles to foreign trade were created. Trade monopolies were created by a web of licences and quotas that controlled trade and access to hard currency. A holding company, called simply 'Ukraine', owned the licence to handle 60–70 per cent of the country's metal exports.

Only in late 1994/early 1995, under pressure from the International Monetary Fund, was there a liberalization of the trade and payments system. Export controls were removed.[13] The result was that a smaller share of foreign trade was conducted illegally. However, since this time Ukraine has continued its practice of continuously changing foreign trade regulations and creating legal inconsistencies.

While in the developed market economies a web of institutions emerged, such as chambers of commerce and banks, promoting foreign economic relations, such an infrastructure is still missing in Ukraine. State institutions even hamper exports. Provincial authorities ban exports of specific agricultural products. A textile manufacturer re-exporting to Western Europe stated that, 'De facto the Ukrainian foreign trade ministry does everything to prevent exports rather than to encourage them'.[14] Regulations for issuing export licences are interpreted too narrowly. For example, the import quota for Ukrainian knitwear to the European Union is set at 1.2 million items per annum. To avoid surpassing the quota, an export licence must be obtained through the Ukrainian foreign trade ministry prior to all exports to the EU. However, in some sub-sectors the quota has been utilized by between 70 and 80 per cent and in others by a mere 15–20 per cent.[15] Nevertheless, the Ukrainian ministry of foreign trade continues its restrictive licencing policy. This is very odd as the EU closely monitors textile exports from Ukraine. The ministry harms the Ukrainian interest. Also, it takes around three weeks to get an export licence, while in rival countries it can be a matter of a few hours.

There has been a steady increase in exports from 1992 to 1996 (Table 7.1). From 1997 onwards exports began to fall. During the first half of 1999, foreign trade was 24.6 per cent down compared to the first half of 1998.[16]

Trade with the 'rest of the world', that is trade with the countries outside the former Soviet Union, has increased sharply since 1992, but slowed down in 1994 and then declined from 1998 onwards. The growth until 1995 is related to the gradual liberalization of foreign trade with the West. However, Ukraine is still a dwarf in the world trade system (Table 7.2). Ukraine, with 50 million inhabitants, had exports valued at US$13.7 billion dollars in 1998. The Czech Republic, with only 10.3 million inhabitants, had exports valued at US$26.4 billion while the value for Denmark, with 5.3 million inhabitants, was US$47 billion (1998).[17]

Ukrainian exports are higher than Ukrainian statistics suggest. Comparable statistics from EU countries show that in 1993 the EU imported 1.76 times more from Ukraine than Ukrainian statistics indicated. In the same year, EU exports to Ukraine were 1.83 times more than Ukrainian statistics indicated.[18] In 1992 only 30 per cent of German exports to Ukraine and only 45 per cent of German imports from Ukraine could be traced in Ukrainian statistics.[19] The mirror statistics from partner countries do not include the coach and carloads of

Table 7.2 Exports and GDP per head of Ukraine compared with other countries (1998, US$)

	Merchandise exports	GDP per capita
Slovenia	4560	9760
Czech Republic	2636	5040
Estonia	3208	3390
Slovakia	2131	3700
Hungary	2294	4510
Lithuania	939	2440
Latvia	906	2430
Poland	674	3900
Bulgaria	534	1230
Russia	503	2300
Belarus	702	2200
Romania	377	1390
Kazakstan	338	1310
Ukraine	**256**	**850**
Moldova	170	410
Uzbekistan	164	870

Source: Based on World Bank (1999).

products imported by the numerous small traders crossing Ukrainian borders.

Since 1994, progress has been made in reducing illegal trade and reporting foreign trade. However, mirror statistics show that Ukrainian data still tend to underestimate the volume of trade flows. The size of this underestimation is by far higher for Ukraine's imports from Europe than for exports. In 1996, Ukrainian customs data on the country's exports to the EU were 6.5 per cent lower, whereas imports were underestimated by as much as 14.3 per cent. The degree of undervaluation in a country-by-country breakdown ranged in 1996 from 3.6 per cent to almost three times on exports and from 3.7 per cent to 2.6 times on imports.[20]

Capital flight has reached enormous proportions. A government agency estimated that in the period 1991–95, US$15–20 billion were illegally exported. In November 1998, President Kuchma blamed the National Bank for failing to prevent massive capital flight.[21]

During 1998 the major suppliers to Ukraine were Russia (49.3 per cent), Germany (6.9 per cent), Belarus (2.8 per cent) and the USA (2.7 per cent).[22]

Table 7.3   Ukraine's main trading partners (1987–98) (country and region percentage shares in merchandise exports and imports)

	1987	1993	1994	1995	1996	1997	1998
Exports to:							
European Union-15			9.0	11.7	10.9	12.1	16.9
Former Soviet Union	86.2	74.8	57.8	54.3	54.1	40.8	35.1
Russia	60.7	45.2	43.1	43.3	38.7	26.2	23.0
CEFTA*			5.5	6.9	7.4	9.4	9.4
Imports from:							
European Union-15			13.3	19.1	14.1	20.4	22.7
Former Soviet Union	71.7	89.3	76.3	67.3	67.8	60.4	56.4
Russia	53.7	62.8	60.6	52.9	48.0	46.7	48.1
CEFTA*			4.4	8.3	6.0	9.5	9.9

*CEFTA stands for Central European Free Trade Zone and comprises Poland, the Czech Republic, Slovakia, Hungary, Slovenia (since 1995) and Romania (since 1997).
Source: Ukrainian Economic Trends, March 1999, p. 72; Boss (1993) for 1987 data.

Ukrainian exports mainly go to Russia (22.7 per cent), China (6 per cent), Turkey (5.6 per cent), Germany (5.1 per cent), Belarus (4.5 per cent), USA (3.9 per cent) and Poland (2.5 per cent) (first 11 months of 1998).[23]

Although trade with the countries of the former Soviet Union has declined sharply, it is still the major trading bloc, with 35 per cent of exports and 56 per cent of imports in 1998 (Table 7.3). The relations with this trade bloc are very vulnerable. With respect to imports, mounting debts create increasing supply problems while lack of convertible currency pushes Ukraine increasingly towards barter deals. The products Ukraine currently delivers to the former Soviet bloc can easily be delivered by other trade partners.

Commodity composition of exports and imports: continuous deterioration

In 1990, 46 per cent of Ukrainian exports consisted of machinery, 21 per cent ferrous metals, 7.5 per cent chemicals and 7.0 per cent food products. Since independence, this export structure has deteriorated. In 1998, 39 per cent of exports consisted of ferrous and non-ferrous metals and 13 per cent of chemicals (Figure 7.2). Machinery and equipment

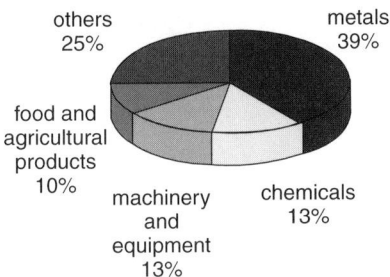

Figure 7.2 Commodity composition of Ukrainian exports, 1998

only accounted for 13 per cent of exports. Most of the metals exported are dumped on the world market. Ukrainian manufacturers can only compete by not paying the full energy bill. Stopping exports of value-subtracting enterprises would mean a sharp fall in exports.

The main reason for the deterioration of the export structure is the fact that since the demise of the centrally planned economy and the Soviet Union, the non-competitiveness of high value added production has become apparent.

Exports of food and agricultural products have declined sharply, from US$3045 million in 1996 to US$1379 million in 1998. Whereas agricultural and food exports accounted for 28 per cent of total exports in 1992, this figure was only 10 per cent in 1998.[24] Exports of iron and steel have gradually increased, from US$3802 million in 1995 to US$5453 million in 1997. However, there was a sharp drop to US$4797 million in 1998 (based on the first nine months), due to lower world market prices and the crisis in Asia.

Military equipment has become an important export product and Ukraine has become the 20th largest arms exporter in the world.[25] Arms exports are mainly to developing countries like Turkey, Iran and Pakistan. Ukraine's major state arms trader, Ukrspetsexport, sold weapons and maintenance services worth US$300 million in 1998, up from US$237 million in 1997. Contracts for modernization of obsolete Soviet-made arms purchased in previous years accounted for about 30 per cent of the company's total contracts in 1998.[26] The increase in arms exports is not so much related to the competitiveness of Ukrainian arms producers but rather to the sale of army stocks.[27]

Services account for an important share of export earnings. At its height in 1996, the service surplus covered almost three-quarters of Ukraine's US$4.3 billion commodity trade deficit. By 1998, however,

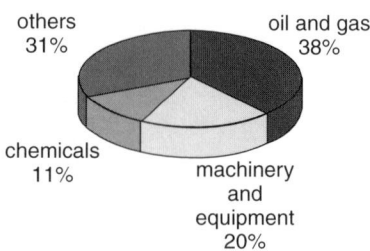

others
31%

oil and gas
38%

chemicals
11%

machinery
and
equipment
20%

Figure 7.3   Commodity composition of Ukrainian imports, 1998

the service surplus had fallen by almost 60 per cent in dollar terms from its 1996 peak, largely as a result of a 30 per cent drop in transit charged for Russian gas.[28] Russia's Gazprom has announced a fall of two-thirds in natural gas transit through Ukraine, related to non-authorized siphoning off of gas by Ukraine. This implies that transit earnings, which amounted to approximately 44 per cent of Ukrainian gas consumption, will be cut commensurably.[29]

More than half of all Ukrainian exports originate from South-Eastern Ukraine, where most heavy industry is located.

Also, the commodity pattern of imports has become very vulnerable. While in 1990, 21 per cent of Ukrainian imports consisted of oil and gas, in 1998 this amounted to 38 per cent (Figure 7.3). While machinery and equipment accounted for 38 per cent of total imports in 1990, this was only 20 per cent in 1998.

The share of chemicals increased from 6.9 per cent in 1996 to 11 per cent in 1998. The share of food and agricultural products decreased from 18.0 per cent in 1992 to 7.0 per cent in 1996 to 6.6 per cent in 1998. The agro-food trade surplus of Ukraine diminished from US$1.6 billion in 1996 to US$0.3 billion in 1998.[30]

Despite the minor role of Ukraine in international trade and low foreign trade turnover compared to countries of comparable size, the import dependence of Ukraine is very high. The ratio of imports of goods and services to GDP amounts to almost 55 per cent. Also, there is a large share of imports in the production costs of Ukraine's main exportable products (steel and chemicals).

Import and import competition

Despite the relatively low level of foreign trade per capita, import competition has contributed significantly to the collapse of domestic producers of Ukrainian consumer goods.

With respect to final products, import competition has been severe. In the West it is argued that import competition may function as a crowbar to break domestic monopolies and to further competition, resulting in higher quality domestic production.

Ukraine seems to be a peculiar case in the sense that adjustment to import competition has been very limited compared to most Central European countries. This is related to the fact that the Ukrainian economy has been marketized to a very limited extent. The lack of response to import competition is also related to the high taxation rate, making it very difficult for domestic producers to compete. Often, imports were not taxed at all. By mid-1998, the average import tariff level was about 15.0 per cent, quite low by international standards.[31] Since then, however, import tariffs have tended to increase and the devaluation of the hryvna since September 1998 has eased the impact of import competition somewhat.[32]

The result of foreign trade policy was that imports were encouraged and exports discouraged. This contributed to a situation in which import competition is killing rather than stimulating domestic producers. The disastrous impact of import competition is related to the slow pace of reform, rather than assumed unfair competition. A few examples are given below to illustrate the problem.

Before the devaluation of the hryvna in September 1998, many food products from Western Europe were offered at Ukrainian markets, of a better quality and lower price than local food products.

Also, labour-intensive products from Western Europe can compete with local products, despite the fact that economic textbooks teach us that countries like Ukraine should have a big comparative advantage in these products.

With respect to comparative advantages, there are also myths surrounding the assumed very low wage level. In early 1993, the average monthly wage in industry was in the range of US$7 a month. By early 1996, the average wage in industry had exceeded US$100 a month. However, this is the net wage, and does not take into account the high taxes and the indirect subsidies of government and enterprises to employees. A private textile factory in Zaporizhzhya, mainly producing for the domestic market, had to pay its employees in 1996 salaries in the range of US$50–80. This is a sector with relatively low wage levels, about US$35 per month. This means that in order to become competitive, the factory had to pay about twice the average salary in the sector. Again, taxes are not taken into account. Of course, wages remain low, but not as low as the statistical office would have us believe.

There is also the example of coal mines, the salaries of Ukrainian miners being very low. But if labour productivity is taken into account, Ukrainian coal appears to be very expensive (see Chapter 5, page 83).

After the devaluation of the hryvna in 1998/99, dollar wages almost halved whereas import restrictions increased. This would imply a boost for domestic producers. Indeed, industrial production picked up with 3.4 per cent growth in 1999. But this was not a boom and the markets remained flooded by labour-intensive products, mainly from Central European countries, which were cheaper than domestic products.

There is also a problem in the quality of labour. Despite the relatively high education level of the population, the average quality of the labour force is rather poor. Low average productivity is not only related to the way labour is organized, but also related to deeply ingrained attitudes. The labour productivity of a private firm, in which the management tries to organize labor in a modern way, does not always lead to similar productivity levels as in the West because the average labour productivity is held back by the general economic environment and deeply rooted attitudes.

Ukrainian authorities tried to discourage imports by imposing their own quality controls, which are much more wide-ranging than international practice. Ukraine insists on subjecting even products widely sold in Europe to its own costly laboratory inspections. The fees, reportedly up to US$250 000 for a case involving standard household cleaning products, seems, according to a report of the Ministry of Economic Affairs and the World Bank, 'designed to cover more than the cost of inspection, and the delays are costly'. Similar problems arise with the customs service. This is 'Ukrainian protectionism', i.e. the 'protection' of the population against domestic and foreign goods.[33]

Disruption of supply chains

Import competition has led to the disruption of supply chains. Often, suppliers had to be sought abroad, in order to guarantee quality. Ukrainian suppliers could, in most cases, not deliver products of the required quality. For example, ZTL, a company from Zaporizhzhya producing food products, imports from Hungary a fruit concentrate for making lemonade. The Hungarian concentrate lasts for one year while the Ukrainian concentrate lasts for only one month. Bolshoi Kazachok, from Zaporizhzhya, exports feathers to Germany where they are cleaned and sorted. Subsequently they are re-imported to be processed for duvets. A factory in Kyiv has the equipment to do the same job, but cannot do so according to the required standards. The Zaporizhzhya textile factory Kora buys all inputs from the West, mainly Germany, in order to guarantee quality. Production is mostly destined for the German market. The picture emerges of enterprises becoming insulated from their regional and national economic environment. New linkages with foreign partners are usually not strong and limited to exchange. The fact that prices of Ukrainian products are often too high is partly a result of the bad debt chain. This induces Ukrainian enterprises to set higher prices and strict delivery conditions for Ukrainian markets.

Disruption of supply chains also occurs in Central European countries. However, due to the slowness of transition in Ukraine, the relatively high production costs in Ukraine and the comparatively low quality standards, the disruption of supply chains through import competition has been much more drastic and has contributed significantly to the sharp decline in industrial production.

A peculiar example of import dependence is that of imports of herbicides, pesticides, high grade seeds and other inputs for the agricultural sector. Since independence many of these materials have been imported. However, a sizeable share of these imports have not been paid for because collective agricultural enterprises could not pay or were not allowed to pay by Ukrainian authorities.[34] Ukrainian agrochemical distributors had by early 1999 US$200 million debts with Western suppliers. As a result the supply of essential farming inputs has been endangered. Imports of plant protection chemicals were 3527 tonnes for the first five months of 1999, compared to 10 216 tonnes for the same period of 1998.[35] The supply of mineral fertilizers fell from 514 000 tonnes in 1998 to 416 000 tonnes in 1999, and the fuel supply fell from 3.6 to 2.9 million tonnes. The Center for Privatization and Economic Reform in Kyiv estimated that the elimination of Western credit sales to Ukrainian farms would result in Ukrainian farms receiving about 50 per cent less Western agrochemical products in 1999, which accounted for about 94 per cent by weight of chemicals by Ukrainian farms in 1998. This would lead to a decline in agricultural export revenues of approximately 30 per cent.[36]

With the collapse of the Soviet Union, many of the supply chains, especially for the all-Union enterprises, were severed and new suppliers had to be found in Ukraine. This appeared to be rather difficult and was hampered by the lack of horizontal communication and the lack of databases.

In the period 1991–96, the decline in trade with Russia as a share of total trade was moderate, compared with the period 1996–99 (Table 7.1). In the first phase of independence, trade links with Russia were primarily hampered by the chaos arising out of the collapse of the centrally planned economy. In the period 1992–95 it was usually a problem of finding suppliers, but since then the problem with trade with other countries of the former Soviet Union has become to pay for supplies.

Nowadays, it is not only trade barriers that lead Ukrainian enterprises to abandon Russian suppliers and look for suppliers elsewhere. Russian suppliers, in many cases, have become too expensive, especially compared to potential suppliers in Central and Western Europe.

Supply chains were also disrupted in another way. The opportunity to trade abroad led many enterprises to break former relationships with Ukrainian clients and suppliers. This has frequently led to the disruption of whole supply chains.

A typical example is the following. A Zaporizhzhya factory has been very successful in exporting leather jackets to the West. However, it became more profitable for the local leather supplier to export leather to the West. The leather jacket manufacturer went bankrupt as a consequence. Subsequently the slaughterhouse found it more profitable to export raw unprocessed leather than to supply the local leather manufacturer. The leather manufacturer went bankrupt. Subsequently agriculture fell into a deep crisis and cattle breeders found it more profitable to export live cattle abroad than to supply the local slaughterhouse. The slaughterhouse went bankrupt.

This is an example of how new export opportunities can disrupt existing supply chains. More often, import competition may lead to the disruption of supply chains. In order to guarantee quality, suppliers had to be sought abroad. Ukrainian suppliers could not, in most cases, deliver products of the required quality.

The fact that prices of Ukrainian enterprises were often too high was also related to a peculiar price setting rule that only applied to domestic trade. This rule was called the principle of cost covering prices, according to which the factory should take into account, when calculating the price of the product, the costs of running the enterprise from the moment that production halted for the last client. This means, for example, that if a factory has not produced for three months and has to start production anew for a new client, this client has to pay for the three months that the factory has not worked. This is an odd rule, but forced enterprises to set high prices for Ukrainian clients. It has the result that steel prices for Ukrainian consumers were 30–50 per cent higher than for foreign clients. This system of price setting contributed to continuing depression in domestic markets and pushed Ukrainian enterprises to foreign producers.

External imbalances and indebtedness

Ukraine's foreign debt amounted to US$12.6 billion in December 1999, US$1.9 billion of which was owed to Russia, US$2.8 billion to the IMF, US$1.2 billion to the World Bank and US$1.8 billion in fiduciary loans. The debt burden is moderate with 30 per cent of GDP in early 1999 (for Russia this percentage was 113) (Table 7.4). This debt burden has been built up since 1991 when independent Ukraine started with a clean sheet. It is worth noting that capital exported illegally from Ukraine by far exceeds the total amount of foreign debt. Also remarkable is that almost all foreign credits are not investment oriented.

The increasing debt service burden since 1996 is related to exceptionally high interest rates on government bonds and the short-term character of most loans. In early 1999, the international reserves of the Bank of Ukraine were only one-third of the internationally accepted minimum level.

In June 1999 the Ukrainian government was unable to repay a Eurobond loan worth US$155 million to ING-Barings. Under IMF pressure, Ukraine managed to convince ING-Barings to 'voluntarily' restructure the loan. Financial experts foresee that without additional financing Ukraine will not be able to meet its debt obligations in 2000 and 2001. In February 2000 Ukraine offered restructuring of US$2.6 billion of loans, while missing repayment of coupons for Eurobonds in March 2000.

Foreign direct investment

Ukraine has one of the lowest per capita foreign direct investments of Central and Eastern Europe, despite the advantage of having a large potential market. In the period 1991–98, US$87.5 billion flowed into Central and Eastern Europe as net foreign direct investment. Only US$2.7 billion dollars went to Ukraine. Cumulative per capita inflows to Ukraine during that period amounted to US$54.[37] In Europe, only Armenia, Georgia and Belarus had lower per capita inflows.[38] Ukraine has 42 times less foreign investment per capita than Hungary, 27 times less than Slovenia and 19 times less than Estonia. In 1999 the inflow of foreign direct investment slowed down and reached only 65 per cent of the 1988 level.[39]

Table 7.4   Ukraine's foreign economic position, 1994–98

	Current account balance as % of GDP	Net FDI (US$ million)	Gross international reserves in weeks of imports	Gross foreign debt (US$ million)	Gross foreign debt as % of GDP	Debt service ratio as a % of exports
1994	−3.1	151	1.8	7167	18.9	11.2
1995	−3.1	257	3.0	8217	22.2	8.0
1996	−2.7	526	4.8	8840	19.8	6.6
1997	−2.7	581	5.6	9555	19.1	7.3
1998	−3.1	747	2.7	11 483	27.1	12.5

Source: Ukrainian Economic Trends, December 1999, p. 73.

Table 7.5 Motives of companies investing in Ukraine and Central and Eastern Europe

Rank	Motive	Ukraine	Central and Eastern Europe
1	Secure potential sales markets	3.65	3.08
2	Develop new sales markets	3.50	3.22
3	Overcome import barriers	2.50	1.36
4	Secure and cultivate existing sales markets	1.70	2.70
5	Enhance competitiveness through primary production in host country	1.58	2.12
6	Lower labour costs	1.40	2.76
7	Lower tax burden	1.10	1.46
8	Better purchasing and procurement possibilities	1.20	1.34
9	Longer working hours	0.68	1.38
10	Fewer administrative impediments	0.55	1.18
11	Longer machine running times	0.54	1.21
12	Less stringent environmental constraints	0.33	0.73

Source: Möllers (1999), p. 145.

The bulk of foreign investment is through the creation of joint ventures with existing partners rather than through privatization. One of the problems with investment through privatization is the fact that enterprises offered for tender are far from being the most interesting ones. The Ukrainian authorities do not give clear information on what is available. There is also a lack of transparency in the privatization procedure itself and finally there is the unpredictability of Ukrainian authorities in the sense that at the last moment, some enterprises may be withdrawn from a list offered for privatization.

Most foreign investment in 1998 went to the food industry (21 per cent), domestic trade (16 per cent), financial services (7 per cent), machine building and metal processing (13 per cent) and the chemical industry (4 per cent).[40] The USA was the most important foreign investor, followed by the Netherlands, Germany and Russia.

Why are foreign investors coming to Ukraine? A survey carried out in 1997 among 21 foreign investors in Ukraine, accounting for more than US$540 million of investments, gave the motives in Table 7.5 (5 means of very great importance while 0 is not at all important; for comparison results from a similar survey in a number of Central and Eastern European countries are given).

It is telling that the factors considered by the Ukrainian government as important for foreign investors do not rank high among foreign investors in Ukraine.

The most important impediment listed by the same interviewees was legal uncertainty: 100 per cent of interviewees confirmed this as an important impediment. The other six impediments most frequently mentioned were 'Unsatisfactory transport infrastructure' (97.5 per cent of interviewees affirmed), 'Government failure to abide by commitments' (90.0 per cent), 'Government control and remnants of command economy as impediment' (80.0 per cent), 'Lack of telecommunications infrastructure' (80.0 per cent) and 'Corruption' (75.0 per cent). Sixty per cent of interviewees denied 'low level of staff commitment' and 'poorly trained labour' as impediment. Also 'unreliability of staff' (50 per cent denials), 'too low workers' quality awareness' (15 per cent denials) and 'organized crime' (10 per cent denials) were not seen as impediments to investment.

A list prepared by US institutions in 1997 of the serious impediments to Western investors in doing business in Ukraine, includes the following:[41]

1. Commercial, tax and land codes are lacking. Related to the lack of a commercial code, Western businesses find that very few business contracts are regarded as final or binding in Ukraine.
2. There is no land market in Ukraine. Land cannot be purchased or sold.
3. Provincial administrations ban grain exports in order to ensure the sale of grain crops under state contract – regardless of whether or not the agricultural producer owned the grain.
4. Tax, laws, customs regulations and specialized licencing procedures are cumbersome and ambiguous, which leads to arbitrary implementation of regulations and to corruption.
5. For almost all licences and infrastructural services, complex and expensive bureaucratic procedures are required. High official and non-official taxes have to be paid.[42]
6. Bankruptcy law does not permit restructuring – it permits companies to accumulate debts and then simply close down.
7. There are limitations on the number of bank accounts (usually to one) and on the amount of cash Ukrainian resident or non-resident companies can withdraw from their bank accounts. Frequent and discretionary 'freezing' of funds in their accounts is common.

8. Corporate profit tax has highly variable and multiple rates. Further, significant tax exemptions exist, which are discriminating. Local tax offices exercise considerable discretion, resulting in abuses.

9. The payroll tax, including various social security taxes, Chernobyl Fund, Pension Fund, and other withholding taxes, is prohibitively high. Further, personal income taxes are also high.

10. Value added and excise taxes are levied on excisable capital (charter fund) contributions and offset of such taxes against other taxes (e.g. corporate profit tax) is not permitted. In practice, refund regulations are non-functioning.

11. Registration procedures for firms and investments are non-transparent and time-consuming, resulting in arbitrary implementation by officials. Procedures and requirements for registration can vary among localities. Often, documents are required that are not envisaged by legislation.[43] High filing fees discourage resort to legal means. Registration of a joint venture may take up to 9 months, instead of the 20 days envisaged by law.[44]

12. Licencing of loans in foreign currency is extremely cumbersome and bureaucratic, hampering foreign financing.

13. Administrative control by the National Bank of Ukraine (NBU) over foreign currency purchases was recently tightened, requiring vetting, registration and prepayment of contracts. Further, additional limitations have been imposed on companies' holding of hryvna settlement accounts. Also, there are short time limits to settle export payments.

14. The Antimonopoly Committee intervenes administratively in broad (and unwarranted) areas of the economy.

15. Real estate laws and lease law agreements (including subleasing) are ambiguous.

16. The law on pledges is inadequate, and the state fee structure for pledge agreements is burdensome.

17. Bidding process state procurement guidelines are unclear and discretionary.

18. Crime and corruption are prevalent.

19. There is no ombudsman (or similar) office that can assist foreign businesses in concluding transactions and sorting out difficulties.

Other surveys add the following obstacles:

- Rapid and reliable transportation of cargo within Ukraine is not possible, due to a dilapidated transport infrastructure.

- Taxation on profits is extremely high.[45]
- Imports and exports are hampered by harassment of customs officials.[46]

According to the OECD, difficulties involved in dealing with Ukrainian authorities top the list of disincentives in almost all investor surveys.[47]

According to the Delegate Office of the German Economy in Kyiv, German investors complained, besides the issues mentioned above, about:[48]

- Slow and expensive visa service[49]
- Long waits at border crossings
- Difficulties with granting employment permits
- Lack of legal stability
- Tax inspectors interpret tax legislation subjectively and ask for bribes
- Successful negotiations with Ukrainian authorities are only possible with the help of the paid service of an unofficial Ukrainian 'coach'

The low level of foreign direct investment in Ukraine is above all related to economic instability and lawlessness. In addition, regulations for direct foreign investment change regularly and sometimes the investor has to pay taxes retroactively, and face financial penalties for past activities that were done perfectly legally at the time. During 1991–96, legal conditions for direct foreign investment changed six times.[50] On some occasions, the president would give foreign investors a guarantee not to pay taxes, while at the same time the parliament adopted a law that obliged them to pay taxes. Enterprises that had registered as joint ventures with foreign shareholdings by 1 January 1995 were promised tax exemption for five years. This was revoked on 1 July 1997.[51] This state of legal flux and uncertainty frightens foreign investors. According to the OECD, one of the main concerns of foreign investors is the quality and consistency of laws. Inconsistent legislation 'opens the door for many interpretations of legislative intent, all equally plausible, and for arbitrary decisions by those in charge of implementation the legislation'.[52]

Apart from the imprecise wording of legal regulations, the enormous quantity of decrees is a problem. For the tobacco industry alone 65 decrees were issued by 12 different state agencies between mid-1996 and mid-1997, while for the cosmetics industry 26 decrees were issued in 1996.[53] A multinational enterprise employs four people 'who do nothing but collate and evaluate the latest legislation. The laws are amended so frequently that the officials themselves are often not familiar with them'.[54]

Legal-regulatory instability, discretionary application of licensing rules, a fragile banking system, and widespread corruption are usually mentioned as obstacles to foreign investment.

There are numerous horror stories of Western enterprises documented in the Ukrainian and Western press. For example, Irina Zubchenko of ICD, a Dutch chemical company, told

> Just to set up a representation office took three months and a packet of documents almost 5 cm thick... the idea was that once we registered the representational office with the ministry of foreign affairs then we would not have to present documents with registered translations from Dutch to English to Ukrainian and to other ministries to do business. But no, now it turns out we have to submit new originals of the same documents to the ministry of finance in order to get a bank account, plus proof of our registration with the ministry of foreign affairs.[55]

Another example is that of Mr Wingate, an American who, after having worked for three years for a US company in Ukraine that wound up its operations, decided to open an American restaurant in Mykolayiv. In November 1997 his company acquired an empty and delapidated building in the centre of town for 21 000 hryvnas. Having finalized the relevant documents and received permission from the city architect for reconstruction as well as a go-ahead from the city public health authorities, Mr Wingate set about renovating the building. However, three months after starting renovation, in April 1998, the problems began. At first, they came from the regional public health office, which in spite of its earlier positive findings, now claimed the building contained dangerous chemicals. After Mr Wingate had carried out the required works, other authorities began to make objections. Among others, he needed special permission to occupy the land on which the building stood. An official approached him to strike a deal, which he refused. Meanwhile, Mr Wingate was offered the option to drop all claims to the building and be refunded 21 000 hrynas. He could not accept this as he had invested US$263 000 in the reconstruction and equipment. As a result, the opening of the restaurant was put off indefinitely.[56]

Another typical example: in 1998 the State Committee on Standardization forced the US company Procter & Gamble to fly a delegation to Belgium to see how the firm made its products and decide if they were good enough for the Ukrainian consumer. In an interview with Tatiania Kyseliova of the Committee, she said that the Ukrainian experts had developed over the last few years over 2000 standards, 60 per cent of which either meet or take into account foreign requirements.

The Wall Street Journal characterized Ukraine as 'a violent, lawless country where greedy, all power bureaucrats prey on American investors with impunity', adding that on the other hand Ukraine is the third largest recipient of USA aid.[57]

It seems that Ukraine is only interested in foreign investments and not in foreign investors.

A telling example is the history of the joint venture between Avtozaz, the only car manufacturer in Ukraine, and Daewoo. This joint venture was seen by Ukrainian authorities, during its inception, as a showcase for Ukraine.

Since 1994, negotiations had taken place with Daewoo, Peugeot, Rover and General Motors. Ukraine, with 52 million inhabitants, is potentially a huge market. Only 62 out of 1000 Ukrainian citizens have a car while the corresponding figure for Germany is 490 and for Italy 425.

According to the Ukrainian press, in March 1996 an agreement had almost been reached with Daewoo. One of the conditions was that most of Avtozaz's management should be replaced. In February 1996, the Ukrainian government dismissed director Kravchuk in order to facilitate the negotiations with foreign investors. However, no break-through occurred.

In September 1996, the Ukrainian press again reported a break-through and some newspapers wrote that a contract had been signed between General Motors and Avtozaz about the joint production of cars.[58]

In mid-September 1997, three years after the search for a foreign partner had begun, a breakthrough seemed to come when the Ukrainian government announced the joint venture between Daewoo and Avtozaz, in which Daewoo would invest US$1.3 billion, up to 2003. That was more than the total accumulated direct foreign investment in Ukraine by early 1997. According to an Avtozaz official, Daewoo would put up half of the venture's US$300 million starting capital, and the 85 per cent state-owned Avtozaz would offer the other half in property.[59] The new joint venture expected to have a capacity of 255 000 cars a year by 2005. Half of its production was destined for export. 150 000 Daewoo cars, 80 000 Tavria cars with Avtozaz engines, and 25 000 Opel cars (General Motors) would be produced every year in Zaporizhzhya.[60] A final agreement was postponed until the Ukrainian government announced the taxation of imported second-hand cars. Also, there were problems between Daewoo and Avtozaz management. Daewoo initially demanded the sacking of Avtozaz director Sotnikov.[61] Wages also posed a problem. Originally Daewoo agreed on US$52 per month. But after Avtozaz refused to reduce the 20 000 personnel, Daewoo and Avtozaz agreed that the average wage should be the same as the average salary of Zaporizhzhya enterprises with more than 2000 workers.[62] Another problem was that Avtozaz promised to prepare assembly lines for the production of five models by the end of 1997. When a Daewoo delegation came to Zaporizhzhya to inspect progress, they noticed that nothing had been done. The argument was that there was no money available to pay the workers that should have prepared the assembly lines. Only 2 March 1998 the founding agreement on the creation of a joint venture between Avtzozaz and Daewoo had been signed. The level of localization should be, by the year 2008, equivalent to a minimum of 70 per cent of the production costs of a single car. The domestic market was further protected by the exemption of Avtozaz and Daewoo cars from VAT and excise duties.[63] Daewoo cars would be assembled not in Zaporizhzhya, but in Ilyichevsk, near Odessa.[64]

It can be seen from this that precious time had been lost due to the negotiation strategy of the Ukrainian government and that Avtozaz management itself constituted a major barrier to foreign investment.

In 1998 the joint venture produced 20 400 cars, of which only 8950 sold and 1999, 24 000 cars were produced, of which 11 000 have been sold.[65] Why were the first two years of the joint venture so disappointing?

Jung-Ho Choi, Daewoo president, noted that the Daewoo plan was contingent on two key conditions, which were not met: a stable economy and effective implementation of the government-imposed restrictions on importing used cars into Ukraine. According to Choi, used-car importers continued to exploit various ways of avoiding the import restrictions. 'According to some statistics, imported used cars accounted for 84 per cent of the car market in Ukraine between January and August of last year ... If it is true, it is natural that the joint venture's sales should slow down and survival itself might be threatened'. Actually, in 1998, 240 000 cars were imported into Ukraine, representing a value of approximately US$1 billion.[66] In 1999, 370 000 cars were registered in Ukraine.[67]

Daewoo's competitors argued that Daewoo cars were too highly priced and poorly advertized. The Tavria continued to suffer from the poor reputation of the Zaporozhets, a cheap mini-car produced by Avtozaz in the Soviet era.

The joint venture slashed prices of its Tavria models from US$3800 to US$2800 in autumn 1998. The prices of Daewoo's Lanos and Nubira models start at US$8200 and US$10 700, respectively. Daewoo produced its own models mainly on the basis of imported parts. Therefore the cut in import duties was incorporated in the joint venture agreement. This caused major problems with the European Union, which threatened to bring the case to court.[68]

When asked in January 1999 if he was pleased with the state of the joint venture, Choi responded, 'This is not the proper time for me to mention here the internal situation of the joint venture itself. Only I would say that everybody knows Daewoo is the most substantial foreign investor for this economy and must be treated fairly by the joint venture partner'. According to the Kyiv Post, Daewoo executives admitted – off the record – that Daewoo and Avtozaz management didn't exactly see eye to eye on many issues, accusing Avtozaz executives of trying to run the joint venture by themselves.[69] Choi stated on another occasion that, 'The joint venture's management has reached a state of deadlock. Both sides cannot execute any decision. That is why we proposed to change the composition of the joint ventures' managing board on both the Ukrainian and Korean sides'.[70]

Questioned about tax privileges he said, 'The benefits that the joint venture receives from tax privileges are barely enough to cover the extra burden that the joint venture is required to shoulder of providing jobs for 20 000 workers and maintaining old plants that were owned by Avtozaz'.[71] Then there was the question of why Daewoo's joint venture in Uzbekistan was doing so much better. 'In Uzbekistan there are no conflicts within the management and the Uzbek government supports Daewoo constantly and continuously.' At the time of the interview Daewoo planned to invest US$500 million in a production facility in the Russian province of Rostov, just across the border.[72]

The Kyiv Post commented that, 'not even the most pampered investor is immune for the well publicized horrors of doing business in Ukraine'.[73]

The joint venture cost Ukraine a fortune. The World Bank estimated the cost of protecting each job at several thousand dollars a month, if price increases of imported second-hand cars and tax exemptions were taken into account.[74]

Marginalization in the world economy

The nature of Ukraine's integration into the world economy and world society differs fundamentally from that of countries in the developed capitalist world. Terms such as multinationalization and globalization are inadequate to describe the sudden introduction of Ukraine in the capitalist world economy.

Distinguishing between internationalization, multinationalization and globalization, with its different underlying logics, it can be said that Ukraine is faced with shallow and one-sided internationalization. There has been a de-multinationalization and de-internationalization with respect to the countries of the former Soviet Union, as there was in many respects a closing down in economic terms since 1991. In terms of total foreign trade turnover, including trade with the former Soviet Union, Ukraine in 1999 is less internationalized than in 1991.

Some internationalization has taken place with respect to the expansion of trade relations with regions outside the former Soviet Union. However, this has remained confined to incidental exchange of products, often with the help of middlemen, without the depth of vertical transnational production integration that has characterized the internationalization processes in the developed capitalist world.

Internationalization has been mismanaged and selective because imports have been encouraged and exports discouraged. Exports of value-subtracting industries surged. In some spheres, internationalization has gone farther than in others.

Ruigrok and van Tulder made a distinction between the globalization of finances, of competition and of technology.[75] The globalization of finances can be described as the deregulation of national financial markets and the subsequent internationalization of capital flows. As becomes evident from the magnitude of capital flight from Ukraine, the international mobility of capital has increased enormously since 1991, when it was virtually non-existent. It is obvious that this increased capital mobility affects investment policy and investment levels in Ukraine. The amount of capital export shows how political and industrial logics in Ukraine became subordinated to the short-term market considerations of financial logic.

With respect to the globalization of competition, Ukrainian enterprises are faced with rivals that are integrated into world-wide corporate networks. These enterprises are cooperating to generate new product, process and organizational technologies (globalization of technology) with which they may out-compete less advanced enterprises such as those in Ukraine. Also lower on the value added chain, in areas such as steel and aluminium production, technological innovations are introduced rapidly. For firms that are faced with lack of investment capital and are excluded from the above mentioned global networks, competition is extremely difficult.

Ukraine has largely stayed aloof from the processes of multi-nationalization and globalization that have transformed the world economy, although Ukraine has been affected by these processes. The mismanaged internationalization contributed to the large-scale destruction of productive capacities in Ukraine.

Since the start of the liberalization of foreign economic relations, Ukraine has been subject to an exposure to foreign competition in which it remained largely passive. Penetration through markets took place rather than an outward dynamism of Ukrainian enterprises. Foreign competition contributed to the steep industrial decline, while industrial enterprises hardly adjusted. There was only an internationalization of markets and not of productive structures. The liberalization of foreign economic relations allowed a kleptocracy to enrich itself on a massive scale by exporting subsidized commodities low in the value added chain, while blocking the emergence of conditions of effective technology transfer that might have enhanced endogenous development potential.

Mainly due to erroneous economic policy, Ukrainian enterprises remained largely defenceless with respect to penetration of foreign products. Import competition, new export opportunities and new trade barriers with the countries of the former Soviet Union led to the disruption of supply chains without creating new and stable supply systems. The increase in exports to the 'far abroad' was mainly based on the export of subsidized iron, steel and aluminium.

As far as internationalization took place, it was largely an internationalization of the bazaar. Many people travelled to foreign, mainly neighbouring countries, in order to trade and profit from price differences. It is international economic cooperation on a very low, possibly the lowest, level. Higher forms of international economic cooperation have hardly occurred. Joint ventures are mainly in trading activities.

Brain drain has become an important phenomenon. Since independence more than 5000 leading scientists have left Ukraine because of difficult working conditions.[76]

Conclusion

Ukraine was faced with a sudden introduction into the capitalist world market while experiencing a breakdown of its economic relations with the former Soviet Union. Adjustment towards import competition and competition on foreign markets hardly took place. Ukraine changed from an exporter of high value added products into an exporter of lowly processed materials such as steel, aluminium and chemical products. The opening up has been mismanaged because exporters were often discouraged to export.

Internationalization was mainly confined to trade in goods and hardly comprised international industrial cooperation. Foreign direct investment is at a very low level. On the other hand, capital flight was substantial, related to the unfavourable investment conditions in Ukraine. Debt service attained high levels at the end of the 1990s.

The commodity composition of imports and exports made Ukraine very vulnerable to price fluctuations in fuels and raw and lowly processed materials on world markets.

8
Regional Economies

An understanding of what is happening at the regional and local level is crucial for understanding the dynamics of economic development in Ukraine. Enterprises are situated in local and regional economic complexes and have to deal with local and regional authorities. Previous chapters have repeatedly referred to the negative role local and regional authorities are playing by harassing enterprises, especially private ones. These authorities are playing an important role in perpetuating parasitic economic mechanisms by focusing their energies on lobbying for government support rather than furthering development potential in the region. In developed market economies, increasingly, coordination by networks, especially at the local and regional level, came to supplement coordination by the market and the state. Structures at the meso-level that furthered competition were also shaped by firms and other non-state organizations. Therefore it is topical to see to what extent in Ukraine governance mechanisms at the local and regional level have developed that may further economic development.

The choice for a centralist state

Without the trouble-shooting of local party officials the Soviet system would be reduced to chaos. Local party officials corrected local and regional disequilibria. Party trouble-shooting was required because the Soviet planning system was organized on functional rather than on regional lines. With weak regional planning, it was up to the local party leader to cross functional boundaries and ensure a more rational regional allocation of resources. In Soviet times, 56 per cent of Ukrainian enterprises were subordinated to the ministries in Moscow, while this percentage was even higher (69 per cent) in the Donetsk Dnipr region, comprising Donetsk, Luhansk, Zaporizhzhya and Dnipropetrovsk, where 53 per cent of industrial production in Ukraine took place.[1] Party and state apparatus comprised a network of strict hierarchical divisions combined with overlapping control over the same areas of activities, and with the right of the local party apparatus to give instructions to parallel state agencies.

With the dissolution of the Soviet Union, Ukraine tried to restore vertical connections with enterprises formerly resorting under the ministries in Moscow through the own industrial ministries in Kyiv. This policy has been a complete failure. At the same time, the consequences of this policy had to be solved by the local and regional authorities. Due to the chaotic situation at the national level, the provinces had more scope to manoeuvre.

In January 1993, there was a decree by the president to give more power to the regions. However, this decree did not change anything. Gradually a situation developed in which the regions began to govern themselves *de facto*, although they did this without any legal basis. By right, the ministries governed.

In August 1994, a presidential decree made local councils and their executive committees ultimately subservient to the president. Heads of provincial state administrations – local representatives of the President – now hold real power in the provinces. According to Article 143 of the constitution and the 1992 Law on Local Councils and Local Self-Governance (amended in 1994 and 1995), territorial communities of villages and towns deal through their Council of People's Deputies with purely local issues such as the establishment of communal enterprises and organizations and control over their activities; development and implementation of local social and cultural projects; and management of communal property. They adopt and control budgets on their territorial unit and establish local taxes. District and provincial councils adopt programmes of social, economic and cultural development, and set and control district and provincial budgets. A local council's power may be terminated by parliament if it decides that the council's actions contradict Ukrainian law.

Local authorities often effectively blocked investment plans of enterprises by withholding the necessary licences.[2] Also, local clans, to which local politicians belong and which often control huge capitals, usually constitute an effective countervailing force for the national government and provincial governors. For example, in Donetsk, the governor and his apparatus are quite isolated.

Nevertheless, the trend since 1994 has been one of centralization. The parliament approved a law according to which municipal and provincial budgets should be approved by the Ministry of Finance.[3] Also, government now has the freedom to act at its own discretion in its relations with provincial budgets and ignore the accepted ratio between central and local budgets (2.33 to 1).

Ukraine consists of 24 provinces, divided into 'cities of province importance' that may consist of several boroughs, and districts (rayons) divided into villages and towns. Whereas the national government collects 19 categories of taxes, local authorities collect 16 categories of local taxes, including communal, hotel, transport and market taxes, that go to local budgets.

Municipal governments are heavily dependent on the state. Approximately 80 per cent of revenues come from the government budget. The provinces have obtained substantial autonomy in the issues of municipal property management, privatization programme implementation, land reform conduct and local budget formation.

The above description refers to the formal institutional set-up. In practice, local and provincial authorities resort to many illegal practices that create major obstacles to market-oriented reform. Also, regular interference by local authorities is mentioned as an important obstacle to foreign direct investment, according to the Ministry of Economy.[4] In our account of the dairy industry (Chapter 5, page 88), it has been shown how provincial authorities illegally interfere in the day-to-day management of Collective Agricultural Enterprises and dairy processors, imposing supply and delivery schemes upon dairy processors and preventing agricultural products from being transported across provincial borders.[5] Corrupt officials at the local level make the life of smaller and medium-sized private enterprises especially very difficult. Local administrative harassment is mentioned in enterprise surveys as an important obstacle.[6] Often, local governments introduce price controls on specific products.

A centralist state was perceived by the ruling elite as a crucial precondition for the cohesion of Ukraine. More so than in countries of comparable size, funds are redistributed to the central budget. Provinces have to lobby for privileges, tax exemptions for enterprises in their provinces and direct subsidies. The idea that some Western provinces are getting preferential treatment is widespread. Only three provinces, Donetsk, Dnipropetrovks and Kharkiv, as well as the city of Kyiv, donate to the state budget, while other regions are net recipients of subsidies from the central government. As far as subsidies to the population are concerned, Western Ukraine profits more than Eastern Ukraine. However, if the stream of open and hidden subsidies to value-subtracting industries is taken into account, another picture emerges. There are many in Western Ukraine who perceive the industrial rust belts in the East as an obstacle to the economic transformation of Ukraine. They also see that despite the sharp industrial decline, living standards in the industrial East are still higher than in the more reform-minded West, although coping mechanisms in the West may be more developed.

However, the lack of financial transparency does not allow identification of the exact direction and size of subsidies across provinces.

The province of Donetsk: captured by the past

The province of Donetsk, located in South-Eastern Ukraine, with 5.064 million inhabitants (1 January 1998) and 10 per cent of the total population of Ukraine, is the most populous province of Ukraine. It produces approximately 20 per cent of Ukraine's industrial production, specializing in heavy industry. The Donbas, the region in which Donetsk is located, has huge deposits of coal, iron ore and manganese. Therefore, it was an ideal location for steel mills. In the late 19th century, the region began to produce a steady stream of pig iron from its first blast furnace. From the time of the first Five Years Plans, from 1928–38, the Donbas began to develop rapidly. It became one of the major coal producing regions in the Soviet Union. In Soviet times Donetsk was a rich province, because miners and steelworkers were among the best paid workers.

However, since 1991, the production decline in Donetsk has been even steeper than in Ukraine as a whole.

All this meant a fundamental shift in the relative position of Donetsk, from one of the core industrial centres of the Soviet Union, a world power, towards a problem border region in a new state that found itself in the impoverished periphery of the new Europe. It should also be recalled that Donetsk, with its majority Russian-speaking population, traditionally was more closely linked to Russia than other provinces in Ukraine.

The Donetsk coal industry has been in decline for several decades. The loss-making coal mining sector is still, for the most part, not privatized and receives huge direct and indirect subsidies. In Donetsk, fifty per cent of mines, all loss-making, produce only 15 per cent of coal output. However, these mines take two-thirds of all subsidies to the coal mining sector.[7] As far as coal is paid, payments are usually in kind. Only 26 per cent of coal sold in Donetsk has been paid for in cash. This contributed to wage arrears.

Some mines have closed, but there are no signs of the restructuring programmes that would soften the social consequences of coal mine closures, even though the World Bank provided assistance for this purpose. During a panel discussion in Donetsk about the regional economy, the participants were totally unaware of the existence of a Coal Mining Restructuring company.[8] It is common for dismissed miners not to receive outstanding salaries.[9] Only 0.4–0.6 per cent of surveyed unemployed in Donetsk received unemployment allowances, which amounted to an average of 35–36.5 hryvnas per month (May 1997). Towns that were totally dependent on coal mines that are now being closed have become ghost towns.

The provincial administration in Donetsk has applied the old methods of the centrally planned economy in order to revitalize the coal industry. In the programme for the social and economic development of Donbas in 1998–2000, the modernization of coal mines is foreseen and an increase in coal production up to 45.5 million tonnes.[10] In the programme there is no mention of a restructuring of the coal sector.

In the meantime the only private mine in Donetsk, Karbon, is harassed by local and regional authorities. This mine is the only one to pay salaries regularly, and provides employment for 1200 miners. The mine is faced with non-payment of coal deliveries by five large consumers in Donetsk. Nevertheless, the director of the Oblast State Energy Company ordered electricity to be cut. The mine did not find any support among local and regional authorities.[11]

Heavy industry and the energy industries accounted for 83 per cent of industrial production in the province of Donetsk in 1996. The metallurgical enterprises in Donetsk belong to the most important in Ukraine. The metallurgical sector in Ukraine did relatively well during the 1990s, due to the fact that it could find a niche in the world market for low quality steel. The Donbas accounts for a third of Ukraine's export income, with the metallurgy industry comprising much of that volume.[12]

The prospects for steel production are gloomy, given rising energy prices, high energy intensiveness of production (open hearth furnaces are common practice in Ukraine) and declining prospects on world markets since the Asian crisis.

Restructuring in Donetsk is blocked by a configuration of interest groups and belief systems. All mayor players in Donetsk, including the majority of the population, think that bankruptcies and redundancies are not acceptable and that the state should continue to subsidize loss-making enterprises in order to preserve 'the social balance' and to avoid unemployment. There is also the widespread belief that value-subtracting industries are in fact value adding. There is a great fear of unemployment. The actual unemployment rate in early 1999 amounted to approximately one-third of the population, while the official unemployment rate was only 3.5 per cent in 1999.[13] Most of the actual unemployed still enjoy some of the privileges of being linked to an enterprise, such as using enterprise apartments, usually without paying the rent. This contributes to the very low mobility of the unemployed.

Many point to the fact that many settlements are dependent on one loss-making mine or steel business. Closure of loss-making enterprises would mean unemployment for whole towns. This is considered unacceptable. There is no alternative employment, especially for miners who do not have any skills that are usable in other professions. It is this problem that legitimizes the present policy of punishing the good enterprises and rewarding the loss making, a policy that may lead to the demise of the whole regional economy.

The dominant attitude among the economic elite is that the causes of the economic crisis are outside their sphere of influence. Many expect that relations with Russia will be restored. The result is a passive attitude, postponing restructuring. The authors of a survey of the economy of Donetsk characterized this attitude as 'the syndrome of being captured by the past'.[14] They noticed 'excessive helplessness in the perception and description of the reality' by workshop participants in Donetsk.[15]

It seems as though Donetsk is caught in a vicious downward spiral with no discernible way out. The situation in Donetsk looks even gloomier than in Ukraine as a whole because Donetsk, with its rust-belt industries, epitomizes the weakness of Ukraine. Moreover, the leftish parties constitute a majority and the communist party is a leading force in Donetsk. Also, Donetsk is one of the most politicized and criminalized regions of Ukraine.[16] The sheer weight of Donetsk, in political and economic terms, combined with the militancy of the miners, exerts considerable pressure on Kyiv for continued subsidies for the regional economy of Donetsk.

Although economic decline is steeper in Donetsk than in the rest of Ukraine, living conditions still appear to be somewhat better because the position of Donetsk at the start of the decline was much better. According to official data, GDP per capita in Donetsk was US$3659 in 1995, while for Ukraine as a whole it was US$2620.[17] However, according to per capita retail trade turnover figures, consumption in Donetsk has fallen below the Ukrainian average: whereas it was 6 per cent above the national average in 1995, it was 4 per cent below it in 1997.[18]

Regional and local authorities do not try to develop a coherent regional economic policy geared at breaking down obstacles to economic development, but focus on concessions from Kyiv. It was thought that a Special Economic Zone could be a way out of the crisis. In Ukraine, Special Economic Zones have often been proposed as a panacea for all problems, and the Donetsk authorities demanded a Special Economic Zone as long ago as July 1992. When the idea was discussed in the Cabinet of Ministers, the Donetsk provincial administration suddenly withdrew its support.[19]

The first Special Economic Zone was set up near Sivash Lake in Northern Crimea in 1996. That was followed by the creation of the Slavutych Special Economic Zone near Chernobyl and the Transcarpathian Special Economic Zone in Western Ukraine.[20] A Special Economic Zone will also be set up in the Ukrainian port of Mykolayiv.[21]

According to the decree adopted by the president in September 1998 and the law adopted by the parliament on 19 November 1998, two Special Economic Zones will be established in Donetsk (in Mariupol, on the shores of the Azov sea, and in the southern part of the city of Donetsk) as well as 19 territories of priority development that encompass 19 industrial towns in Donetsk. Enterprises in these zones and territories get tax privileges and are exempted from the payment of import taxes. According to the law 'the investment projects, which are realized on the territories of priority development, are priority for granting the credits which are given by foreign states, international financial organizations, foreign banks, other financial credit establishment under state guarantees'.[22]

One of the main reasons for establishing Special Economic Zones and areas of priority development in Donetsk is the attraction of foreign direct investment. Per capita foreign direct investment in Ukraine is one of the lowest in Central and Eastern Europe. Up to 1 January 1998 Donetsk attracted only 5 per cent of total foreign direct investment in Ukraine, which amounted to US$106 million.[23]

The question is whether some tax concessions may attract investors if the general economic environment does not change. During a conference about Special Economic Zones in Kyiv (28 January 1999) representatives of the World Bank warned that Ukraine will not solve its nationwide investment deficit by creating Special Economic Zones with special investor privileges, and may only make matters worse by doing so.[24] According to John Hansen of the World Bank, 'Gifts to investors are of no importance if general economic problems in the country are not addressed'. He also warned that tax breaks given to Special Economic Zones often result in costly budgetary losses. If the main problems for foreign investors, such as regulatory hassles, poor enforcement of basic law and order, vague tax laws and the prohibition of land ownership, are not tackled, investors will not come. However, politicians in Donetsk see the Special Economic Zone as a way out of the economic crisis.[25]

The law on Special Economic Zones is rather vague and fails to deal with many of the issues that have to be resolved. The management of the Special Economic Zones and territories of priority development is rather complex. The administration of the zones have the power to intervene radically into enterprise activity and extended licencing requirements are in place. It seems that the whole set-up provides ample opportunities for abuse.

On 16 December 1998, the president vetoed the law adopted by parliament.[26] The reason cited for the initial veto was unwarranted benefits granted to investors, which will not efficiently stimulate industrial production in the region. This move, embarrassing for the president because he had earlier issued a decree allowing the Special Economic Zone, was most probably inspired by the international financial organizations, which opposed it. However, on 24 December 1998, the president signed the law.

Donetsk has had some opportunities for large investments. For example, British Petroleum was planning to invest US$50 million into developing a gas field in Ukraine's Dnipro-Donetsk basin.[27] According to the results of preliminary surveys, the field holds 500 billion m^3 of gas, with perhaps over twice that amount still not prospected. BP officials expressed confidence that by 2015 the field could be producing 50 billion m^3 per year – over half Ukraine's present annual consumption of gas – provided the proper investment conditions and appropriate technologies were present. The development of the Dnipro-Donetsk basin would require a total investment of US$22.5

million, according to State Geology Committee Chairman, Serhy Hoshovsky.

Although the state announced plans to exempt companies involved in exploration and operation of oil and gas deposits on the Black and Azov Seas shelf from corporate income tax, provided the money saved is reinvested in the same projects, British Petroleum renounced its plans because investment conditions were not favourable enough.[28]

During a visit by the Alabama State Oil and Gas Board to Ukraine in late 1998, it was said that they could provide Ukraine with the technical expertise to develop its huge methane resources. In Donetsk's abandoned coal mines, methane production could be profitable. However, inadequate methane distribution methods and a heavy tax on production prevented any investments in Ukraine.

The province of Zaporizhzhya: missed opportunities

Zaporizhzhya is a province in Eastern Ukraine, neighbouring Donetsk. It is a major industrial centre built around a large hydroelectric power station in the Dnipr. The power industry is important to Ukraine and the largest nuclear power station in Europe can be found in Zaporizhzhya. The core of the regional economy is made up of steel and aluminium enterprises. Many high value added industries can be found, in particular Motor Sitch, producing plane engines, Avtozaz, the major car producer in Ukraine, the Transformer enterprise, the only producer of transformers in Ukraine, and the Magnesium and Titanium enterprises.

Enterprises in Zaporizhzhya hardly functioned in the context of a regional economy. In Soviet times, most enterprises functioned under the supervision of the branch ministries in Moscow that organized all inputs and distributed all outputs. These ministries did not take into account a rational utilization of productive forces in a spatial context and neglected the advantages of intra-industry trade. It often happened that some inputs came from the Far East in the Soviet Union, while the very same inputs could have been provided by an enterprise in Zaporizhzhya, but which happened to be subordinated to another ministry.

In 1991, Transformer enterprise imported 22 300 tonnes of steel, 4800 thousand tonnes of copper and 5.7 tonnes of aluminium from Russia and 27 200 tonnes of copper from Uzbekistan. Note also, and this is typical, that large quantities of inputs have been imported, like steel and aluminium, that are also produced in Zaporizhzhya. Avtozaz imported 22.5 tonnes of steel from Russia, while there are huge steel factories in Zaporizhzhya. The Melitopol motor factory imported 676 tonnes of steel and 392 tonnes of rolled steel from Russia. The picture arises of a region that was highly integrated into the Soviet economy, but with a limited regional coherence. However, the regional economy has been designed as a coherent complex, centered on the hydroelectric power station and given the local natural resources.

With respect to output, similar data as for inputs are not available, but it is known that most large enterprises produced for the Soviet market as a whole and many of these enterprises were even monopolists. For example, Avtozaz was the only producer of cheap cars for the entire Soviet Union. Motor Sitch, which was incorporated in the military-industrial complex, delivered to the aviation industry located elsewhere in the former Soviet Union. Eighty per cent of engines for Soviet military transport planes were made in Zaporizhzhya.

With the falling apart of the Soviet Union many links with the republics of the Community of Independent States were severed and this contributed to a large degree to the economic decline of Zaporizhzhya. Many links are still there, as is reflected in the geographical composition of exports and imports, but at a much lower level than in 1991.[29] Another problem is that with the falling away of former links, few new links within the region have been established. This is, among others, related to the fact that horizontal networking between firms is not developed. Zaporizhzhya society is rather fragmented and the various clans barely communicate with each other. Secrecy is paramount and even the most trivial data, such as the bulletins from the statistical office of the provincial administration, are kept classified and are not even accessible to local researchers.

With a 10-point manifesto for the development of a regional policy, in 1992 the (former) provincial administration of Zaporzhzhya went to neighbouring provinces. A coordinating committee had been formed by the provinces of Donetsk, Dnipropretovsk, Luhansk and Zaporizhzhya. One of the results of this initiative was that coal supplies for the electric power generating stations were organized. Another result was that on 26 November 1993, the president of Ukraine, then Kravtshuk, gave Dnipropretovsk, Donetsk, Zaporizhyzhya and Luhansk substantially more scope for self-governing. However, one problem that remained was that of unclear competencies of regional administration and national ministries. Many initiatives were thereore blocked.

Nowadays, the Zaporizhzhya provincial administration has no more scope to manoeuvre than other provinces. The opportunity, given at the end of 1993, has not been seized. The years 1992–93 constituted a short interlude of increased autonomy for the regions. Since then the central administration has once again gained more powers.

The Zaporizhzhya provincial administration has not developed a genuine regional policy, although a good regional policy would seem to be urgent in view of the economic and social crisis. Nowadays, the approach to regional problems has more of an ad hoc nature, trying, like a fireman, to run from one fire to another, and not taking the time to get an overall view. It is also significant that no research on the regional economy has been done, and that such research is even hampered by the provincial administration. The approach towards regional problems has been of an administrative-command nature rather than facilitative. The newly established Regional Development Agency has not played any role in the development of a regional policy. The regional development plan, elaborated by Coopers and Lybrand in 1993 for the price of US$400 000,[30] has remained a piece of paper. Also, the numerous initiatives supported by Western donors, like the Business Communication Center, did not have the expected results. The Chamber of Commerce mainly organizes missions abroad and has little to offer to its members.

One of the most significant missed opportunities in Zaporizhzhya was the joint venture between Avtozaz and Daewoo, which promised a total investment of US$1.2 billion and which almost came to a standstill in early 1999 (see Chapters 6 and 7). Another missed opportunity was that of Motor Sitch, which in 1995 negotiated with BMW/Rolls Royce to develop the joint production of an aircraft engine. In the negotiations about the US$100 million project, the technical design was not a problem. The main problems concerned marketing aspects, and, above all, quality control. The directors of Motor Sitch also refused to discuss long-term strategy. In the meantime, BMW/Rolls Royce had found a partner in Russia. Another example: it was announced that a foreign investor, Washington Foundations, had won a tender for shares in the Ferroalloys enterprise, which holds a domestic monopoly for the production of metallic manganese. The factory was doing relatively well. However, domestic bidders united and succeeded in annulling the bid, the second time that this had happened.[31]

An interesting initiative has been the agreement of cooperation between neighbouring districts in Ukraine and Russia, in which Zaporizhzhya also participated (27 January 1995). It appears that cooperation is easier at this level than at government level. However, since its announcement nothing has been heard about this initiative.

The most recent initiative from the Zaporizhzhya provincial council, renowned in Ukraine for its initiatives, came early in 1999, with an anti-crisis plan. The plan addressed the crisis situation in the energy sector. It observed that in Zaporizhzhya, with its many energy-intensive producers, the energy bill has become, following increases in energy prices, three to four times as high as its Western competitors. Moreover, it has been noticed that 30–45 per cent of energy is lost as it is transported over the energy grid.[32]

In Zaporizhzhya almost half of industrial production is accounted for by heavy metallurgy and another 11 per cent by metal processing enterprises, all heavy energy consumers. Industrial firms only pay 5 per cent of the electricity bill in money, while households pay 60–70 per cent of the energy bill in money. Given the unfavourable ratio of industrial to household users in Zaporizhzhya (only 6 per cent of energy is consumed by households, in Ukraine as a whole 18 per cent), the energy producers in this province lose more money than energy producers elsewhere in the country. For the first nine months of 1998, Zaporizhzhya nuclear power station received only 6.8 per cent of income in money (the average for Ukraine is 16 per cent). Although labour productivity at the Zaporizhzhya nuclear power station is the highest in the country, the average salary is lower than the national average salary for the sector and went down from 416 hryvnas in 1996 to 400 hryvnas in 1997. Large salary payment arrears emerged.

The Zaporizhzhya provincial administration claimed that Zaporizhzhya nuclear power station should get four times more money than it actually got in 1998.

The anti-crisis plan encompasses a lowering of the energy price for enterprises in Zaporizhzhya province and transfer of funds from other power stations. In a decree entitled *About measures to stabilize and economic and social development of Zaporizhzhya province* (5 April 1999) the president of Ukraine supported the anti-crisis plan.[33]

Despite the missed opportunities mentioned, Zaporizhzhya is doing better than most other Ukrainian provinces, due to the high share of power production and heavy metallurgy in total production.

Conclusion

Characteristic of both Zaporizhzhya and Donetsk is the secrecy in public life that is much more pronounced than in Kyiv. It is much easier to obtain basic information about the economy of these provinces in Kyiv than in these provinces themselves. This secrecy is furthered by provincial authorities that stick to communist-style information policies.

In the set of parasitic mechanisms that paralyses the Ukrainian economy, the blocking role of local and provincial authorities constitutes an important element. Instead of furthering endogenous development potential, local and provincial authorities focus on lobbying for additional funds or privileges with national authorities. The non-transparent cross-subsidization of provinces and the fact that more than 80 per cent of local and provincial funds originate from the central budget, constitutes an important leverage for national government.

The example of Donetsk shows how the weakness of Ukraine is epitomized in this province. The dependence of many localities on one or a few value-subtracting enterprises makes restructuring extremely difficult. Many cannot believe that the market can create new jobs and many do not admit that coal and steel industries are often value-subtracting. These beliefs underpin an economic system that devours its own economic base.

The example of Zaporizhzhya shows the collapse of the Soviet division of labour, without being replaced by a more developed division of labour within Ukraine and the region. Above all high-technology production, for which Zaporizhzhya was known, declined during the 1990s. A coherent regional economy is still absent. Also a coherent regional economic strategy is absent, despite efforts to this end by Western donor organizations. Networking among firms is at a very low level. There is a range of missed opportunities, the most important being the failed Avtozaz–Daewoo joint venture.

Initiatives of both the provincial authorities in Donetsk and Zaporizhzhya were focused on Kyiv, with the aim of redistribution of resources at the national level, be it in the form of tax exemptions (Special Economic Zones), direct subsidies or special price policies (Zaporizhzhya).

9
Social Change: Economic Implications

In Chapter 3, the Ukrainian polity was analysed and the question addressed of how power, especially in relation to economic processes, is organized. The focus has been on the functioning of the political system and the state bureaucracy. However, the state, political system and bureaucracy are all part of society and socially embedded, although a prominent feature of the Ukrainian polity is the enormous division between the polity and the population.

In Chapter 2 it was shown how specific social practices, such as 'beating the system' by squeezing public property and lax labour ethos, helped to undermine the communist system, but erecting at the same time formidable obstacles to social and economic progress under post-socialist conditions.

This chapter analyses the interdependence of social and economic change. It is shown that anti-modern practices at all levels prevent modern institutions, including a modern market economy, from developing.

An anti-modern society against 'modern' institutions

The people, in 'beating the system', were much more ingenious than 'the system' and the socialist system finally disintegrated under its own weight. Socialism had created a disincentive system that discouraged people from working for the common good. However, the disrespect for the public good and the spread of parasitic attitudes and mechanisms worked as a boomerang once the old system was abolished.

Richard Rose described Soviet society as an hour-glass society.[1] There was a rich social life at the base, consisting of strong informal networks based on trust between friends, relatives and other face-to-face groups.

The state tolerated those networks as long as they did not affect the interests of the Nomenklatura. At the top of the hour-glass there was also a rich political and social life, in which elites competed for power, wealth and prestige. Exchanges between top and bottom were very restricted. Whereas in modern societies an intermediate level exists, that of civil society with numerous autonomous interest-representing organizations, this intermediary level was missing in Soviet society. This relative isolation of the elite and blocked feedback mechanisms produced increased inefficiencies. As described in Chapter 2, people increasingly succeeded in circumventing 'the system' (meaning the formal organizations of society, the upper half of the hour-glass), by creating their own, informal mechanisms of redistribution.

The anti-modern tactics of the population undermined the modern facade of Soviet society and also undermined economic and social development of this society. Imposed modernization was interrupted when the communist system was abolished. A modern society can be conceived as a society with large, impersonal and transparent bureaucratic organizations that are rule-bound and function in the context of the rule of law. It is obvious that the former Soviet Union was not modern in this sense although it had some attributes of modern society, such as large physical output and high levels of human capital.

With the abolishment of the party-state and the partial withdrawal of the state from social and economic life, suddenly a Pandora's box opened in which anti-modern practices could easily spread. It was not only the population at large, but above all the elite who used anti-modern and parasitic mechanisms. The creation of a 'freedom from the state' further undermined the functioning of modern organizations like the state and enterprises. In modern societies people, in principle, do not need to develop a repertoire of tactics for dealing with formal organizations. The behaviour of formal organizations is predictable. In modern societies organizations function like a kind of vending machine, i.e. if a person inserts an entitlement or money then the expected good or service will be delivered.[2] Organizational failure in Ukraine prevented this from happening and this failure contributed further to fostering anti-modern tactics, aimed to get round modern organizations.[3]

As the Ukrainian state failed even to deliver the most elementary services, a legitimacy crisis deepened. A hidden war between citizenry and state developed, partly as a result of non-payment of a number of services and taxes. Also, as in Soviet times, Ukrainian citizens do not respect state property.

Thus, the failure of the state to deliver, or, generally, organizational failure of 'modern' organizations, is not only related to bad management and a kleptomanic elite, but also to general attitudes of the population. The peculiar nature of the pseudo-modern superstructure of Ukrainian society can only be properly understood in the context of specific social practices that sustain it.

Many observers of Ukraine agree with the observation that specific attitudes of the general population constitute obstacles to social and economic progress. However, little research has been done in order to test the validity of this observation. Here, it is maintained that changes in the social habitus occur more slowly than political and economic changes, and differences in time-scales in these spheres cause major disfunctionalities. It is stated that anti-modern practices in Ukrainian society prevent pseudo-modern organizations from transforming into modern organizations and prevent modern organizations from preserving their 'modern' character.

The (post) Soviet socio-psychological syndrome

Here it is argued that Stalinist rule, and more broadly, the communist and Tsarist past, has produced a system of values, norms and behavioural patterns that is quite persistent and that is able to replicate itself. This coherent system of values is called the '(post) Soviet socio-psychological syndrome'.

This syndrome will be described below. Emphasis will be placed on the interrelationships between its component parts.

The cult of power

Although parliamentary democracy has been formally introduced in Ukraine, the political system and society at large is still very much authoritarian.[4] Power in Ukraine is generally not countervailed. Bureaucrats and enterprise directors reign in their domains as absolutist monarchs. Exercise of power in Ukraine has absolutist traits as power in Ukraine was always, in Soviet and in Tsarist times, absolutist. There is no tradition of challenging power because this has been severely punished in the past. Asking people in Ukraine why they tolerate unbearable circumstances at their workplace or in their town, the usual answer is: the choice is between slavery and dismissal, or between slavery and civil war.

Power is exercised in an absolutist and arbitrary way and this is reinforced by the way the ruled react. This is not to say that the people of Ukraine are to be blamed for the way they are governed. However, the way power relations are reproduced in Ukraine is partially rooted in the acceptance or tolerance by the subject people. In the words of Simon, there is an incomplete separation of ruler and state, of public and private. 'The bond between the people and the ruler/state was always forged by subjugation and reward, but not by mutual rights and duties'.[5]

Absolutist power and the totalitarian power of the communist party-state created a cult of power.[6] The attribute of power became so over-whelmingly important in the totalitarian state, where almost everything was subordinated to the will of the central power, that power, and therewith the lack of it, became of overriding importance in everyday life.

Absolutist and totalitarian power meant that those in power wanted to control as much as possible the behaviour of their subordinates. A control mania is visible in all areas of life.

The availability of absolutist power generates the desire to use this power. This is visible with the functionaries of public administration who are usually quite rude towards their clients. It is the powerlessness of the individuals faced with absolutist power that nurtured the rudeness of officials. It generally furthers the contempt for the feelings or the rights of individuals.

Due to the nature of power as is exercised in Ukraine the very notion of power as such, and politics in general, becomes discredited. Power is not used to facilitate but rather to block initiatives coming from below. The usual attitude of bosses in Ukraine is that everything that happens in their domain should be controlled by them. Independent initiatives are incompatible with such an attitude. It means that exercise of power in Ukraine is often paralysing. At the same time there is a refusal to delegate power.

It was the cult of power described above that enabled people in power on all levels to abuse their positions during the transition to a market economy, when the power of the state weakened, in order to appropriate state property on a massive scale.

Power is not intended to be used in a constructive way, although in communist times there was a typical developmental ideology that helped the Soviet economy to increase production. With the abolishment of the party-state, old communists, who usually stayed in power, lost all interest in the common good. Apparently, the previous developmental facade was imposed by the party and not internalized by many communist bosses.

Because of the way power is exercised and the long history of absolutist power, people have generally become very compliant and accept almost everything that is imposed on them. Therefore Ukraine can be ruled with impunity. Rulers hardly have to take the general interest into account, although politicians love to speak about 'preserving the social balance'.

Totalitarian power and oppression deterred trust and the development of horizontal cooperation networks in society. Ukrainian society, as a low trust society, is still very much fragmented. Only the small circle of family and friends can be trusted.[7] Ukrainian society can be considered as a conglomerate of small groups of families and clans that barely communicate with one another. Sharing knowledge with people who do not belong to the same clan is uncommon.[8]

Attitude towards the state and the public sphere

A peculiarity of Ukraine is the thinking in terms of dichotomy where it concerns the state and the public sphere. This dichotomy has a moral undertone: the nation (good) versus the state (bad), 'us' (good) versus 'them'(bad), people (good) versus the rulers (bad). It is in this context that stealing state property is not considered as a serious offence. 'Beating the system' is considered as a virtue. Although 'the state' has a negative connotation, the state is held responsible for providing a wide range of services. At the same time the state can be blamed for all personal failures.

Related to this peculiar attitude towards the state is the absence of solidarity that goes beyond the small circle of family and friends.

The culture of dependence and reluctance to assume responsibility

The cult of power, typical of all countries that belonged to the former Soviet Union, with the possible exception of the Baltic states, has led to a culture of dependence. Independent behaviour has always been punished.

Within larger or traditional organizations, like (previous) state-owned enterprises, the state bureaucracy and schools, this aversion to independent behaviour is still very much present. This attitude produced a deep-rooted lack of or fear of taking the initiative.

Extreme passivity is also characteristic of many inhabitants of Ukraine, although not immediately visible. The attitude is that the world, even the immediate environment, cannot be changed. If you put forward concrete proposals for cooperation for people in Ukraine, the first reaction usually is to enumerate scores of reasons why such a project is not possible. The second reaction is that the Western partner should do everything. It is an attitude of 'learned helplessness' – A deeply rooted attitude that is very difficult to unlearn.

The culture of dependence not only produces a lack of initiative, but also a lack of willingness to assume responsibility. Generally, people do not feel responsible for the tasks allotted to them. Their superiors do not credit them with competence, so there is no scope to assume responsibility. Assuming responsibility for something may have negative consequences. In Soviet times, people were only expected to follow orders, not to show initiative, although people found many ways to silently circumvent the orders imposed from above.

Of course, such an attitude has very negative consequences for labour ethos in general. Industriousness, discipline and efficiency did not rank high with most Ukrainians. One of the most notable traits in Ukraine was the lax national work ethic.[9] This is not to say that people in Ukraine do not want to do a good job. However, circumstances often prevent them from doing so. Usually, in order to make sure that they work, people have to be supervised constantly.[10]

The culture of dependence and the cult of power created a general inertia in society and individuals. One seldom finds an enthusiasm to undertake something, although with small industrial entrepreneurs one can find quite another attitude. But they are rare in Ukraine.

Generally, Ukrainian society can be described as a 'victim-society', a society in which the overwhelming majority of people feel themselves victims of their situation. The idea of shaping one's future by determined action and initiative is alien to most people. Most people are inclined to complain about the circumstances imposed upon them, without taking any action.

Related to the culture of dependence is the inclination to blame all deficiencies in one's own environment to external factors. It is at the same time a legitimation not to change anything. Conspiracy theories are quite common in Ukraine.

The marginalization of intellect

The fact that intelligent and competent people are often marginalized in society and the economy is very conspicuous in Ukraine. Ukrainian society is far from being a meritocracy. Being competent and intelligent is a major obstacle to obtaining positions of influence.

Compliance with those in power is a first requirement for influential positions. All other abilities are secondary. The result is an elite that is very incompetent. And incompetent people cannot tolerate competent people in their immediate environment. Thus, with the exception of some enclaves of privately owned enterprises and scientific centres of excellence, the specific recruitment mechanisms for influential positions in Ukraine prevent the development of competence.

Generally, and this is typical of Ukrainian and Soviet history, the intelligentsia eschewed power. In their eyes, power is corrupt and something evil. Talented people have usually sought a career in science or arts, rather than in politics. Creative intelligence in society was not only oppressed but channelled in directions that were not threatening to those in power. Nowadays, despite the introduction of parliamentary democracy, not much has changed in this respect.

No questions

People were never asked to think independently. In the educational system they have never learnt to analyse. It was geared towards the reproduction of facts rather than towards developing the ability to theorize or to analyse independently. This is still a basic characteristic of the educational system. Students have an overloaded program of classes. There are practically no seminars in which texts are discussed and students have hardly any time in the curriculum for independent research or writing.

Soviet society and the Soviet educational system produced a world outlook that was very simple. The 'laws' of society and economy were laid down in the classics of Marxism–Leninism and the only problem was to interpret them in the right way, which meant the interpretation of the party-state. Of course, the official world outlook and that of citizens differed but Soviet propaganda has had a profound impact on the world outlook of citizens. Also, the fact that almost everything in the individual's life was planned by the party-state, from professional career to the place where one lives, had an enormous impact. Citizens had very limited scope for manoeuvre in planning their lives. Consequently they did not learn to plan or to analyse the future in terms of alternative development paths. They also often lack the ability to think in terms of hypotheses.

A peculiar phenomenon observed by Westerners lecturing in Ukraine is that students usually react to theories or suggestions proposed by the lecturers by asking 'is it right or wrong', or 'is it good or bad'. Usually, students cannot envisage that the world may be interpreted in different ways, or that one particular theory may be partly adequate and partly inadequate in explaining a specific phenomenon.

This is related to the specific forms of exclusion that were predominant in Soviet thinking. In political life, the adage has been 'who is not with us, is against us', instead of inclusive thinking, namely 'who is not against us, is with us'. This attitude penetrated science as well. For example, existentialist philosophy was not in line with the party-state ideology and therefore bad. This official, exclusionist way of looking at the world of ideas had a profound impact upon the world outlook of citizens. Related to these mechanisms of exclusion is the propensity to be intolerant towards deviant opinions.[11]

A corollary of this simplistic world outlook is the fact that questions are seldom posed, reflecting the general lack of curiosity.[12]

The (post) Soviet socio-psychological syndrome as a comprehensive mechanism

As Scheme 9.1 shows, the constituent elements of the (post) Soiet socio-psychological syndrome form an interrelated whole, reinforcing each other. This is why it is so tenacious. The system described above is a system of negative feedbacks. No features are described that can be interpreted as positive. The negative feedback mechanisms can be seen as a kind of tumour in Ukrainian society. Understanding this phenomenon is crucial for grasping the essence of the present crisis in Ukrainian society.

The collective programming of the minds of individuals in Ukraine has been described here. It does not mean that the above description depicts adequately the average Ukrainian citizen. Such an average citizen does not exist. People in Ukraine are as diverse as they are in any other place in the world. Nevertheless, the assertion is that the majority of Ukrainians are affected by the syndrome as described above, but this does not imply that most Ukrainian citizens share each element of the syndrome.[13] The idea of the (post) Soviet socio-psychological syndrome should be seen as a hypothesis.

Some elements need explanation. One is the problematic relationship to truth. Under communism lying was a means of survival. In many enterprises, managers had to manipulate figures and cheat the authorities. This legacy may have contributed to the widespread practice of cheating in economic life.[14] Connected with this is the generalized lack of trust in society. A related phenomenon is the widespread opportunistic behaviour.

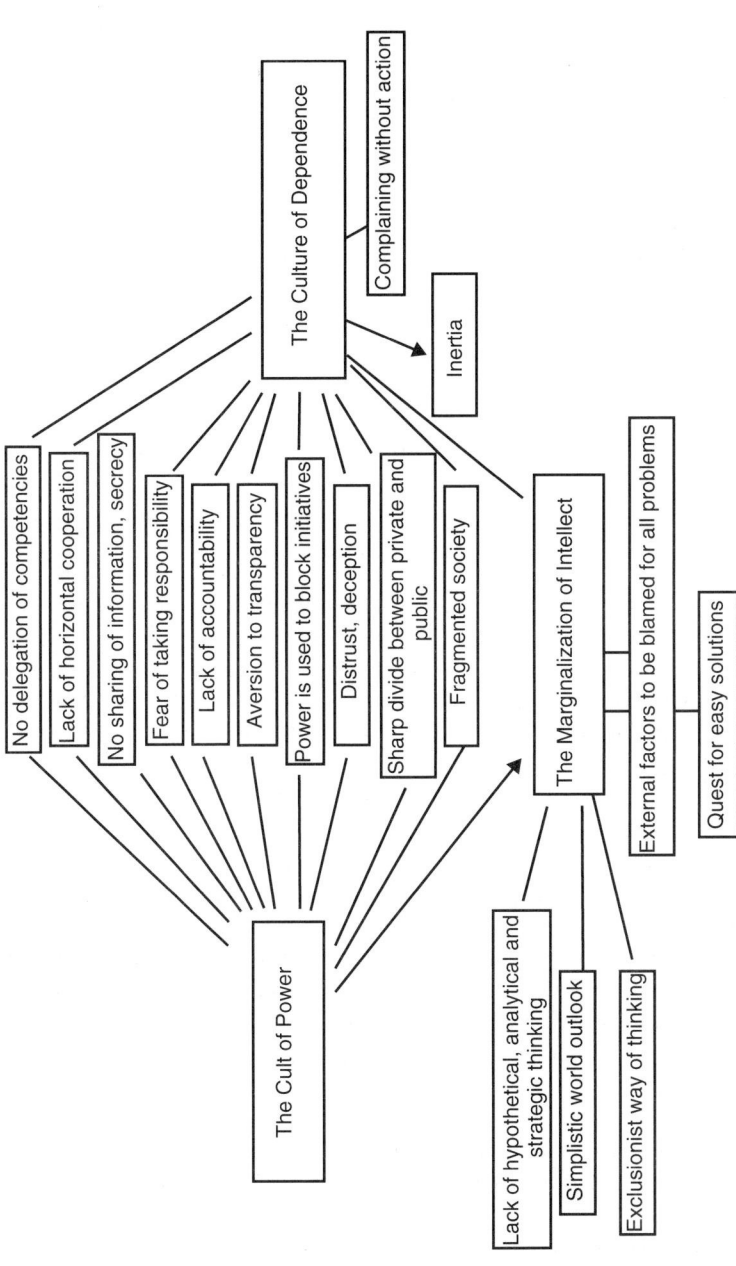

Scheme 9.1 The (post) Soviet socio-psychological syndrome as a comprehensive mechanism

Of course, the argument surrounding the syndrome is built upon subjective impressions. Also, some attitudes are not discussed that can be considered as an asset. There is, for example, the value attached to education, resulting in many attending higher education, even under difficult economic circumstances. However, this is not activated in social practices that may further economic development.

The properties attributed to the (post) Soviet socio-psychological syndrome became most pronounced in Stalin's time, although many of these properties had already developed in Tsarist times and have been described in 19th century Russian literature. Almost one decade after the demise of communism it appears that this syndrome is very persistent and that *Homo Sovieticus* is still very much alive.[15]

The (post) Soviet socio-psychological syndrome should be understood in the context of specific social practices. The term 'social practice' captures attitudes and behaviour in a social context and points to the pervasive character of it.

Implications for economic development

Economic behaviour constitutes a social practice that cannot be understood solely by referring to formal economic institutions. Economic development and economic institutions can be seen in the context of the nature of social interaction in a given society. Institutional economists now generally accept the idea that well functioning markets can only be conceived in the context of specific generally accepted and enforced norms. Douglass North wrote:

> In the modern Western world, we think of life and the economy as being ordered by formal laws and property rights. Yet formal rules in even the most developed country make up a small (although very important) part of the sum of constraints that shape choices ... In our daily interactions with others, whether within the family, in external social relations or in business activities, the governing structure is overwhelmingly defined by codes of conduct, norms of behavior, and conventions.[16]

For example, trust is a basic norm underpinning the well functioning of markets in developed market economies. As North pointed out,

> How effectively agreements are enforced is the single most important determinant of economic performance.[17]

It is obvious that in Ukraine, where cheating in business is common practice, trust is often lacking in economic life.[18] It seems that a minimum of trust is needed to allow all kind of transactions to take place. Also other behavioural patterns, conducive to economic development, may be stabilized and expanded once relations of trust have been established. Favourable for the furthering of trust are, according to Messner, organizational structures that, for instance, are characterized by relationships based on the rule of law, transparency of information, institutionalized monitoring mechanisms, consultations, high communication density, and reflexivity.[19] It is obvious that the Ukrainian government has not even begun to try to transform the country into a high-trust society. Of course, it is an illusion to think that this can happen in the short or medium term. But the problem has to be addressed by policy-makers. Hitherto, government policies furthered mechanisms that breed distrust.

Here the issue of the interrelationship between cultural change and economic change emerges. Generally, this interrelationship is neglected by economists, who often assume the existence of *Homo Economicus*. Generally, few believe that values and attitudes can shape a mode of production.[20] On the other hand, it is generally recognized that the changeover from a traditional economy to a modern industrial economy implies major value change. The industrial revolution also meant an industrious revolution, in which a new kind of man came to the fore: rational, ordered, diligent and productive. The widely studied transformation of peasant economies into modern agricultural economies in Western Europe took a long time, during which traditional values, attitudes and social practices constituted a major obstacle. David Landes showed in his 'The Wealth and Poverty of Nations' how much culture matters in economic development.[21]

In the most developed economies, innovation is at the core of economic progress. Networking within and between firms enables the sharing of knowledge and diffusion of innovations. The lack of horizontal cooperation and the closed character of clientele networks in Ukraine inhibit innovations and the diffusion of innovations. As far as innovations occur, it is above all 'parasitic innovativeness', i.e. the creativity in all kinds of illicit trading, smuggling, tax and duty evasions. It is elaborating the 'grab-and-run' practices.

Transformation into a modern society can also be analysed in terms of problem-solving capacities. Ukrainians learned during ages of despotic rule to live with problems while not solving them. Conflict and problem-solving mechanisms are weakly developed. Modern market economies entail a search for most efficient solutions at the micro-level involving a social engineering that is largely absent in Ukraine. Modern societies are learning societies. However, collective learning, by trial and error, is very difficult in Ukraine.

In Ukraine lack of accountability permeates the economy, related to the lack of horizontal differentiation and a concomitant delineation of responsibilities. Few feel responsible and few can be held responsible. Related to this generalized lack of accountability is an omnipresent control mania, especially obvious in the functioning of the state bureaucracy, and an associated deep aversion to control.

It is not only squeezing practices of the bureaucracy and Mafia that prevent small enterprises from developing, it is also lack of initiative that pushes the general population in more defensive portfolios of economic activities.[22]

Transaction costs are enormous in Ukraine, compared to developed market economies, given the fact that agreements are often not honoured and that the law is not enforceable. Corruption is omnipresent and political and bureaucratic power is used for private enrichment rather then for the public good. The development and persistence of such practices is enabled by a passive population that accepts almost everything that is imposed. There is a symbiosis between the victims and the benefactors of the present situation. A kleptocracy could develop because the thieves were not restrained.

The (post) Soviet socio-psychological syndrome and its associated social practices undermined the functioning of the Soviet system from within. It functioned as a kind of time-bomb under the system. It helped to pave the way for the emergence of the semi-feudal robber capitalism, preventing economic and social progress.[23]

Social preconditions for a modern industrial society are missing

At first sight, looking at some aggregate Human Development Indicators, Ukraine is a modern society. Ukraine ranks high with respect to literacy rates and number of doctors and teachers. Although this may be considered as an asset, in many respects Ukraine is still a traditional, or even anti-modern, society.

The modernization of Ukraine has been imposed, partial and superficial. The communists squandered huge resources on building the physical facade of an industrialized society, while neglecting the social fabric of it. The result was that Ukrainian society was, initially, very good at producing large quantities of iron and steel, less so in high value added products. As innovation and collective learning was very difficult in a centrally planned economy, the Soviet economy lagged increasingly behind modern industrial economies.

In modern economies, there is a complicated horizontal differentiation within society and economy in which various actors have clearly demarcated competencies and tasks. The differentiation occurs within enterprises, between enterprises and between all institutions that are part of industrial society. There is a high degree of insulation of institutional spheres from each other and a limited convertibility of status attributed from one sphere to the other.[24] Agency in industrialized societies is institutionally encapsulated.[25] In the words of Elster *et al.*, 'modern industrialized societies have a well institutionalized social order in which the (contingent, 'non natural') rules according to which political and distributional conflicts are carried out are relatively immune from becoming themselves the object of such conflict. There is, in other words a solid hiatus between rules and decisions.'[26] It is obvious that Ukraine is missing this horizontal differentiation and hiatus between rules and decisions(see also Chapter 3).

Transformation from a centrally planned to a market economy can be conceived as the splitting up of encompassing and multi-functional institutional compounds into smaller and functionally more specific units.[27] This transformation should not only be conceived in terms of organizational patterns. Gradually, in Western economies network coordination became more important besides the coordination mechanisms of the market and hierarchies. Network structures exist within and between firms and organizations and are linked to public authorities. According to Messner, networks are social innovations, institutional inventions for solving complex problems in view of which both market-like allocation (due to the production of negative externalities, a lack of long-term orientation, insufficient redundancy relations) and hierarchical forms of decision making (due to rigidity, a lack of flexibility, imperfect information, a lack of variety) prove dysfunctional.[28] In Ukraine, these innovative networks are absent. It can be said that Ukraine is not only faced with market failure and state failure, but also with network failure.

While in the developed capitalist countries a complex social fabric emerged to sustain economic development and industrialization, in the Soviet Union it was the vertically structured party-state that organized industrialization in an authoritarian way. While in developed market economies a horizontal organizational differentiation occurred in which new institutions got a large degree of autonomy that enabled collective learning, in the Soviet Union, technological progress was conceived in a linear, top-down way.[29]

A major problem arises here for Ukraine, because the country never has known such a deepened horizontal organizational differentiation. Moreover, informal institutional legacies of the past hinder the transformation towards a modern society and economy. While industrializing, in Ukraine basic perceptions of agrarian society could survive as they underpinned Soviet power. As Elster *et al.* put it, 'the coercively imposed industrialization did not go along with cultural and political modernization'.[30]

One can argue that Soviet power has meant, in a certain way, the modernization and civilization of society. One can point to the spread of mass education and a range of public services, to the spread of hygienic habits, as well as the internalization of a range of formerly externally imposed rules.[31]

At the same time, and Ferge pointed to this paradoxical process for the case of Hungary, there was a de-civilizing impact of communist rule.[32] In Ukraine, the upper class and traditional intelligentsia were largely destroyed and therewith its cultural traditions. Rude manners became generalized and intellect became even more marginalized compared to Tsarist times, despite the fact that so many obtained higher education. The destruction of the old social texture of society had a negative impact on the formation of social network capital that might have been conducive to the modernization of the country. Social capital is defined by Putnam as, 'features of social life, networks, norms and trust – that facilitate cooperation for mutual benefit'.[33] As Rose has pointed out, pre-modern societies also have social capital, and social capital can also be mobilized against another social group, as in the case of Northern Ireland, or against society as such, as in the case of the Mafia in southern Italy. From an economic perspective, social capital takes a negative form when it distorts the rule-bound allocation of goods and services. In the case of Ukraine, social capital exists but assumes pre-modern forms and anti-modern tendencies.[34]

Ukrainian social networks are usually internally homogenous and cohesive, but interactions outside the networks are weak. This resulted in an atomization of groups, not individuals.[35]

The peculiarity of Ukrainian society is that anti-modern network capital predominates while organizational capital, characteristic of modern societies, is very weak. Organizational capital is a society's stock of organizations that are formal, i.e. legally recognized by the state, rule-bound, bureaucratic, and hierarchically coordinated.[36] Organizational capital is weakened by anti-modern networks. The lack of rules governing social relations and relations between institutions, resulting in high barriers to cooperation, in all spheres, can be considered as one of the major obstacles to social and economic development in present-day Ukraine. This is reflected in the diminishing civic engagement of the population. While in 1991 65 per cent of Ukrainians did not belong to a civic organization, this percentage was 88 per cent in 1997.[37] Although the situation of the population deteriorated during the 1990s, civil disobedience had less support.[38] One can speak about intensifying political alienation in Ukraine.

With the collapse of communism a particularization of society took place that implied the emergence of an archipelago of social networks.[39] A division between inside and outside morals, typical of pre-modern societies, became more pronounced. Also, as in pre-modern societies, universal and impersonal mechanisms of social integration are very weak. Against this background of social disintegration the 'war of all against all' developed, a Hobbesian nightmare in which only the brute power of the strongest counts.

Srubar (1991) described how the privatization of the state under socialism as well as the spread of state influence over the economy produced a social structure whose integration was based on a texture of networks that redistributed the state's resources. That encompassed a shift from a universalistic ascriptive pattern to a particularistic ascriptive pattern. The latest phase of socialism saw a particularization and insulation of socialist society. An increasing divide appeared between 'we' and 'us'. Only the group members became moral subjects. This implies a return to a traditionalist society. However, there are important differences. The social structure is not sanctioned by religious beliefs and traditional value-generating institutions have disappeared or weakened. It seems that the most negative elements of traditional society come to the fore in what can be characterized as current 'neo-traditionalism'.

The mechanisms of exclusion

Ukrainian society also became polarized. The gap between the small group of extremely rich and the larger impoverished part of the population widened. The Gini coefficient, as based on official figures, stood at 22 for Soviet Ukraine at the end of the 1980s. By 1997, it has increased to 38, almost the level of the US.[40] However, as most of the income of the new rich is usually unreported, the Gini coefficient based on real income differences must be much higher.

In 1998, 80 per cent of the Ukrainian population was insolvent and the majority of the population spent most of their income on food. The calory intake per capita in Ukraine dropped from 3597 kilocalories in 1990 to 2567 kilocalories in 1997, while the protein consumption fell in the same period from 105.3 grams to 75.4 grams.[41]

Real disposable income of the average Ukrainian more than halved during the 1990s. According to the World Bank, in 1997 about three-quarters of the Ukrainian population were living below the poverty line (on a purchasing power parity basis). The poverty line was fixed at US$4 a day, which is higher than the poverty line used in low income countries in the developing world, because transition countries like Ukraine are more urbanized and have colder climates.[42]

The level of destitution is also exemplified in unemployment figures. Half of all households in Ukraine have at least one unemployed. Only 36 per cent of those polled in early 1998 had a full-time job, 23 per cent were pensioners, 5 per cent were not employed (students, house-wives), 8 per cent were employed part-time, 1 per cent were self-employed, 4 per cent were pensioners and employed, 14 per cent were unemployed without state benefit, and 3 per cent were unemployed while receiving state benefit. The remaining 5 per cent had no job but received an income maintenance grant.[43] It should be noted here that the official statistics only count the unemployed receiving state benefit.[44]

Many employees are sent on administrative leave. In the first half of 1998, 2.2 million workers, accounting for 17 per cent of formal sector employment, were on administrative leave. Also, 1.8 million workers were engaged in part-time employment.[45]

Those who are employed and actually working often do not receive their salary. In late 1999, wage arrears equalled 6.5 billion hryvnas (about 6 per cent of GDP). More than three-quarters of the wage debt was more than three months overdue, one of the highest levels among transition countries.[46]

In the context of Western societies this situation would not be sustainable. As can be seen in many countries of the South, in the context of a pre-modern society deep polarization, extreme inequality and permanent exclusion of a larger part of the population is sustainable (Pakistan, Mexico, India). In contradistinction with most countries in the South, Ukraine witnessed a sudden and sharp drop in living standards and social degradation for the overwhelming majority of the population.

Many expected that the Ukrainian middle class would gradually expand during the transition process. However, the middle class largely disappeared.

The abolishment of the party-state and economic decline meant for most Ukrainian citizens a downward social mobility. In Kharkiv, Eastern Ukraine, respondents were asked in an opinion poll 'In your opinion, what is your place in society now, which step on the social staircase do you occupy?' While in 1986, 85 per cent of respondents reckoned themselves to be middle class, by 1996 this had declined to 39 per cent. While 6 per cent of respondents reckoned themselves in 1986 to be lower class, this percentage was 49 per cent in 1996. This means that in terms of self-ascribed social status, the social stratification of the population of Kharkiv deteriorated enormously. The authors of the report noticed that values which used to determine the respondent's social status, such as level of education and moral and human qualities, dropped considerably in their view, whereas such factors as level of income, personal connections and business qualities become more and more important.[47]

Most of the poor seem to be sinking away in passivity and despair. The longer they stay in poverty, the more difficult it will become to regenerate the economy. Sustained mass poverty generates mechanisms that perpetuate the downward vicious circle of destitution and deprivation. Desperate people are usually not energetic or entrepreneurial.[48] If new opportunities arise, these people often do not seize them.

'Civic behaviour' cannot spread as 'modern organizations' fail to deliver. Because enterprises and state organizations fail to pay regular wages, theft of enterprise and state property has become widespread. Due to lack of money, an increasing share of the population no longer pays for rents or supplied electricity and gas.[49]

As a result mainly of the deteriorating socio-economic situation, birth rates have dropped and mortality rates increased.[50] Therefore the population of the Ukraine started to decline from the early 1990s onwards, from 51.9 million inhabitants in 1991 to 49.8 million in late 1999, and the population age structure deteriorated. If current trends persist, by 2056 there will be only 0.5 workers supporting each pensioner, compared with 1.6 in 1999 and 2.0 in 1990, placing an impossible burden on the working population.[51]

Also, many people have emigrated. On a net basis, more than 400 000 people left Ukraine between 1990 and 1997.[52]

Ukraine became an experimental ground for those who were inclined to take risk and provided numerous opportunities for those who were reckless. Rather than developing into a modern society with citizens, Ukraine remained a society with subjects to an unaccountable regime.

How to foster modernization of society and economy

In the Western world, since the crisis of social democracy unfolded and especially since the weaknesses of the neo-liberal approach became more obvious, old political categories have been reassessed, especially in the context of the discussion about a Third Way. One of the tenets of the new Third Way is that the old dichotomy between the left and right about the state is not relevant anymore. The question is not about more or less state, but about creating adequate governance mechanisms in state and society. Within the sphere of public authorities there is a shift towards subsidiarity, that is the principle that state tasks should be executed at the lowest level possible. This led to devolution of state power. Since neo-liberalism has come to the fore, the role of the state in economic life has certainly not diminished, despite the wave of privatizations of state enterprises. The state did a lot to promote industrial innovation. The role of industrial and regional policy gradually changed, with a shift of focus from the redistribution of resources, to the benefit of poorer industries and regions, to the fostering of industrial innovation and endogenous development potential.

Given this shift in the role of state and the discourse about it, the discussion about the role of the state in Ukraine does not reflect these new insights at all. The left in Ukraine, dominating the political spectrum, furthers more state in the form of more state ownership and redistribution of state funds to poorer industries and regions. The right pleads for less state. However, the question is to what extent less state and more liberalization leads to more market economy. In those segments of the economy where the state withdrew and liberalization proceeded farthest, like in the shadow economy or in small-scale industrial production, economic development is hampered by many factors. One of the major hindrances is the lack of adequate governance mechanisms.

Messner noticed that for the most developed economies, 'a multiplicity of new patterns of organization and governance has emerged beside hierarchical governance of society by the state'.[53] A new socio–echnological–

organizational paradigm appears to be gaining ground, characterized by a complex organizational and governance pluralism.

In Ukraine, the emergence of such a paradigm is hindered by the general lack of trust in society, the lack of cooperative attitudes among enterprises and organizations and the obstructive attitude of the state towards non-state organizations. Ukraine is actually moving away from above-mentioned paradigm.

Ukrainian-style networking contrasts sharply with the emerging 'network society' in the developed capitalist world. It is not the phenomenon of networking as such that distinguishes the Ukrainian economy and society from that of the developed capitalist world, but the character of networking, as explained above.

The International Monetary Fund and World Bank have started to address issues of state governance. In 1997, the World Bank started an initiative on Defining, Monitoring and Measuring Social Capital, while in late 1998 the IMF listed the reform of Ukrainian public administration as one of its conditions for issuing a new tranche (see Chapter 4).

Conclusion

Changing the economic system in Ukraine involves not only changing the set of formal economic institutions and creating new rules of the game at the macro-level, but also changing society and deeply ingrained social practices. Disdain for the public good, general passivity and lack of initiative, lack of trust, widespread cheating and lack of accountability and transparency are all characteristic of present-day Ukrainian society. In fact, the state is currently furthering these attitudes and social practices. It seems that in many ways, Ukraine is moving from a pseudo-modern society to a pre-modern or even anti-modern society. Social network capital in Ukraine has a pre-modern character and holds back the development of organizational capital. The low level of civic engagement is diminishing even further. Like in a pre-modern society impersonal norms of social integration are very weak and there is a sharp distinction between in-group and out-group. This runs counter to the organizational needs of a modern economy with its highly complicated horizontal differentiation. Also, in its social stratification and mechanisms of exclusion, Ukraine is moving away from modernity, not to mention the new techno-economic paradigm that is spreading in the most advanced economies.

It is the pre-modern characteristics of Ukrainian society that makes the rapid disintegration and continuous decline of the Ukrainian economy socially and politically sustainable. Economic development without social integration is not feasible.

There is a mismatch between the formal institutional framework and social practices. Social practices cannot immediately be influenced by state policies. A major contribution the state can make in the creation of attitudes that are better geared to modern economic development is the overhaul of state institutions, i.e. administrative reform, creating conditions for the rule of law, combating corruption as well as furthering the self-organization of society.

10
Path Dependency and Development Prospects

Is it possible, after nine years of 'transition', to delineate the contours of the new socio-economic formation emerging in Ukraine? The question is not so much to put an adequate label as rather to detect the operating mechanisms of the new socio-economic system. The question is policy relevant as the answer may point to major issues to be tackled in order to achieve social and economic development. It is argued that a set of parasitic mechanisms at all levels of society and economy prevent economic regeneration.

Comparative analysis of other countries with similar characteristics allows the delineation of alternative development paths. Major factors and actors are identified as well as driving forces behind the socio-economic development in Ukraine.

Western perspectives and Ukrainian realities

When communism was abolished in Central and Eastern Europe, it was the naive assumption of many in the West, particularly the international institutions such as the IMF, OECD, World Bank and EBRD, that capitalism could be introduced by decree. They stated in 1990 that:

> A recovery from the reduced level of output should be able to get underway within two years or so...further, strong growth of output and rising living standards could be expected for the remainder of the decade and beyond.[1]

They expected a quick fix that did not require any structural changes. They expected that the market could function as a lever to impose economic rationality upon society and economy. They implicitly assumed the prevalence of *Homo Economicus* making rational choices.

Soon afterwards, it became obvious that Ukraine and other countries of Central and Eastern Europe were not only faced with a transformational recession, in which wasteful and value-subtracting activities were eliminated, but also with a 'normal' recession, caused by systemic transformation and the collapse of the socialist division of labour. By 1999, it can be said that in the case of Ukraine that much more was involved.

In this book it has been shown that many other factors contributed to the continuous economic decline of Ukraine during the 1990s. Most factors are structural and related to the institutional legacy that comprises ingrained social practices. It was often informal constraints that constituted impediments to the emergence of a more efficient economic system. It is shown that path dependency prevented a quick and easy transformation towards a modern industrial capitalism.[2]

Despite a qualitative break with the falling away of the party-state in 1991, the new socio-economic formation developed organically out of the old. Ukraine was in 1991 no *tabula rasa*. A reconfiguration of elements from the former economy and society led to a new configuration of social and economic interests. It was as if with the abolishment of the party-state, a world that was hitherto hidden, came to the fore and imposed its rule over society.

It has been described how the state retained its patrimonial character. Clientelism spread and the state–society divide deepened further. Although a state apparatus was built up from scratch, the new state was predatory in character and used by the ruling elite as a feeding ground. At the same time the state was disintegrating and the problem of governability came to the fore. The peculiar character of the self-destructive state and its institutions is at the core of the new socio-economic formation and prevents social and economic development.

The new socio-economic formation crystallized under President Kravchuk (1991–94). Hyperinflation and lawlessness allowed a kleptomanic elite to enrich itself on a massive scale. The new banks functioned as a channel for both money laundering and, initially, for government-sponsored easy loans instead of an instrument for financially disciplining enterprises. Privatization usually did not lead to change in corporate governance because the general economic environment did not change. Also, actual control over property often did not change significantly. The position of collective agricultural enterprises, which became formally autonomous and independent, shows this clearly. The semi-feudal setting in which they operated did not change. Major sectors of the economy, such as the energy complex and steel production, are still state dominated and profit from subsidies.

The system of subsidization has become less transparent. Nowadays it is quite difficult, through payment arrears, barter trade and shadow activities, to determine which enterprises are loss-making and which are profitable. Generally, lack of transparency is characteristic of the new socio-economic formation that emerged in Ukraine. For example, the complicated and contradictory system of laws and decrees and the lack of an independent judiciary make the legal environment very uncertain. Contracts are generally not enforceable.

This is not a flaw that could easily be overcome: it is at the core of the socio-economic system. Generally, deeply entrenched anti-modern practices complicate the emergence of modern and effective organizations.

The specific way in which Ukraine opened its borders allowed capital flight on a massive scale to take place. Import competition destroyed domestic producers and prevented international industrial co-operation from developing. However, it allowed value subtracters to export their products.

In hindsight, it is easy to show how all new trends and properties fit easily together. It is also obvious that the market cannot function as a *deus ex machina* in the economy and that markets are socially embedded.

The legal reforms, aimed at introducing a market economy, did not provide a change in social property relations and property rights remained poorly defined. They did not secure a separation of enterprises from the state and their subordination to market competition. Policy makers and their Western advisers ignored the fact that social relations predetermine the impact of markets.

With respect to the role of the state, Western advisers ignored the fact that the aim of politicians, and the state as such, was power maximization and not the extension of welfare, or enhancement of economic efficiency. The state was rent-seeking instead of market facilitating. Paradoxically, reform supposed by the donor organizations to reach 'the market-facilitating state' is exactly what was pushing Ukraine into creating a rent-seeking state.[3]

In Ukraine, and in most other states of the former Soviet Union, it was not the state privatizing state-owned enterprises, but rather the state owned enterprises privatizing the state. The state transformed into an organization that did not promote modernization and transition to market economy, but fostered anti-modern tendencies in society and economy.

Not a market economy but a virtual economy

The description of economic change so far shows how developments in various spheres of society and economy fit together to form a movement towards a new socio-economic formation, beyond market and plan, consisting out of a set of parasitic mechanisms that leads to an economic system that eats its own economic base.

Westerners are often impressed by the expansion of a network of fashionable shops in the centres of large towns, the opening of new restaurants and the higher level of services offered. However, it is the modernization of the facade of the country, hiding the marasma of the core economic sectors.

Deception is at the core of the economic system. Gaddy and Ickes introduced the term 'Virtual Economy' to describe the newly emerged economic system in Russia.[4] This economy is non-market in nature and its inefficiency will ensure, according to Gaddy and Ickes, continued economic decline and future crises. The roots of the Virtual Economy lay in the largely unreformed industrial sector inherited from the Soviet period. At the heart of the phenomenon are the large number of enterprises that still produce goods but destroy value. Enterprises can operate without paying their bills. This is possible because value is redistributed from other sectors of the economy. One way this is done is through tax arrears, which are in effect the continuation of budget subsidies in a different form. In the case of Russia, the authors argue, a much more important form is the redistribution of value from the resources sector to the value subtracting industry. The process of redistribution is difficult to analyse due to the fact that many transactions are not registered. Thus, what appears on the surface and in the statistics is quite different from what happens in reality.

The case of Ukraine is similar to that of Russia in that so-called 'reform' did not lead to, but from, 'the market'. For many reasons, participants in the Ukrainian Virtual Economy want little transparency and they stay away from cash. There is for instance the practice of the state taking money from enterprise accounts in cases of tax arrears (the Kartoteka 2 rule) and high interest rates. Also, deception can be found at all levels of the Ukrainian economy. Even in the bazaar, one kilogram weights only 800 grams, and everybody accepts this. Falsification of statistics is still common. A major difference with Russia is that Ukraine is not resource rich. In fact, the coal sector is value subtracting. This is one of the reasons why during the 1990s economic decline has been much steeper in Ukraine than in Russia.

Virtualization appears to be a greater threat to market-oriented reforms than government budget deficits and high inflation. It is both the cause and effect of inconsistent, incomplete, unfinished and unenforceable reforms.

Gaddy and Ickes' argument is that on all accounts, the Virtual Economy is performing, on paper, better than the actual economy. On paper, it often seems that the value subtracting industry is actually value adding. On paper, wages and pensions are much higher than they really are, because wage arrears are usually not reflected in the average wage and pension.

The belief that the value subtracting industry is value adding is a major force sustaining the Virtual Economy. Too many people want to believe this fiction.

Although in Ukraine many registered economic activities are actually value subtracting, it cannot be said that on paper the Ukrainian economy functions better than in reality because approximately 60 per cent of the real economy is in the shadow economy and is not registered, and many shadow activities are value-adding.

Belief systems underpinning parasitic mechanisms

Old belief systems are very persistent. It is extremely difficult to explain to someone who grew up in Soviet times the basics of a market economy, to explain that a coal mine should be closed if it produces coal whose cost price is two or three times higher than the world market level. It would create massive unemployment in the mining regions. A Westerner would respond, with a well functioning market economy in mind, that the process of closing loss-making mines should be gradual and that new value-added activities will create new employment. The market will create that. However, people who grew up in Soviet times cannot imagine how this could happen. They would say 'ideal norms are bad criteria for judging real world phenomena'. Their only certainty is the experience of a centrally planned economy. Their instincts are based on this experience. If something goes wrong, the central planner should intervene and increase controls.

Although the present economic system produces further economic decline, most people in influential positions continue to act against market-oriented reform. The overwhelming majority of the political and economic elite have no experience of a market economy and have a very simplistic and distorted notion about how modern market economies function. They do not see the core of the problem and are therefore unable to devise a strategy to emerge from the current crisis.

Most politicians are unable to think in terms of economic rationality. It is alien to them. Those who ran a centrally planned economy had an engineer's mentality. Problems of production are, in their view, basically technical. Still, the core of the problem is not seen as economic in nature. This is one of the major reasons why state owned enterprises have hardly restructured.[5]

At the political level, it is mainly survival networks that are represented and less so entrepreneurial networks. An entrepreneurial network is interested in furthering the market economy and sees prospects in a situation of free competition. The survival network can only survive by siphoning off funds from the state and is therefore not interested in market-oriented reforms. By early 2000, survival networks in Ukraine were far more influential than entrepreneurial networks. This resulted in government policies and practices of the state bureaucracy that squeezed citizens and healthy enterprises to the benefit of the value subtracting industries and the state bureaucracy. Survival networks are not interested in involving Western enterprises in production because the Ukrainian side fears that the Westerners may impose rules based on economic rationality that may threaten their position. There are many examples of management of Ukrainian enterprises that successfully blocked the takeover or participation by Western enterprises (see also problems with Avtozaz–Daewoo, Chapter 7).

A typical example is that of Oriana, a chemical plant in Ivano Frankivsk province. In October 1997 the government granted Shelton, a private Ukrainian company with a foreign stake and the biggest private oil importer, a 50 per cent plus one share in Oriana. The government did so after Oriana became a significant burden on the budget. When Shelton took over control of the plant, employing 17 000 workers, it launched a consolidation programme, closing down unprofitable operations and investing in profitable ones. Oriana managed to make a profit of 446 million hryvnas in 1998, compared to a loss of 29.4 million hryvnas in 1997. However, production and total revenues were down considerably. This worried the provincial administration and they started lobbying President Kuchma. On 10 July 1999, Kuchma ordered the cabinet of ministers to return the Shelton stake in

Oriana to the provincial administration, annulling the state's privatiz-ation contract with Shelton.[6] The case is exemplary for the belief that enterprises should not make a profit but should produce as much as possible and maintain employment. The case also reflects the disdain for contractual obligations.

The above-described belief system is shared by both the majority of the ruling elite and the larger part of the population.[7] It is this belief system that sustains the present system of involution, that is an econ-omic system that eats its own economic base.[8] It prevents the emer-gence of monetary transparency and organizational reform because these issues are seen as non-issues.[9]

Western advisers and their Ukrainian counterparts usually have a dialogue of deaf, starting from totally different assumptions. The Western adviser starts with the idea that economic rationality should govern the economy. The task of the state is to sustain the economic rationality of the economic sector, while correcting in the case of unwanted distortions. For the Ukrainian counterpart it is usually not possible to disentangle political and economic rationality (Scheme 10.1). Basically, economic problems are dismissed as non-existent, because they turn a blind eye to it. Capitalism is not accept-able because they see the law of value operate against their interests. Letting the blind force of the market, the invisible hand, go its own way, means in their view the closure of almost all factories, and no guarantee that alternative employment will be created. Many Ukrainians believe that capitalism cannot work in their country. They cannot imagine a self-regulating economy.

It is this belief system that legitimizes the attempts of Ukrainian public authorities to resist 'the market', at the same time allowing the further demise of the Ukrainian economy.

Some elements in Scheme 10.1 need clarification: procedural ratio-nality refers to the primordial importance of the application of a special agreed-upon set of rules. In Ukraine it is not the way in which an outcome has been brought about but the outcome itself that counts. Typically there is an aversion to clarifying and codifying behavioural rules and procedures.

The widespread tendency to blame economic failure on external factors is conspicuous in Ukraine . In the provinces government policy is often blamed. At the national level, it is often the Russians, and increasingly Western states, donor organizations and multinational enterprises that are the culprits. Conspiracy theories are still very popular in Ukraine.

Scheme 10.1   State and economy: Western and Ukrainian models

	Western model	Ukrainian model
Economy and politics	Clear distinction between spheres of economy and politics.	No distinction between spheres of economy and politics
Law of value	Law of value should be driving force in economy (economic rationality)	Law of value rejected. Primacy of political rationality over economic rationality. Administrative decisions should govern the economy
Rule of law	Rule of law	Mores are more important than laws
Demarcation of competencies and the issue of accountability	Horizontal differentiation within and between organizations, clear demarcation of competencies	Opaque borders between and within organizations. Wheeling and dealing. Economic transactions based on personal trust.
	Contractual obligations are important.	No accountability
	Hiatus between rules and decisions (Procedural rationality)	No hiatus between rules and decisions
Enterprises	The function of an enterprise is profit maximization	The function of an enterprise is to maximize output and to guarantee employment
	Enterprise headed by entrepreneur/manager	Enterprise headed by 'chozjan' (lord)
	Networking in and between enterprises important Social engineering through sophisticated management methods	Top-down hierarchical management methods
Role of state	State as facilitator, provider of basic public goods such as education	State has a role to pay in the organization of production Where enterprises fail, the state should intervene
	Soft governance mechanisms are important	Rule by decree
	State rules over citizens with mutual right and obligations	State rules over subject-people Bonds between rulers and ruled forged by subjugation and reward

Scheme 10.1 Continued

	Western model	Ukrainian model
Approach to economic problems	Economic rationality, analytical approach, transparency Economic calculation possible.	Political rationality. Lack of transparency. Economic problems ignored. Economic calculation very difficult. External factors often blamed for economic problems
	Methodical rational acquisition	Aversion against 'book-keeper mentality'

The above-mentioned belief systems are linked to mental constructs that change very slowly. It is these mental constraints that evolve an ideology that not only rationalizes the society's structure but also accounts for its poor performance.

Feudal property systems and Ukraine

When advising the transition countries to privatize state-owned enterprises, Western financial organizations assumed that private ownership of the means of production is at the core of the capitalist system. When studying the Ukrainian economy it is appropriate to study property systems in a broader context.

Brenner (1985) looked at both property structures and balances of class forces in various European regions, during the crisis of feudalism. Brenner's argument started with the assertion that

> the feudal social–property system established certain distinctive mechanisms for distributing income, and, in particular, set certain limits on the development of production, which led to economic stagnation and involution. It did so, most crudely, because it imposed upon the members of the major social classes – feudal lords and possessing peasants – strategies for reproducing themselves which, when applied on an economy-wide basis, were incompatible with the requirements of growth. In particular, reproduction by the lords through surplus extraction by means of extra-economic compulsion

and by peasants through production for subsistence precluded any widespread tendencies to thorough specialization of productive units, systematic reinvestment of surpluses, or to regular technical innovation. The system wide consequence of this structure of reproduction – especially given the tendency to long term demographic increase – was a built-in secular trend towards declining productivity of labour and ultimately to large scale socio-economic crisis.[10]

It is obvious that Ukraine's specific social property system restricts the economic actors to certain limited options and strategies, in order to best reproduce themselves, that is to maintain themselves in their established socio-economic position.

The growth of the market is not associated with the growth of competition through which enterprises would be subjected to the law of value. The emergence of the banking sector has not subjected enterprises to 'hard budget constraints'.

A comparison with feudalism is instructive. Feudalism saw at a very early stage of its development the emergence of money and commercial capital, but this capital was for a long time parasitic on, and subordinate to, feudal social relations of production. What emerges now in Ukraine looks like a kind of parasitic 'merchant capitalism' in the context of a Byzantine polity and semi-feudal relations in major sectors of the economy (state-owned enterprises and agriculture). Parliamentary democracy seems to be a facade for 'democratic despotism'.

As in so many countries in the world, 'rulers devised property rights in their own interest and transaction costs resulted in typically inefficient property rights prevailing'.[11] It is the existence of poorly defined property rights that prevents economic growth. Related to this is the problem of enforcement of contracts. Again, North can be quoted: 'The inability of societies to develop effective, low cost enforcement of contracts is the most important source of both historic stagnation and contemporary underdevelopment in the Third World'.[12]

The plunder of economic resources that is characteristic of present-day Ukraine is historically not unique. One can even say that economies that are not based on plunder are historically the exception. As Hilton noticed, plunder was for centuries a feature of surplus extraction in early feudal society. He also noticed that 'social conflict in medieval towns often seems to be no more than factional struggle within oligarchies...'.[13] This is reminiscent of the Ukrainian situation where popular unrest has hitherto been avoided.

Criminalization of economy and state

According to a report written for President Kuchma in 1996, organized crime poses an immediate threat for the stability of the state. The criminal subculture has penetrated all levels of the state apparatus. Organized crime has its parallel power structure and the population has to pay for these structures. On average, organized crime makes products 20 to 30 per cent more expensive.[14] Few firms can escape organized crime; about 90 per cent of firms are under its influence.[15]

Some authors suggest that in transition economies, the Mafia should not be viewed entirely as a social pathology.[16] Rather, it is a market accommodation to the failure of the state to deliver an attractive combination of taxes and public goods.

The problem is that with the criminalization of the state, state power becomes a function of private, often criminal, interests and that the public good becomes subordinated to those private interests. It is nowadays difficult to make a clear distinction between organized crime and the state. It is not only that Mafias find protection by the state, as is the case in many countries, but that organized crime can instrumentalize the state.

It means that there is not anymore a 'raison d'état'. The state as a semi-autonomous institution has ceased to exist. The state has transformed into an entity that is acting against the public good, in the interests of a kleptomanic, criminalized elite.

Coping mechanisms of the population and social exclusion

The present socio-economic formation not only leads to economic decline, but also to extreme income inequalities and an impoverishment of the overwhelming majority of the population. Social exclusion is part and parcel of the new socio-economic formation. Historically new is that there was a rapid changeover from a rather egalitarian society, in which social mobility was high and mass poverty unknown, towards a society in which most of the population is marginalized and impoverished by a predatory ruling elite.

As the 'modern' economy is less able to produce goods and services, Ukrainian citizens are increasingly pushed into pre-modern economic activities in order to survive. It is noticeable that most Ukrainians have developed defensive portfolios of economic activities, such as cultivation of the kitchen garden and providing services for friends and family (see Chapter 9, page 164). Most Ukrainians retreat into a largely non-monetary economy. It should be recalled that a large part of the population does not have a permanent job.[17] However, traditional coping mechanisms are becoming less effective, as stealing of crops from kitchen gardens becomes more widespread, and one can count less on the help of relatives and friends as they are becoming poorer.[18] It means that the protective buffer of the pre-modern informal economy is becoming weaker.

On the other hand, the passivity of the population and the general lack of interest of mediating organizations in Ukrainian society allows a predatory elite to continue to act with impunity.

Factors contributing to involution

Ukrainian-style involution, i.e. an economic system that eats its own economic base, is determined by the following factors.

1. *Economic mechanisms of the Virtual Economy.* All major players in this economy are interested in the perpetuation of the present situation in which economic sectors are cross-subsidizing. They are opposed to the dominance of economic rationality and the introduction of the law of value. This is underpinned by a lack of transparency.

2. *Lack of transparency.* A lack of transparency is at the core of the virtual economy. Due to a lack of transparency, it is almost impossible to show where the crucial weaknesses of the present system are and so to undermine the dominant belief system. Also, a lack of transparency with respect to rules laws and competencies, allows the widespread lack of accountability to persist. It allows the continuing malfunctioning of the state apparatus and enterprises.

3. *Social practices.* As is described in Chapter 9, anti-modern social practices of the population at large and of the ruling elite in particular, prevent economic rationality from coming to the fore and sustains the present system of involution.

4. *Belief systems.* Dominant belief systems, ignoring and rejecting economic rationality, are deeply rooted in Soviet and Ukrainian traditions.

5. *Mechanisms of exclusion that allow a predatory ruling elite to act with impunity.*

6. *Nature of the state.* A predatory state and a parasitic bureaucracy are at the core of the set of parasitic mechanisms that paralyses the Ukrainian economy.[19] Local and regional authorities reinforce

parasitic practices of the state bureaucracy at the national level (Chapter 7).
7. *The Ukrainian mode of internationalization.* The specific way in which Ukraine opened up, that means allowing capital flight to take place, enabling the export of subsidized products on a massive scale, preventing international industrial cooperation from developing and allowing import competition to destroy domestic enterprises rather than creating the conditions under which they could perform better, was an important element in the emergence of involution.

Is the Ukrainian model unique?

It is often assumed that the expansive logic of the emerging market sector, combined with the positive example of Western market economies and pressure from international institutions, may give the market sector a dynamism that pushes aside the non-market sector. It is a Darwinist assumption that is widespread among economists. However, the emerging market sector is inserted into a kleptocratic system that prevents a productive capitalism from developing. The face of the emerging capitalism is that of robber capitalism, or primitive merchant capitalism, inserted into a semi-feudal political context.

The 'Wild East' of the 1990s is often compared with the 'Wild West', i.e. the USA of the 19th and early 20th centuries. However, the 'Wild West' knew an economic dynamism, was not faced with a parasitic state bureaucracy and was a new settler economy.

The situation may be compared with Sicily, where social and economic development is structurally retarded by criminalization of society and economy. The vicious circle of underdevelopment is perpetuated in Sicily by a more or less stabilized socio-economic formation, although functioning in the context of the market-oriented institutional environment of the Italian state.

Also, similarities with Pakistan and Nigeria are striking. Pakistan has a kleptomaniac elite, but Pakistani society is largely agrarian and the presence of the state is less pervasive than in Ukraine. In Nigeria a kleptomaniac elite squandered oil resources and robbed the country. A major difference with Ukraine is that it is urbanized and industrialized, the population is well educated and the role of the state is much more pervasive. Also, a comparison with Indonesia is relevant, a crony capitalism that had, until the Asian crisis struck, a dynamically developing market sector. Again, in Indonesia the state is less pervasive compared to Ukraine.

A comparison with China seems to make more sense because it is also undergoing extraction from a centrally planned economy. However, in China the mode of interaction state-society is of a fundamentally different nature. Although corruption is rampant and the presence of the state bureaucracy overwhelming, the market has penetrated the state and has introduced competition within the state apparatus. In contradistinction to Ukraine, where the state is disintegrating, in China effective state management was a precondition for successful reforms and under the leadership of the party-state a transformation towards state guided capital accumulation has taken place. In China there is still the primacy of politics whereas in Ukraine there is the chaos of clan interests. In China, a gradual decentralization has taken place, while the government still has control over the political and economic process. The regions can no longer lobby for subsidies and they are rewarded for enhancing the productive potential of their regions. In Ukraine, the regions nowadays have more interest in lobbying for subsidies from Kyiv than in enhancing endogenous development potential because the latter does not appear to be in their benefit, given the redistributive mechanisms. In China the redistributive state is gradually withdrawing (see Table 10.1).

In Mexico, an underdeveloped economy where for many decades a kleptomaniac elite was in power and where the state played an important role in economic life, is an interesting case because industrial development recently took off in the context of Mexico's membership of the North American Free Trade Arrangement. Also, the kleptomaniac elite appeared to become more interested in economic development. The history of Mexico is reminiscent in many respects of the

Table 10.1   Ukraine and China compared

	% of GDP (average for the period 1990–97)	
	Ukraine	China
Expenses for economy/subsidies	10.9	3.9
State expenses	35.6	14.5
Budget deficit	7.7	1.8
Foreign direct investment	0.8	4.6
Taxes	28.3	11.6

Source: Heets (1998).

present situation in Ukraine.[20] However, the proximity to the huge prosperous US market is an important factor for Mexico that is absent in the case of Ukraine.

The above comparisons show that Ukraine has a distinct mode of state–society and state–economy interaction. Ukraine has a long history of despotic rule, where the state has had an overwhelming role in society and the economy.

The Ukrainian mode of state–economy/society interaction is characterized by the following elements:

1. Overwhelming role of the state in the economy.
2. The state exhibits a control mania. Related to this is the bureaucratization of the economy.
3. There is rule by uncertainty.
4. Absence of the rule of law.
5. Rampant corruption in the state apparatus.
6. Very weak structures that mediate between society and the state. This resulted in deep divisions between the state and society. This produced distrust towards the institutions of the state. Civil society is hardly developed and does not pose a countervailing force for the state.
7. The state furthers anti-modern social practices.
8. The state allocates resources according to political and not economic criteria
9. The state pushes the economy into the shadow sector.
10. The state fails to provide basic services. Delivery failures contribute to the disintegration of state structures.
11. The state is not interested in reproduction of the basic functions of the state. The state contributes to its own demise.
12. The state is dominated by private interests of the ruling clans. The privatization of the state prevents emergence of a developmental and facilitative state.
13. The legitimacy crisis of the state is enhanced by the fact that the Ukrainian statehood is weakly established.

Path dependency of Ukraine

The account given of the history of the Ukrainian political economy shows the many constraints that policy-makers face and how they themselves were shaped, in their world outlook and behaviour, by the society that produced them. Socialism created a legacy that is still very much alive. It is this legacy that determines path dependency. According to North, path dependency is a way to conceptually narrow the choice set and link decision-making through time.[21] Path dependence is the key to an analytical understanding of long-term economic change.[22]

In this section, the path dependency of Ukraine will be outlined in the context of the constraints in which the Ukrainian economy is likely to develop. Given these constraints it is possible to exclude certain development paths. For example, it is safe to say that it is unlikely that Ukraine will develop in the medium term into a country that resembles the developed capitalist countries in its political, social and economic system.

A predatory state, a parasitic bureaucracy, the lack of adequate governance mechanisms and a low level of organizational capital are all constraining and structural factors that are obstacles on a path that leads to social and economic progress.

It has been shown how post-socialist developments in Ukraine fit into tendencies that had already emerged in Soviet times. Despite dramatic change, continuity at the micro level is very prominent. Typical behavioural patterns can even be traced back to Tsarist times. For example, the functioning of the bureaucracy is reminiscent of Tsarist times. Traditional passiveness of the masses allowed a predatory elite to develop a kleptocracy. The network of semi-feudal fiefdoms has its roots in the patron–client relationships that developed under socialism as well as in the informal economy that grew in scope. The state in Tsarist Russia and the Soviet Union have always been patrimonial and the nature of power exertion absolutist. It is in this tradition that a predatory state and parasitic bureaucracy could develop. Elements from Western market economy models have been introduced as far as they did not endanger historically grown interest configurations.

North argued that path dependence is also related to the increasing return mechanisms that reinforce the direction once on a given path.[23] This is confirmed by the case of Ukraine, where the predatory behaviour of the ruling elite has been rewarded and reinforced by the development of an institutional infrastructure that neatly fitted the interests of those in power, who perceived their interests in function of established belief systems and dominant social practices.

A major driving force nowadays seems to be the greediness of a predatory ruling elite that only has a short-term perspective. The ruling elite is diversified in its interests. The bosses of big industrial enterprises seem to be interested in limited market reform so long as it does not contravene their interests, i.e. the stream of state subsidies. The representatives of banks that live off government bonds and enterprise transactions, are parasitic in character but have an interest in monetary stability.

However, no major forces that are interested in market-oriented reform can be identified in the Ukrainian polity. Overwhelming are the forces that are parasitic in character, to begin with the state bureaucracy. However, the major source of path alteration of Ukraine is through changes in the polity.

The major factors that determine Ukraine's development path are:

- low level of organizational capital;
- anti-modern social practices of the population and in particular the elite;
- passivity of the population and strong exclusion mechanisms, allowing a predatory ruling elite to act with impunity;
- the strength of belief systems that underpin the system of parasitic mechanisms;
- the strength of survival networks in the economy;
- the criminalization of the state;
- control mania and the parasitic character of state bureaucracy.

What about the international factors?

1. *The dependence on Russia.* Much depends on future developments in Russia because this country is by far Ukraine's most important trading partner. Basically, the same socio-economic formation has emerged there. A likely development is the emergence of a more protectionist, nationalist and anti-reform Russian government. However, prospects for developing economic ties with Russia are gloomy because the institutional framework for furthering economic ties is underdeveloped. Nevertheless, Ukraine's dependence upon Russian energy and related indebtedness gives Russia powerful leverage. Russia exerts pressure on Ukraine to pay off gas debts with state property.
2. *The influence of international financial institutions.* Ukraine is vitally dependent on assistance from these institutions. There is also the competitive pressure of the international system at large.

Here it should be recalled that economic ties with the Western world in terms of trade relations and foreign direct investment are rather weak. It should also be recalled that IMF leverage in Ukraine has hitherto hardly led to market-oriented reform.

The provinciality of the Ukrainian polity may lead to a Belarus scenario – means isolation from world society and the world economy. It may mean further rapprochement with republics of the former Soviet Union. However, the Ukrainian elite has an interest in keeping the Ukrainian state viable, in order to pursue their rent-seeking activities. This acts as a brake upon too close relations with Russia.

The economic policy pursued so far, i.e. stalling market-oriented reforms, the legal chaos that enabled the elite to enrich itself, a policy aimed at fostering value subtracting industries and creating disincentives for agricultural producers, will inevitably lead to further economic decline and impoverishment of the masses.

All these factors push Ukraine in a direction of continuing and deepening economic and social hardships.

With respect to Ukraine's place in the world economy, the processes of marginalization are likely to intensify. Ukraine focused on the export of value subtracting industries such as steel, aluminium and chemicals. Many of these products increasingly face dumping procedures and the Asian crisis showed that these products are very sensitive for economic conjuncture. Moreover, value subtracting becomes more difficult in a shrinking economy. With few other export options, it seems that Ukraine will become more irrelevant for the world economy.

Politically, Ukraine will remain important as a counterweight to Russia, which increasingly behaves like a pariah state with mass destruction weapons at its disposal.

Social and economic developments in other republics of the former Soviet Union, except the Baltic republics, point in a similar direction, which is divergent from most of the rest of Central and Eastern Europe where the market economy is attaining a critical mass. Apparently, a new dividing line is emerging in Europe, alongside old cultural civilizational divides coinciding with the border between Western and Eastern Christianity, or the borders of the former Turkish and Russian empires.

Almost all major actors and factors mentioned so far push Ukraine into a doom scenario. What about forces that may support social and economic progress, in whatever guise? What about the young professionals and young new entrepreneurs? Analysis of the behaviour of civil servants showed that younger and better trained young civil servants are not less corrupt than their colleagues. Generally, young professionals are pushed into behaving according to the rules of the present socio-economic formation. However, generally, youngsters are less touched by the post Soviet socio-psychological syndrome and show more initiative.

Small and medium-sized industrial enterprises are so weakly represented that they do not constitute a significant pro-reform force.

Motyl argues that a creeping institutionalization may increasingly entangle the elite 'in the tentacles of growing democratization and rule of law'. He also says that there is a physical limit to parasitism and that 'even thieves may want to put their booty to productive use at home'. On the other hand, he argues, the Third World shows that long-term economic decline is perfectly compatible with bureaucratic corruption. However, all in all, Motyl expects that Ukraine may transform from a 'nuisance state' into the West's geopolitical partner.[24]

What about the public at large, which suffers enormously under the misery produced by the current socio-economic system? The popular feeling may be expressed in elections.

First of all, public opinion has never been in favour of market-oriented reform and this support has dwindled even further since the advent of President Kuchma to power. A larger part of the population blames 'the reformers' for the hardships they endure.[25] In a survey in early 1998, 90 per cent of those questioned preferred the old economic system and only 10 per cent approved the present one.[26] Of course, popular attitudes towards reform greatly complicate economic reform.

Alternative development paths

Alternative development paths are limited given the constraints of Ukrainian society and economy as described above. Usually, scenarios are given in the form of high growth, medium growth or low growth scenarios, or, more geared towards Ukraine: a competitiveness, status quo and protectionist scenario. Here the point of departure is not economic policy ideals (see competitiveness/protections scenarios above) but real-world models in the form of country-models. It is not to suggest that Ukraine might follow the path of Mexico, Pakistan and Belarus (Scheme 10.2). Differences are too great. But crucial elements in their development paths may characterize Ukraine's prospective scenario.

The Pakistanization scenario refers to feudalization of the social and political system, not to Islamic fundamentalism. A strong national identity as a cohesive force, as is the case in Pakistan, is not likely to develop in the short and medium term. However, passivity of the

Scheme 10.2 Alternative scenarios for Ukraine

	Mexicanization Liberalization	Belarussification Pan-slavism, state-centred development	Pakistanization Feudal/ mercantilist scenario
Economic system	Market economy attains critical mass	State-centred development, rent-seeking state and rent-seeking economy	Rent-seeking state and rent-seeking economy
Economic policy	Further liberalization and privatization	Strong protectionism, Some revitalization of state-run industries. Some restoration of division of labour in former Soviet Union	Selective protectionism, further privatization
Polity	Slow democratization. mercantilist class transforms into bourgeoisie	Autocratic government. End of parliamentarism. State power remains source of all wealth	Autocratic government. Ukrainian nationalism more pronounced. Prominent role of military. Semi-feudal mercantilist class rules with impunity
Society	Emergence of strong middle class. Mass poverty diminishes gradually	Mass poverty. Strong anti-Western tendencies	Mass poverty
International relations	Inclusion in European Free Trade Area. Close relations with EU. Strong Western influence	Inserted into Russian sphere of influence. Russian-dominated bloc has pariah status within the international community. Isolation from world market. Russian exerts influence primarily through economic leverages	West buys compliant foreign policy. Increasing debt service burden

population may enable such a scenario to materialize. There is a striking resemblance of the functioning of the suq and the practices of exchange in the Ukrainian economy. The driving force of the Pakistanization scenario is the stabilization and institutionalization of the present semi-feudal power structure.

The driving force of the Belarus scenario is Slavic unity, nostalgia for the past and submission to new Russian expansionism, assuming the form of a new Russian sphere of influence. This scenario means isolation from world society and the world economy, autocratic power and a rent-seeking state, softened by pseudo-social policies. Protectionism and the redistributive state keep inefficient enterprises afloat. The driving force of the Mexicanization scenario is the transformation and stabilization of the ruling elite, perceiving the introduction of Ukraine into the world economy and the stabilization of the economy as in its long-term interest. It means gradual liberalization and marketization. Ukraine will be included in a free trade zone centred around the European Union. This scenario is supported by Western financial institutions.

The Mexicanization scenario is economically the most optimal scenario. This may be surprising for those having Ukraine's high value added production in mind, producing, albeit nowadays in minimal numbers, plane engines and even rockets. However, Ukraine in 1999 was, in terms of GDP per capita, between China and India. GDP purchasing power parity per capita was US$8190 in Mexico while it was US$2000 in Ukraine.[27] Ukraine has fallen behind most Central and Eastern European countries. It should be borne in mind that GDP PPP per capita was in Russia US$3950 (1998), in Hungary US$6730 (1996), in Slovakia US$7560 (1996) and in Poland US$6740 (1998), according to the World Bank.

An obvious reference point is neighbouring Poland, that has developed since the mid-1990s into the fastest growing European economy (on a par with Ireland). However, we did not elaborate a Polonization scenario because this is unlikely to materialize during the coming decade. The development paths of Poland and Ukraine, compared in Scheme 10.3, are too differrent.

Policy recommendations

Ukraine increasingly resembles a typical stagnating Third World economy. Pervasive inefficiencies persist in all spheres of life. The path dependency approach helped to explain the emergence of an

Scheme 10.3   Development paths of Ukraine and Poland compared

	Ukraine	Poland
Pre-socialist history	almost no experience with capitalist development very weak civil society no experience of independent state new nationalism strong collectivism/ weak individualism	industrialization in South-West civil society more developed experience, although short, with nation state old nationalism weak collectivism/ strong individualism experienced epochal changes of Renaissance and Enlightenment
Socialist history	70 years communist experience for arger part of Ukraine post (Soviet) socio-psychological syndrome isolation from world society/economy totalitarianism integration in Soviet economy enterprise centre of social and political life	40 years communist experience more open compared to Ukraine more links with developed West authoritarianism significant private sector (agriculture, second economy) countervailing force of Catholic Church history of economic reforms
Economic system	state dominated, bureaucratically controlled economy shadow economy 60 per cent of economic activity corruption involution	critical mass of market economy evolution
Economic structure	agriculture: 12 per cent of GDP 38 per cent of imports energy (1998) industrial enterprises	agriculture: 7 per cent of GDP industrial restructuring,

Scheme 10.3 Continued

	Ukraine	Poland
Economic structure continued	hardly adjusted 25 per cent of industry used to produce for military large share of intermediate products heavy emphasis on heavy industry	corporate restructuring
Economic policy	control mania of bureaucracy aliberal policy Ukrainian style 'social market economy' no commitment to reform	liberal import policy liberal economic policy market economy shock therapy
Economic environment	very weak state very low level of economic competence GDP decline 97/89 66 per cent impoverished population deindustrialization very low level of social capital	GDP growth 97/89 8 per cent economic dynamism industrial regeneration
International environment	partnership agreement EU far away from prosperous markets Ukraine very weakly inserted in European institutional set-up Ukrainian products not competitive on OECD markets no protection for import competition very low level of FDI high debt service, very dependent upon IMF support conflict potential with Russia low level of trade with OECD	association agreement EU prospective EU member bordering EU gradually integrated into EU prospective markets EU import competition furthers domestic competition moderate level of FDI moderate debt burden much trade with OECD

economic system that eats its own economic base. Socialist and Tsarist legacies created a complex of social practices and belief systems that greatly delimit the development prospects of Ukraine. The specific mode of state–society interaction is a crucial element in the newly emerged socio-economic formation.

By early 2000 there were no significant forces discernible that may implement market-oriented reform. This makes policy recommendations an exercise in thin air. However, it can be said that the reform of the state administration is a precondition for social and economic progress. The state should create the conditions to govern effectively. This means introducing transparency, clear demarcation of competencies and imposing accountability. It also means combating crime, corruption and nepotism. Only in these circumstances can institutional conditions for market economy be created. In these circumstances a civil society may develop that may push back the predatory elements of the current Ukrainian state.

Notes

1 Introduction

1. GDP per capita PPP in 1998 was US$3220 in China, US$1700 in India and US$8190 in Mexico (World Development Report, 1999–2000).
2. Only Belarus and Tajikistan were rated lower.
3. Twenty-nine per cent of the population were pensioners in 1997.
4. Over the last 13 years US$11 billion have been spent on dealing with the consequences of the Chernobyl nuclear disaster. These expenditures constituted 5.7 per cent of the Ukrainian state budget in recent years (BBC, Summary of World Broadcasts, FSU, 15 April 1999). On 1 January 1996, 3 146 500 people were registered as victims of the Chernobyl disaster (Cornelius and Lenain, 1997, p. 131). Under pressure from the IMF, the Chernobyl tax was abolished in January 1999.
5. Merton, 1976, p. 169, as quoted in Sztompka, P., 1995, p. 61.

2 Independence: Euphoria and Disillusionment

1. Ukrainian territory increased by 35 per cent between 1939 and 1954 (the Crimea was added in 1954) (Shen, 1996, p. 7).
2. Karl Marx characterized Russia as a strongly centralized form of despotism. Frederick Engels labelled the Russian socio-economic formation as oriental despotism (Wittfogel, 1957, p. 423).
3. Manning, 1953, 'Ukraine under the Soviets', New York: Record Press, as quoted in Shen (1996) p. 133.
4. See Koropeckyj (1991) p. 127; Shen (1996) p. 43.
5. See van Selm and Wagener (1993).
6. See Crowley (1995) p. 44.
7. See Motyl (1993) p. 245
8. See Harris and Lockwood (1997).
9. Whereas in 1926 only 18 per cent of the Soviet population lived in towns, in January 1939 this percentage had increased to 33 per cent.
10. See Koropeckyj (1991) p. 12.
11. Forty-six per cent of the population speaks Russian at home, but this figure increases to 57 per cent for 15–19 year olds (Russia Today, 12 August 1998).
12. See Shlapentokh (1989) p. 52.
13. See Shlapentokh (1989) p. 67.
14. As quoted in Shlapentokh (1989).
15. Ledeneva (1998) p. 182. 'There was a kind of fundamental caring by everybody for everybody, all acquaintances helped each other.' Blat subverted the Soviet economic system at the same time as it sustained it. See also Srubar (1991).
16. Solnick (1998).
17. Srubar (1991) p. 421.

18. Castells (1998) p. 10. According to Lukin (in Koropeckyj, 1992, p. 43), based on national statistics, the average annual increase of national income produced was 6.7 per cent in 1966–70, 4.6 per cent in 1971–75, 3.4 per cent in 1976–80, 3.4 per cent in 1981–85 and 3.0 per cent in 1986–89. According to Gregory and Stuart (1998, p. 227), unofficial Soviet/Russian estimates of economic growth, taking into account inflation, amongst other things, were 5 per cent for 1951–60, 4 per cent for 1961–65, 3.8 per cent for 1966–70, 3 per cent for 1971–75, 0.8 per cent for 1976–80, 0.5 per cent for 1981–85, and 0 per cent for 1986–88.
19. See Gärtig (1993) p. 319.
20. See Kakwani (1996) p. 49.
21. See Knabe (1998a).
22. Seventy per cent of the population voted for the preservation of the Soviet Union in March 1991.
23. Melnyk calculated that from 1959 to 1970, before oil became an important factor, capital transfers from Ukraine amounted to 19.9 per cent of the reported national income of Ukraine (Melnyk, 1973, p. 163). The only source that warned against an overestimation of Ukraine's potential was Goskomstat (the Soviet planning agency) which calculated that, if valued at world market prices, Ukraine would have been the third largest net receiver of external aid within the Union, and not, as is thought, the second largest net payer. (See also Castells, 1998, p. 44.)
24. The situation can be compared with 19th century Italy on the verge of unification. The Sicilian aristocrat Lampedusa wrote 'If we want things to stay as they are, things will have to change'.
25. See Hague (1995) p. 422.
26. See Havrylyshyn (1997) p. 31.
27. Miller *et al.* (1997) p. 605.
28. In March 1994, 40 per cent of Ukrainians wanted reunification with Russia (Clement *et al.*, 1996, p. 33). In May 1997, in a Gallup opinion poll 46 per cent supported the policy of reunification of the former Soviet republics (Ott, 1998, p. 22).
29. See Wittkowsky (1997) p. 581.
30. Ibid. p. 583.
31. Ibid. p. 594.

3   Politics, State and Bureaucracy

1. In parliament, only half of the members are elected on party lists. During the elections of March 1998, the communists got by far the most votes, with 119 seats out of 450. 171 seats were for other left-wing parties (including socialist, peasant party and progressive socialists), the nationalist Rukh got 47 seats, Hromada 39 seats, the social democrats 24 seats, the Greens 24 seats and the People's Democratic Party (President Kuchma's party) 84 seats.
2. President and government demonstrated dissatisfaction with the state of affairs. In November 1998 President Kuchma complained that some 750 documents were awaiting consideration by parliament, including 646 laws. He added that parliament had viewed only 1 out of 21 draft laws he had

submitted in 1998 as a matter of urgency, in order to deal with the economic crisis (Radio Free Europe, 16 November 1998).

3. This is exemplified in speeches by President Kuchma, which are often a hodgepodge of contradictory texts. For example, in November 1998 Kuchma said at one point that the government must cancel all tax privileges to ensure greater budgetary revenues, and at another, he called for agricultural producers to be granted tax holidays. In one part of the speech Kuchma promised that Ukraine would create equal conditions for domestic and foreign investors, and in another, he called for stricter policies toward non-residents on the Ukrainian securities market. After complaining about the lack of cash in circulation and repeatedly calling for cash emissions, Kuchma said the money supply shouldn't grow any faster than it did in 1997.

4. The bank accounts of Oleksandr Volkov, the man behind Kuchma and his chief re-election campaigner in 1999, worth US$3.5 million, had been frozen in Belgium. Several prime ministers who served under President Kuchma have been charged with corruption. Swiss authorities think that former prime minister Pavel Lazarenko (1996–97), siphoned off US$72.1 million from Ukraine. Former prime minister Y. Zviahilsky left Ukraine for Israel after stealing US$22 million from the state (Kyiv Post, 17 June 1999).

5. Sundakov (1997) p. 115.

6. Ministry of Economy *et al.* (1999).

7. By February 1999, there were 48 executive bodies (18 ministries, 13 state committees and 17 other institutions) (Ukrainian Economic Trends, February 1999, p. 3).

8. Sundakov (1997) p. 113.

9. Sundakov (1999) p. 112.

10. In October 1998, the parliament rejected a government proposal to abolish electricity privileges for a large part of the Ukrainian population, some 5.6 million Ukrainian residents, according to which they would get reduced tariffs. Electricity companies were not compensated for this (IntelNews, 26 October 1998).

11. Ministry of Economy *et al.* (1999) p. 2–5.

12. Orsmond (1997) p. 39.

13. Memorandum of Economic Policies, 16 March 1999.

14. Finance Week, 13, 1999.

15. HIID-CASE/OR/May 3, 1999.

16. Russia Today, 15 March 1999.

17. For example, on 22 February 1999, a Council of Exporters was created to form the legislative environment and supervise export activities of Ukrainian enterprises.

18. BBC Monitoring, Summary of World Broadcasts, 22 March 1999.

19. HIID-CASE/OR/May 3, 1999.

20. Sundakov (1999) p. 115.

21. There is a committee for gardening and wine making, a committee for veterans of war and foreign military conflicts and a state committee for repatriation of cultural values.

22. In 1998, consolidated budget expenditures on maintenance of executive authorities amounted to 154 per cent of what was approved in the budget,

while actual local budget expenditures for this purpose were 426 per cent of the approved amount (HIID-CASE/OR/May 3, 1999, p. 2).

23. Radio Free Europe, 3 June 1998.
24. OECD (1997a) p. 11.
25. See Beetham (1987).
26. Hirszowicz (1980) p. 16.
27. Ledeneva (1998) p. 77.
28. Ibid. p. 78.
29. Ibid. p. 79.
30. Solnick (1998).
31. Fleron (1998) p. 50.
32. Crozier (1964) p. 299.
33. Although the Ukrainian government opted to transform from a centrally planned economy into a market economy and to decentralize decision-making in a number of fields, the size of the state bureaucracy increased considerably. Whereas in 1990 only 287 000 people worked in public administration, this number had increased to 574 000 persons by 1996 (Statistical Yearbook of Ukraine for 1996, p. 395).
34. Piirainen (1997) p. 28.
35. IntelNews, 16 May 1998.
36. IntelNews, 28 September 1998.
37. Miller *et al.* (1997) p. 605.
38. Kaufmann (1997) p. 246.
39. Radio Free Europe, 25 February 1999.
40. Radio Free Europe, 25 February 1999.
41. The Day, 10 April 1999.
42. Miller *et al.* (1999).
43. The newspaper wrote that diplomats complain that 'the new breed of apparatchiks, or communist style bureaucrats, increasingly brazen in dishing out the nation's meager wealth to cronies'. The paper wrote that 'bureaucrats from competing political clans have even been gunned down in drive-by shooting from passing police cars. The Prime Minister narrowly survived a car bombing only days after he distributed 11 billion dollars in lucrative gas distribution concessions last year'.
44. Ledeneva (1998) p. 205.
45. Ekonomika Ukraini, January 1997, p. 11.
46. EBRD (1997).
47. Zerkalo Nedeli, 13 March 1999, p. 6.
48. Ministry of Economy *et al.* (1999) p. 2–13.
49. GLS Research *et al.* (1997).
50. Some challenge this view. According to an American, quoted by James Mace in Kyiv Post, 23 June 1999, 'The problem is not corruption. The problem is that they don't stay bought, and when somebody else offers them more money, you have to buy them all over again'.
51. EBRD (1997) p. 38.
52. As quoted in Evans (1995) p. 29.
53. Ibid.
54. Ibid.
55. Ibid. p. 248.

56. World Bank (1997b) p. 3.
57. Ibid.
58. The absence of the rule of law is reflected in the fact that in 1996, 99 per cent of all cases to reach the courts resulted in convictions (Havrylyshyn, 1997, p. 26).
59. See Burawoy (1996).
60. Markwick (1999) p. 120.
61. Ibid. p. 121.
62. See Knabe (1998a).
63. Zerkalo Nedeli, 10 February 1996, p. 6.
64. Hirschman (1999) p. 289.
65. Ibid. p. 295.
66. Ibid. p. 301.
67. Messner (1997).
68. Giddens (1998).
69. Shlapentokh (1996).
70. Stark (1990).
71. This happened in Soviet times. Both Stalin and Khruschev used institutional reorganizations and the rotation of personnel to strengthen their position and advance their political programme. Under Brezhnev the elite got more certainty as rotation became less frequent. The Nomenklature developed into a caste with ever widening privileges. Brezhnev's Dnipropretovsk group helped to form a nucleus for a large coalition that governed the Soviet Union for nearly two decades.
72. Willerton (1992) p. 7.
73. According to Kuzio (1998a), the positive side of patronage was, in the context of the building of a new and weak state and in the absence of genuine political parties, that it provided coherence to the political process. In Kuzio's view it functioned as an adhesive, binding individuals and groups together, bridging various organized interests. However, the lack of transparency and generally accepted rules for resolving conflicts led to elite infighting and neglect of the public good.
74. Ledeneva (1998) noticed a move from patronage, predominant under socialism, towards corruption. 'What could be done in the Soviet system simply from loyalty or sympathy, is now calculated in terms of short-term costs and benefits.' (p. 201) 'Connections still function, but their 'social' charge seems to have been overtaken by their 'functional' (calculated) core.' (p. 201). In other words, 'connections in the socialist economy were predominantly value oriented (rhetoric of friendship, requests for others) while now they are driven by considerations of self-interest and mutual profit.' (p. 195).
75. Motyl (1998) p. 10.
76. As quoted in Motyl (1998).
77. Kyiv Post, 20 October 1998. BBC/SWB, FSU, part 1, 18 November 1998. The Dnipropetrovsk clan has always been powerful. Brezhnev installed during his long rule many fellows from Dnipropetrovsk to key positions in the Kremlin. Dnipropetrovets V. Shcherbytsky's reign in Ukraine lasted from 1972 until 1989. A team of researchers commissioned by M. Gorbachev to study Ukraine in 1990 found that 53 per cent of Ukraine's executive officials came from Dnipropetrovsk (Kyiv Post, 16 February 1999).

78. Kyiv Post, 10 November 1998.
79. The five oligarchs are: Ihor Bakai, head of state oil and gas company Naftogaz; Viktor Pinchuk, head of Interpipe, dealing in gas and steel pipes; Hryhory Surkis, who controls the Slavutych holding company, which deals mainly in oil, electricity and metals; Vadim Rabinovich, who runs the Swiss-based holding company Rico Capital Group; and Oleksandr Volkov, who controls the TV channel Gravis (Kyiv Post, 15 April 1999). In June 1999 Rabinovich was forbidden to enter Ukraine for a period of five years.
80. Kyiv Post, 18 March 1999.
81. Kuzio (1998a) p. 37.
82. Hare *et al.*, in Kuzio (1998b).
83. Holmes *et al.* (1997); Kyiv Post, 4 January 1999.
84. North (1990) p. 99.

4 Economic Reform

1. See Van Atta (1999).
2. The state's budget increased from 61.7 per cent of national income in 1992 to 85 per cent in 1994 (Shen, 1996, p. 65).
3. As quoted in Shen, 1996, p. 25.
4. Ibid. p. 73. The real wage declined by approximately three-quarters between January 1992 and late 1994 (p. 70).
5. However, Hirschhausen asserts that 'retail and wholesale price controls zigzagged between 80 per cent and almost 0 per cent', (see Zviglyanich,1996, p. 14). The problem is, according to Sundakov *et al.* (1994, p. 411) that the distinction between controlled and 'free' prices was not clear (in 1992).
6. Sundakov *et al.* (1994) p. 414.
7. The first round of price deregulation that began in January 1992 covered items affecting two-thirds of consumer expenditure: prices of select consumer goods increased between 500 and 1000 per cent in a matter of days (Shen, 1996, p. 75).
8. EBRD (1997) p. 209.
9. Shen (1996) p. 75.
10. Shen (1996) p. 76.
11. World Broadcasting Service, BBC, 18 December 1998.
12. Zerkalo Nedeli, 24 April 1999.
13. Hare *et al.* (1998) p. 188.
14. The hryvna-denominated bonds which Odessa issued at a high interest rate could not be repaid in 1998 with the result that the government had to take over this debt (Duchêne, 1998, p. 7).
15. See Duchêne (1998) p. 6
16. Economist Intelligence Unit, Country Profile Ukraine 1999–2000, p. 28.
17. Ukrainian Economic Trends, November 1998, p. 7.
18. Ukrainian Economic Trends, November 1998.
19. Gros and Steinherr (1999) p. 205.
20. Kyiv Post, 6 November 1998.
21. From August to September 1998, during the Russian financial crisis, the bank's liquid assets plummeted by 32 per cent, while short-term liabilities fell by only 29 per cent.

22. Eastern Economist, 22 March 1999.
23. Radio Free Europe, 31 July 1998.
24. Ukrainian Economic Trends, April 1999, p. 4.
25. Gros and Steinherr (1999) p. 210.
26. Ministry of Economy *et al.* (1999) p. 2–2.
27. Ibid.
28. Ukrainian Economic Trends, June 1999, p. 38.
29. Zerkalo Nedeli, 6 February 1999, p. 7.
30. Ibid.
31. Ukrainian Economic Trends, June 1999, p. 38.
32. The Day, 20 July 1999.
33. In the memorandum that the government signed together with the World Bank, USAID and the European Union on behalf of the donors (1999), general objectives for the mass privatization programme were described: 'The objective of mass privatization in Ukraine is to (1) distribute shares rapidly and equitably to the citizens of Ukraine, (2) develop capital markets and capital market infrastructure and (3) rapidly create a critical mass of privately owned enterprises to allow necessary restructuring and modernisation to proceed under the direction of the new private owners.' The Memorandum also states that 'many other economic factors – external to mass privatization – are critical to the success of the privatization program and privatised enterprises. Progress retarding these factors must occur in parallel to mass privatization.'
    As to the why of privatization, a government web site states that in late 1994 there was a general vision among Ukraine's leaders as to the path of reform to be pursued:
    • state-ownership, state management and official corruption had resulted in political mismanagement of the country's resources and the eventual collapse of the Soviet economy
    • recovery and growth would require radical new initiatives to create an environment which encourages competition, investment and risk-taking by the private sector while discouraging official corruption
    • Ukraine's future lies in a liberal, market economy with expanding ties to new markets in Europe and other regions in the world.
    It is doubtful whether these views really represent a consensus among policy-makers in late 1994. Ukrainian leaders had to articulate such views in order to obtain financial assistance from the West. The above presented views are not the product of mature consensus that emerged within the Ukrainian polity. Quite the opposite is true. There has always been a solid majority, within the parliament and the Ukrainian polity at large, against the above view.
34. Hare *et al.* (1998) p. 191: Until 1995 the main features of the privatization process were the following: the working collective (managers and workers) chose whether to privatize. The 'value' of the firm was apparently set externally. The collective needed to raise the funds via their own privatization vouchers. Most privatizations (70 per cent) were in fact buy-outs, in which the future profits of the firm were mortgaged to pay for shares.
35. Ministry of Economy *et al.* (1999) p. 5–10.
36. von Hirschhausen (1996) p. 21.
37. Kyiv Post, 29 July 1999.

38. Von Hirschhausenn (1996) p. 17.
39. According to Hare *et al.* (1998) p. 191.
40. The following is an example of the confusion over the privatization process. 'Kuchma signed a decree, July 1998, requiring the State Property Fund to report to the government following a court decision to invalidate a law giving parliament responsibility for the fund.' (Russia Today, 8 July 1998).
41. Statistical Yearbook 1997, p. 361.
42. Ibid. p. 361.
43. Lyakh and Pankow (1998) p. 36.
44. Kyiv Post, 28 March 1999.
45. News Agency UNIAN, 7 December 1998.
46. See Ukrainian Economic Trends, December 1998, p. 93–101.
47. Conrad (1997) p. 194.
48. Vinogradskaia (1999) p. 37.
49. Transition Report 1997, p. 208. The Small and Medium Sized Business Union claims that 1.7 million Ukrainians work in small and medium-sized enterprises (Kyiv Post, 16 October 1998). Vinogradskaia claims that in early 1999, 1 million people worked in small enterprises (p. 37).
50. Conrad (1997) p. 194.
51. Vinogradskaia (1999) p. 37.
52. Statistical Yearbook 1997, p. 323.
53. Ibid. p. 325.
54. Business Central Europe, June 1997.
55. Business Central Europe, June 1997.
56. Pryor and Blackman (1998) p. 40.
57. Kaufmann (1997) p. 239.
58. Fifty enterprises were surveyed in 1996. Unofficial payments amounted to US$176 for enterprise registration, US$42 for each visit of the health and fire inspector, US$87 for each visit of the tax inspector, US$984 for each telephone line installation, US$123 for each export licence/registration, US$278 for each import licence/registration, US$211 for each border crossing (lump sum). The border crossing 'unofficial payment' amounted to 3 per cent of the value (Kaufmann, 1997, p. 242).
59. Vinogradskaia (1999) p. 40.
60. Kaufmann (1997) p. 240.
61. Ministry of Economy *et al.* (1999) p. 2–13.
62. Kaufmann (1997) p. 253.
63. Conrad (1997) p. 204.
64. Cornelius and Lenain (1997) p. 156.
65. Gärtig (1993) p. 312.
66. Ben and Sychenko (1999).
67. Ministry of Economy *et al.* (1999) p. 2–13.
68. Ibid.
69. From the early 1960s to the end of the 1980s the shadow economy of the former Soviet Union grew by 30 times, and attained approximately 20 per cent of national product (Ekonomika Ukraini, January 1997, p. 5).
70. Ukraine has one of the largest shadow economies in Central and Eastern Europe. The share of the shadow economy in the total economy was estimated at 36 per cent in Bulgaria (1995), 11 per cent in the Czech Republic

and 13 per cent in Poland, while it amounted to 49 per cent in Ukraine. In the countries of the former Soviet Union this share is estimated at, on average, about 40 per cent, and in Latin American countries at about 30 per cent.

71. Ministry of Economy *et al.* (1999) p. 2–12.
72. Ekonomika Ukraini, January 1997, p. 11.
73. The Day, 30 March 1999.
74. See Vorovev and Timchenko, in Ekonomika Ukraini, October 1998.
75. The World Bank has committed some US$2.8 billion in loans to Ukraine and disbursed US$1.8 billion of that amount since 1992, according to bank officials (Kyiv Post, 17 June 1999).
76. Gaddy and Ickes (1998).
77. Gould-Davies and Woods (1999).
78. Sundakov (1999).
79. The Day, 16 February 1999.
80. It seemed that the IMF and the World Bank were supporting Kuchma in the presidential elections of 1999. The IMF approved just before the election additional tranches of an Extended Fund Facility loan, due, it was said, to progress in macro-economic stabilization. The World Bank approved in early September 1999 a US$100 million loan that was used, according to Prime Minister Pustovoytenko, to pay off some wage and pension arrears. (Radio Free Europe, 6 September 1999).
81. See Duchêne (1998).

5 Structural Change in the Economy I: Sectoral Analysis

1. Ukrainian Economic Trends, December 1999, p. 22.
2. Ibid.
3. The share of agriculture in GDP decreased from 24.5 per cent in 1990 to 11.9 per cent in 1998 (Lukas, 1999, p. 7).
4. Ukrainian Economic Trends, December 1998, p. 20.
5. Ukrainian Economic Trends, March 1999, p. 54.
6. Electricity consumption in 1993 was 227 billion kWh, and in 1997 it was 190 billion kWh (Statistical Yearbook, 1997).
7. Fixed investment as a percentage of GDP in 1995 was 23.3 per cent in Ukraine, 32.5 per cent in the Czech Republic, 20.0 per cent in Hungary and 16.9 per cent in Poland (Economic Survey of Europe, 1998, no. 1, p. 99).
8. Statistical Yearbook (1997) p. 210.
9. Lindner (1998) p. 924–5.
10. According to Tedström (1991). Ukraine's defence plants produced about half of the Soviet Union's tanks and missiles. They produced half of the Soviet armed forces' optical and radio based management systems. Estimates of the share of defence production in total industrial production vary, rising to as much as 50 per cent. Credible evidence suggests that it is at least 25 per cent. According to former Prime Minister V. Masol, a quarter of Ukrainian industrial output is in the defence complex and 40 per cent of total scientific and technological potential. (Transition, World Bank, Vol. 5, No. 7, September 1994).

11. Weissenburger and Hirschhausen (1997) p. 124.
12. Economist Intelligence Unit, Country Profile Ukraine 1999–2000, p. 27.
13. EIU country report Ukraine, 1st quarter 1999, p. 19.
14. DIW (1998). In Ferroalloy enterprise (Zaporizhzhya) per unit electricity consumption rose between 1990 and 1996 with 26 per cent for ferro manganese and by 34 per cent for silico manganese.
15. Ibid.
16. Levine and Bond (1998) p. 157.
17. Ibid.
18. Ekonomika Ukraini, April 1999, p. 77.
19. Ibid.
20. Reuters, 25 February 1998. Aleksei Nogovitsin, an official from the Ministry of Industry, said that between 1992 and 1997 more than US$1.8 billion was spent on modernizing production facilities but that the investment was far too small – US$3.5 billion was needed in total.
21. Levine and Bond (1998) p. 152.
22. During the first quarter of 1999, metal exports to the Community of Independent States almost halved compared to the first quarter of 1998 (Ukrainian Economic Trends, June 1999, p. 6).
23. According to Kyiv Post they vary from 20–25 per cent in Asia and Latin America to 50–80 per cent in Western Europe to more than 100 per cent in the USA (Kyiv Post, 16 November 1998).
24. Kyiv Post, 16 November 1998.
25. EIU country report Ukraine, 1st quarter 1999.
26. Kyiv Post, 10 February 1998.
27. Ibid.
28. Clement *et al.* (1993) p. 136.
29. IntelNews, 12 July 1998.
30. Naftogaz Ukraine announced that it could boost domestic gas output to 31 billion m^3 by the year 2010 (Kyiv Post, 17 June 1999).
31. According to Mr Skorik from the World Bank office in Kyiv, 1 June 1999.
32. World Bank (1999) p. 248–9.
33. von Hirschhausen *et al.* (1997) p. 159.
34. Kyiv Post, 28 March 1999.
35. Economist Intelligence Unit, Country Profile Ukraine 1999–2000, p. 37, Ukraina v tsifrax, p. 38. Ukrainian miners extracted 67 million tonnes of coal during the first ten months of 1999 (BBC/SWB, 12 November 1999).
36. Subsidies to coal mining amounted in 1992 to 2.29 per cent of GDP, in 1993 to 3.36 per cent of GDP, in 1994 to 3.02 per cent, in 1995 to 0.66 per cent, in 1996 to 1.55 per cent and in 1997 to 2.01 per cent (Zerkalo Nedeli, 6 February 1999).
37. Marples (1991) p. 178.
38. Kyiv Post, 28 March 1999.
39. BBC/SWB, 5 January 1999.
40. According to Agence France Presse (11 January 1999), in 1998 350 miners died.
41. von Hirschhausen *et al.* (1997) p. 155.

42. Lovei and Skorik (1999) p. 343.
43. Vincentz and von Hirschhausen (1999) p. 384.
44. Kyiv Post, 30 December 1998.
45. According to a report by the European Investment Bank, The Guardian, 17 February 1999. According to Kyiv Post 6 April 1999, 18 per cent of industrial enterprises pay their energy bill in cash. Only half of the delivered energy remained unpaid. According to BBC/SWB, FSU, 26 March 1999, during January–February 1999 power stations paid for only 1.6 per cent of the value of coal consumed.
46. In 1996, residential natural gas prices were at 77 per cent of international prices, residential coal prices at 85 per cent and industrial coal prices at 93 per cent (World Bank, 1996, Ukraine – The Real Economy and its Sectors; Kyiv).
47. BBC/SWB, FSU, 12 March 1999.
48. Radio Free Europe, 3 June 1998.
49. Lindler (1998) p. 922.
50. BBC/SWB, FSU, 22 January 1999.
51. Memorandum, p. 11 (point 45), 'By December 1998 we will terminate the provision of production subsidies to non-viable mines in category 1.'
52. Radio Free Europe, 16 January 1998.
53. EIU, Country Report Ukraine, 1st quarter 1999, p. 23.
54. von Hirschhausen (1999) p. 404.
55. Radio Free Europe, 12 January 1999.
56. Radio Free Europe, 29 April 1998.
57. Financial Times, 27 October 1998.
58. Zerkalo Nedeli, 8 May 1999.
59. There are no indications that waste has been reduced since independence. EU-TACIS estimated in the mid-1990s that due to bad harvest and transport techniques, 18.5 per cent of grain production (excluding corn) had been lost (von Cramon-Taubadel and Koester *et al.* 1997, p. 140).
60. World Bank (1994) p. 6.
61. Ibid.
62. In 1989 Ukraine, which accounted for only 15 per cent of the Soviet Union's arable land area, produced 26 per cent of its total grain output, 53.3 per cent of its sugar beet output, 26.7 per cent of its potato output, and more than 20 per cent of its total livestock production.
63. Ukrainian agricultural production is extremely low by comparison with Western Europe, with grain and sugar yields at less than half of those in the UK and France (World Bank, 1994, p. 99).
64. International Monetary Fund (1997) p. 97.
65. Ukraina v tsifrax. 1997, p. 119.
66. Csaki and Lerman (1997).
67. Ibid.
68. For example, Volodomyr Honcharenko, a private farmer near Sumy city, said his neighbours viewed him as a enemy when he left the collective farm. His wife, working as a nurse in a nearby town to supplement the family income, would not tell anyone her husband was a private farmer

for fear of earning derision reserved for 'capitalists' (Kyiv Post, 26 May 1998).

69. The overall caloric intake of animal products was, in mid-1998, barely half of its 1990 level.

70. In 1997, the milk yield per cow in Ukraine was 2000 litres per year, compared with 2941 litres a year in 1990. Respective figures for the USA and Germany (1993) are 6494 and 4802 litres a year (World Bank, 1994, p. 104, Lukas 1999). See also Baker (1998) p. 9.

71. Cow numbers decreased from 9 million in 1985 to just over 6 million in 1997. However, real decline has been sharper as Collective Agricultural Enterprises have an interest to over-report (see Baker 1998).

72. Farm managers and workers have an incentive to pay in kind and to sell at production costs to workers. Lower prices for products sold to workers give rise to lower profits and reduce the profit tax. The prices paid by workers for grain is on average 32 per cent of the procurement price, and for oilseeds 42 per cent of the procurement price (Koester and Striewe 1999, p. 268).

73. Perotta (1998) p. 5.

74. Baker (1998) p. 3.

75. Baker (1998).

76. Perotta (1998) p. 6.

77. According to von Cramon-Taubadel and Koester *et al.* (1997, p. 138) traders in Ukraine take 20–25 per cent of the grain price, while internationally approximately 5 per cent is usual.

78. International Herald Tribune, 10 April 1997. According to von Cramon-Taubadel and Koester *et al.* (1997), the world market price was US$163 per tonne, while the producer price was US$115 (2 February 1996).

79. Striewe and von Cramon-Taubadel (1999) p. 299.

80. Radio Free Europe, 21 May 1998. According to Don Van Atta, heading the Kyiv-based Center for Agriculture and Rural Development, Ukraine's low grain harvest of 1998 will be entirely used to pay off state debts. According to Van Atta, the government and private sector rely on barter to keep grain flowing into the state monopoly, Khlib Ukrayiny. But the grain monopoly has hurt farmers by losing billions of hryvna on the world market. 'Khlib Ukrayiny managed to buy grain at the highest price in the last two years, and to claim it was paying that price and to sell grain at this year's price. It's lost millions, if not thousands of millions of hryvna for the Ukrainian state. The only thing worse than a monopoly is a monopoly that does not work.' (Kyiv Post 4 February 1998).

81. IntelNews, 14 December 1998.

82. IntelNews, 18 January 1999. The parliament decided to subsidize the production of combines in Kharkiv for the amount of 100 000 hryvnas per harvester (Eastern Economist, 3 August 1998).

83. Radio Free Europe, 21 May 1998.

84. World Bank (1994) p. 99.

85. EIU, Country Report Ukraine, 1st quarter 1999.

86. Baker (1998) p. 5.

87. Ibid.

88. Economist

89. Zerkalo Nedeli, 13 March 1999.
90. Lukas (1999) p. 3.
91. Ibid.
92. Von Cramon-Taubadel and Koester (1997) p. 128, EIU country report Ukraine, 1st quarter 1999.
93. Statistical Bulletin, 1st quarter 1999, p. 120.
94. Ukrainian Economic Trends, March 1998, p. 84.
95. Csaki and Lerman (1997).
96. Lerman (1999) p. 48.
97. Koester and Striewe (1999) p. 263.
98. Csaki and Lerman (1997).
99. Ibid.
100. Ibid.
101. CPER Newsletter. Survey of the Press, No. 13 (93), 6 April 1999.
102. World Bank: Agriculture Report Ukraine, 1994.
103. Van Atta (1998) p. 614.
104. Perotta (1998).
105. Van Atta (1998).
106. Van Atta (1998) p. 611.
107. Radio Free Europe, 21 May 1998.
108. Ukrainian Economic Trends, March 1998, p. 84.
109. Ministry of Economy *et al.* 1999, p. 4–9.
110. Ibid. p. 32.
111. International Monetary Fund (1999), p. 39.
112. The Day, 23 February 1999.
113. World Bank (1997c).

6 Structural Change in the Economy II: The Micro-level

1. Clarke (1992).
2. Clarke (1992) p. 6.
3. Fallon *et al.* (1997) p. 88.
4. International Monetary Fund (1997) p. 23, TACIS, Pryor and Blackman (1998).
5. Ibid. p. 39.
6. Estrin and Rosevaer (1999).
7. IMF (1997) p. 23.
8. Pryor and Blackman (1998) p. 36.
9. Harris and Lockwood (1997).
10. The number of bankruptcy cases has gone up from about 5000 cases in 1996 to 8000 in 1997 and to 9000 in 1998 (IMF, 1999, p. 27).
11. Ukrainian Economic Trends, December 1999, p. 10.
12. Ukrainian Economic Trends, March 1998, p. 65.
13. von Hirschhausen (1996) p. 23.
14. von Hirschhausen (1996) p. 19–20.
15. In 1998 Nissan Sunderland became Europe's most productive factory with 105 cars produced per employee. The Guardian, 18 August 1999.
16. The Guardian, 18 August 1999.

7   Opening Towards the World Economy?

1. Shen (1996) p. 139.
2. Thiessen (1997) p. 213.
3. Äslund (1995) p. 127.
4. Shen (1996) p. 132.
5. Thiessen (1997) p. 213.
6. Gregory and Stuart (1998).
7. Eastern Economist, 24 February 2000.
8. Shen (1996) p. 135.
9. Makarenko, in Shen (1996) p. 136.
10. EIU, Country Report Ukraine, 2nd quarter, 1994.
11. World Bank (1994) p. 47.
12. Ibid.
13. IMF (1997b) p. 51.
14. Möllers (1999) p. 155.
15. Ibid.
16. Radio Free Europe, 13 August 1999.
17. World Bank (1999).
18. Zviglyanich (1996) p. 132.
19. Clement *et al.* (1993) p. 11.
20. Ukrainian Economic Trends, March 1998, p. 71.
21. Radio Free Europe, 23 November 1998.
22. Radio Free Europe, 14 July 1999.
23. BBC/SWB, 22 January 1999.
24. World Bank (1994) p. 44.
25. Russia Today, 25 June 1998.
26. IntelNews, 9 February 1999.
27. Ministry of Economy *et al.* (1999) p. 5–26.
28. Economist Intelligence Unit, Country Profile Ukraine 1999–2000, p. 32.
29. Eastern Economist, 29 February 2000.
30. Lukas (1999) p. 6.
31. Ministry of Economics *et al.* (1999) 5.26.
32. By early 1999, the import tariff for agricultural and food products was 27 per cent and for industrial products 8 per cent. Lukasz, 1999, p. 24.
33. Zerkalo Nedeli, 6 February 1999.
34. Agrochemical distributors rely on grain received from farms in exchange for their product to generate hard currency to pay back Western suppliers. In July 1998 the Ukrainian government froze the movement of grain and gave a select group of state input providers preference for settling debts (Kyiv Post, 18 February 1999).
35. Kyiv Post, 15 July 1999.
36. Kyiv Post, 17 February 1999.
37. Havlik *et al* (1999) p. 25.
38. Economic Commission for Europe, 1997.
39. Ukrainian Economic Trends, December 1999, p. 52.
40. Economist Intelligence Unit, Country Profile Ukraine 1999–2000, p. 33.
41. Kaufmann (1997) p. 243–4.

42. The official license for establishing an enterprise, for a period of two years, costs 200 dollar. Customs officers have to be bribed. Large amounts of money have to be paid for electricity and telephone connections (Thiessen, 1997, p. 240–1).
43. OECD (1997) p. 15.
44. Thiessen (1997) p. 241.
45. According to a detailed calculation in the newspaper 'Golos Ukraini' (28 November 1995), the addition of 15 different taxes caused Ukrainian enterprise to pay taxes amounting to more than 70 per cent of profits (Thiessen, 1997, p. 241).
46. There are numerous horror stories about dealings with Ukrainian customs. One of the most revealing stories is that of a truckload of copiers send from Germany to Odessa. All the required documents were present. The only problem was that there was only one copy of the invoice. The shipment was confiscated and criminal procedures against the company started. The enterprise instigated a costly procedure against the customs and the copiers were only returned to the owner one and half years after they were confiscated. No charges were brought against the customs officers involved (Kyiv Post, 29 September 1998).
47. OECD (1997) p. 20.
48. Thiessen (1997) p. 241–2.
49. Visa costs are US$150 or more (Thiessen, 1997, p. 241).
50. Ekonomika Ukraini, January 1997, p. 37.
51. Möllers (1999) p. 152.
52. OECD (1997) p. 11.
53. Möllers (1999) p. 151.
54. Ibid. p. 150.
55. Kyiv Post, 11 September 1998.
56. The Day, 16 February 1999.
57. Wall Street Journal, 23 April 1997.
58. Avtomobil, nr. 23(50), 1996, p. 5.
59. Radio Free Europe/Radio Liberty Newsline, 17 September 1997.
60. The production of OPEL cars never materialized.
61. Both Avtozaz directors Kravchuk and Sotnikov were unwilling to cooperate with Daewoo. Daewoo representative Kim U Djung said that he only wanted to cooperate with Daewoo if Sotnikov was replaced. Only after a meeting with Prime Minister Pustovoytenko was this demand dropped (Zerkalo Nedeli, 24 April 1999).
62. Ibid.
63. BBC Monitoring, Summary of World Broadcast, part 1, 13 March 1998.
64. Interfax News Agency, 30 March 1998.
65 Zerkalo Nedeli, 21 January 2000.
66. Kyiv Post, 10 March 1999.
67. Kyiv Post, 3 February 2000.
68. Kyiv Post, 18 January 1999. In February 1998, the EU issued a press release that stated the law granting fiscal advantages to Daewoo made it 'virtually impossible for anyone else to sell cars in Ukraine'.
69. Kyiv Post, 18 January 1999.

70. Kyiv Post, 15 March 1999.
71. Ibid.
72. Kyiv Post, 10 March 1999.
73. Kyiv Post, 18 January 1999.
74. Ukrainian Economic Trends, December 1999, p. 53.
75. Ruigrok and Van Tulder (1993) pp. 29–34.
76. Zerkalo Nedeli, 3 April 1999.

8   Regional Economies

1. Koropeckyj (1992) p. 127
2. For example, in 1992, an American businessman planned to build an office complex in Kyiv. In 1996, after four years of struggle, he obtained all the necessary licences from Kyiv City Council. Then the security council, which owned a complex nearby, made objections and half of the office complex had to be abandoned. The process of obtaining licences started anew and by mid-1999, the businessman still did not have all the licences (Zerkalo Nedeli, 15 May 1999).
3. Lyakh and Pankow (1998) p. 23.
4. BBC/SWB, 19 February 1999.
5. Kaufmann 1997, p. 243, describes how provincial administrations ban grain exports in order to ensure the sale of grain crops under state contract – regardless of whether or not the agricultural producer owned the grain. See also Eastern Economist, 21 July 1999.
6. Ibid. p. 239. In a survey, in March 1996, this obstacle was rated 3.8 on a scale of 1–5 (1 meaning no impediment, 5 maximum severity).
7. According to P. McInally, a coal mining engineer working as consultant for TACIS in Donetsk, 30 January 1999.
8. Lyakh and Pankow (1998) p. 177.
9. Lyakh and Pankow (1998).
10. Tretiakov (1999) p. 5.
11. The Day, 3 August 1999.
12. Kyiv Post, 10 November 1998.
13. According to Tretiakov, the vice-governor of Donetsk, 30 January 1999. Fifty-eight of those polled in a survey in Donetsk in May 1997, did not have a permanent job. (Lyakh and Pankow,1998, p. 35).
14. Lyakh and Pankow (1998) p. 78.
15. Ibid. p. 177.
16. Lindler (1998) p. 929.
17. Human Development Report Ukraine, 1997, table 1.2. In reality, given non-payment of wages and other distortions, the difference may have been smaller.
18. Statistical Yearbook 1997, p. 272.
19. According to Minister Tulub, in Zerkalo Nedeli, nr. 52, 1998, p. 1.
20. Kyiv Post, 2 February 1999.
21. BBC/SWB, Weekly Economic Report, FSU, 30 October 1998.
22. Donbass Invest, January–February 1999, p. 7.

23. Makogon, 1999, p. 17, forty-one per cent of foreign direct investment in Donetsk originates from the USA, 8 per cent from Germany and 7 per cent from Great the UK (1 January 1998); 24 per cent was invested in commercial structures; 11 per cent in foreign trade; 9 per cent in machine building and metallurgy and 8 per cent in the chemical sector.
24. Kyiv Post, 2 February 1999.
25. See interview with V. Ribak, Member of Parliament, in Zerkalo Nedeli, nr. 40, 1998, p. 2.
26. Ukrainian Economic Trends, January 1999.
27. According to State Geology Committee chairman Serhy Hoshovsky, Kyiv Post, 19 December 1997.
28. IntelNews, 12 July 1998.
29. In 1998, 29 per cent of Zaporizhzhya exports went to the former Soviet Union, and 45 per cent of imports originated there (Zaporizhzhya Statistical Yearbook, 1998).
30. Zerkalo Nedeli, 29 May 1999.
31. IntelNews, 29 June 1998.
32. The average percentage of electricity losses during transport in the energy grid is 25 per cent for Ukraine, according to the Ministry for Energy.
33. Zerkalo Nedeli, 10 April 1999.

9 Social Change: Economic Implications

1. See Rose (1998a).
2. The comparison is from Rose (1998a) p. 11.
3. Often, organizations that appear to act as interest-representing organizations, are not. An example is the Federation of Ukrainian Trade Unions, an umbrella organization of 42 branch and 27 regional unions, that claims a membership of around 20 million. It claims to represent both the interests of the employees and the employers. As in Soviet times, the trade unions are more a tool of management than a worker's organization.

   The Union of Industrialists is a more powerful player and exercises great power over government policies. They have pushed for trade liberalization, currency liberalization and improved conditions for foreign direct investment. However, critics accuse the Union of being anti-reform because it competes unfairly with a nascent private sector in trying to get government funds.

   Political parties are gathered around personalities rather than ideologies or specific social groups, although each party has its specific regional or social background. For example, the liberal party is mainly based in Eastern Ukraine, primarily organizing directors of state enterprises turned capitalist. Ukrainian politics rest more upon elite bargains with elite beneficiaries than on support from below.
4. In early 1998, the populations in eleven Central and Eastern European countries were surveyed about alternatives to the current regime. Only 24 per cent of polled Ukrainians rejected all authoritarian alternatives, while the mean for seven Central European countries was 66 per cent. Fifty-

one per cent of polled Ukrainians agreed strongly or to some extent with the communists in power as an alternative. The mean for seven Central European countries was 20 per cent (Rose and Haerpfner, 1998, p. 19). Authoritarianism can be related to the power distance index as elaborated by Hofstede (1994). In his survey, Ukraine got 70 points on a 100 point index (100 means very high power distance). Only India ranked higher (77 points). Sweden got 31 points, the USA 40 points, Poland 52 points and France 68 points.

5. Simon (1998) p. 131.
6. This has been analysed by Etkind and Gozmann, 1992.
7. H. Smith (1990) noticed for Russia that 'within the trusted tribal ring, the bonds are strong but outside it, the frictions are abrasive and the mistrust corrosive' (p. 182). Trust in the small circle of family and friends is relative as there is almost an absence of delicacy with respect to matters of privacy. Usually, people have not learnt to be careful with personally entrusted information.
8. Secrecy is paramount everywhere in Ukraine. The author encountered wide-spread secrecy in his field research in Zaporizhzhya (see van Zon *et al.*, 1998). The higher in the hierarchy, the less likely interviewees were to give information. Even the Statistical Yearbook of the province is not public and difficult to get hold of. Polish researchers in Donetsk also complained about the reluctance to share information: 'Our Ukrainian partners from the Renaissance Foundation were not able to share information while empha-sizing their independence of the state administration.... Furthermore, even our potential allies from the Donetsk chapter of the Sörös Foundation were withholding from us basic information concerning the regions major prob-lems.' (Lyakh and Pankow, 1998, p. 171).
9. Many Ukrainians would not agree with such a statement. When asked by what traits four countries can be characterized (industriousness, laziness, unpredictability and punctuality) most polled Ukrainians characterized Ukraine by industriousness, while Russians were characterized by unpre-dictability and Germans and English by punctuality (Zerkalo Nedeli, 22 May 1999).
10. This assessment is based on interviews with Dutch investors in Ukraine, during a seminar of the Utrecht Chamber of Commerce, October 1995.
11. Custine pointed to the deep intolerance he encountered in Russia in 1839 (Custine, 1975, p. 48).
12. Many journalistic accounts of life in the Soviet Union and Russia point to this phenomenon. Kapuscinski, (1996) noticed that 'gradually, the art of formulating questions (for it is an art!) vanished, as did even the need to ask them ... A civilization that does not ask questions... is a civilization standing in place, paralyzed, immobile. And that is what the people in the Kremlin were after, because it is easiest to reign over a motionless and mute world.' (p. 145).
13. Surveys confirm this for at least part of observed attitudes. Comparative research between Russia, Ukraine, the Czech Republic and South Korea showed that Russians and Ukrainians are very similar and differ from Czechs as well as Koreans. 'Ex-Soviet citizens are four times more likely to turn to anti-modern behavior to get a youth into university, two to three

times as likely to use corruption or connections to get a better flat, almost twice as likely to use anti-modern methods to get prompt hospital treatment.' The same research showed that the Soviet experience is most likely to foster anti-modern social capital networks (Rose, 1998a).

14. Ledeneva argues that in everyday dealings with authorities lies come out almost automatically. 'One does not lie always blatantly or tell the uncomfortable truth. People have learned to mix the two into credible stories to resolve bureaucratic problems.' Ledeneva stresses that these lies should be perceived as practices of creating exceptional cases, rather than dishonesty, as an ability not only to live with the contradictions of their society, but also to manipulate them creatively (Ledeneva, 1998, p. 79). Shlapentokh (1996) sees the lie as an institution of the privatization of the state. Lying is a means of survival. 'People easily protect their private life because they are forced to lie regularly in their professional work' (p. 159).

15. The term 'Homo Sovieticus' is used with reluctance here as many of the characteristic behavioural patterns and values described here and usually labelled with the term 'Homo Sovieticus' were already visible under Tsarist rule (see Custine, 1975).

16. North, (1990) p. 36.

17. Ibid.

18. Rose (1997) pp 16–20. Amongst a group of seven surveyed Central and Eastern European countries (Bulgaria, Czech Republic, Slovakia, Hungary, Poland, Romania, Slovenia, Belarus, Ukraine), Bulgarians and Ukrainians appeared the most distrusting, not only towards state institutions, but towards all major institutions of society. Popular distrust was lowest in the Czech Republic.

    In this context, the division into characteristic-based, process-based and institutional-based trust becomes important. Institutional-based trust is tied to formal structures and depends on individual or firm-specific attributes or on intermediary mechanisms. It includes standardization, regulation, formalization or legislation as common denominators for how to settle specific exchange expectations. In the absence of institutional-based trust, it is replaced by characteristic-based and process-based trust. Characteristic-based trust is tied to a person and his or her specific traits as ethnicity, profession or family background. This kind of trust is found in regional economic networks in, for example, Northern Italy. Process-based trust is tied to past or expected exchange. Reciprocity and reputation generate process-based trust. Process-based trust was the linchpin of Soviet informal exchange activities.

19. Messner (1997) p. 278.

20. It is mainly sociologists that pointed to the interrelationships between cultural and economic change (Hofstede, 1994; see also Max Weber).

21. Landes (1998).

22. According to a survey done in Russia (Rose, 1998c, p. 27), 56 per cent of 2002 persons interviewed in early 1998 resorted to defensive portfolios, i.e. earnings from regular jobs, benefits at place of work or pension is the second or most important and growing food, repairing the house or helping friends and relatives or using free connections is the second or most important activity. Sixteen per cent had vulnerable portfolios, that

means earnings from regular job, benefits at place of work, pension are the only important economic activities. Fourteen per cent had marginal portfolios, that means growing food, repairing the house, helping of friends and relatives using free connections are the most important economic activities, or respondent does not know what activities are important. Only 14 per cent of respondents had enterprising portfolios, that means income from additional jobs, getting paid for doing favours and dealing with foreign currency.

We may assume that in Ukraine, the portfolio patterns do not differ much from those in Russia.

23. Sztompka (1995, p. 63) pointed to the boomerang effect of the 'socialist habitus'.
24. Elster *et al.* (1998) p. 31
25. Ibid. p. 27.
26. Ibid. p. 28.
27. Ibid. p. 31. This is exemplified in the problem of splitting up the gigantic state enterprises that have autarchic inclinations, produce a lot of sideline products and have an extended social sphere (see Chapter 6, page 101).
28. Messner (1997) p. 180.
29. Elster *et al.* (1998).
30. Elster *et al.* (1998).
31. Hygienic habits have spread since the 1950s, as living conditions of the populations started to improve.
32. Ferge (1998).
33. Putnam (1993) p. 35.
34. The concept of social capital became very popular during the second half of the 1990s. The concept has been criticized for being vague and chaotic (see Fine, 1999). Social capital is about the non-economic, or non-market factors that make the economy function better. Fine criticizes the concept as ignoring aspects of conflict and power. He quotes Evans as saying 'if a community is riven by conflicting interests, the nature of meaning of social capital becomes more complicated...if conflict codetermines the notion of social capital, why not take conflict and its theoretical underpinnings as the starting point rather than social capital which is rendered both ambiguous and redundant' (p. 14).
35. See Gibson (1998).
36. Rose (1997) p. 12.
37. O'Loughin and Bell (1999) p. 243.
38. Ibid. The percentage of respondents who ruled out actively taking part in any form of protest – whether legal or illegal- increased from 31.9 to 37.3 per cent between 1991 and 1997.
39. Srubar (1991) p. 28
40. Ministry of Economy *et al.* (1999) p. 1–7.
41. Statistical Yearbook 1997, p. 422.
42. Ministry of Economy *et al.* (1999), p. 1–6.
43. Rose (1998b) p. 34.
44. Of 600 persons polled in Donetsk in May 1997, 58 per cent did not have a permanent job. Sixty-three per cent of surveyed persons cannot provide for their basic needs (Lyakh and Pankow, 1998, p. 35 and 39).

45. Ministry of Economy *et al.* (1999) p. 4–2. According to the Statistical Yearbook 1997, in 1997 33.1 per cent of those employed in industry were on administrative leave, and 22.6 per cent worked part-time (p. 393).
46. Ibid.
47. TACIS.EDUK. 9402.
48. Among interviewees polled in Donetsk province (May 1997), 72 per cent believed that there was no possibility of overcoming their difficulties. (Lyakh and Pankow, 1998, p. 49).
49. In 1998, more than one-third of all housing and utility bills were unpaid. In some provinces, like Zaporizhzhya, only a tiny part of the populations pays these bills (Radio Free Europe, 3 February 1999). In 1996, only 20 per cent of the Zaporizhzhya population paid the gas bill. See Bagratian and Gürgen (1997).
50. The average death rate rose from 13.4 per 100 000 people in 1992 to 15.4 in 1995 and 14.9 in 1997 and is now more than 50 per cent higher than in the European Union. In 1995, life expectancy at birth was just 65 years, compared with more than 77 years in the European Union. Birth rates fell from 15.0 per 10 000 in 1985 to 12.7 in 1990 and 9.0 in 1997 (Ministry of Economy *et al.* 1999, p. 1–8).
51. Ministry of Economy *et al.* (1999), pp. 1–7.
52. Ibid. pp. 1–8.
53. Messner (1997) shows that economic development and creation of competitiveness are, contrary to the view dominant among neo-liberal economists, not based solely on liberal economic policies and a strengthening of market forces. The development of efficient industrial locations and competitive economies constitutes a challenge to society as a whole and it ability to focus its governance and problem-solving potentials.

10 Path Dependency and Development Prospects

1. IMF *et al.* (1990) pp. 18–19.
2. Path dependency is determined by the structure of the historically grown social and economic system, implemented policies and the impact of the changing international environment. See van Zon, 1996, p. 44.
3. See Harris and Lockwood (1997) p. 629.
4. Gaddy and Ickes (1998).
5. A World Bank poll among 140 experts in government and non-governmental organizations showed that society and political and economic elite is not ready for fundamental institutional changes (Zerkalo Nedeli, 18 May 1999).
6. Kyiv Post, 29 July 1999.
7. In 1999, 35.2 per cent of polled people (1000 interviews) thought that loss-making enterprises should not be subsidized, 22.8 per cent thought they should while 26.7 thought 'yes, partially'. Sixteen per cent did not know (Kyiv Post, 17 June 1999).
8. The term involution is used here in the interpretation of Burawoy (1996) and differs from the term as used in the natural sciences and by Clifford Geertz is his 'Agricultural Involution'. The Process of Ecological Change in

Indonesia'(1963) in which he described how the Javanese economy, faced
with external pressure from the economic demands of the Dutch colonial
regime and internal pressure from a rapidly increasing population,
intensified existing forms of agriculture rather than changing.

9. The directors of Avtozaz said in interviews with the author (1996 and
1997), that the major problem for the enterprise was lack of capital. 'The
foreign investor should provide capital, we know how to make cars', was
the adage, ignoring the fact that few wanted to buy the low quality Tavria
car. The low quality of the Tavria was attributed to lack of modern machinery.

10. Quoted in Aston and Philpin (1985) p. 214.

11. North (1990) p. 7.

12. North (1990) p. 54.

13. Hilton (1984) p. 91.

14. Zerkalo Nedeli, 10 February 1996, p. 6.

15. Ibid.

16. Johnson *et al.* (1997).

17. In a poll in Donetsk, covering 600 residents in mining districts, 58 per cent
of those polled did not have a permanent job (Lyakh and Pankow, 1998,
p. 36). Most people live on old age and disability pensions, benefits or plots
of land and help of relatives.

18. Sixty-two per cent of 600 persons polled in Donetsk (May 1997) have to
count on own resources (Lyakh and Pankow, 1998). Mutual help among
people is decreasing.

19. The nature of the Ukrainian state is also perceived by international donor
organizations as a major obstacle to reform. The representative of the World
Bank in Ukraine, Mr Jedrzejczak, stated that the main failure of Ukraine is
the absence of central and local administrative reform (The Day, 16 March
1999).

20. The following characterization of the institutional environment of nine-
teenth century Mexico, by John Coatsworth, is telling: 'The interventionist
and pervasively arbitrary nature of the institutional environment forced
every enterprise, urban or rural, to operate in a highly politicized manner,
using kinship networks, political influence, and family prestige to gain privileged access to subsidized credit, to aid various strategems for recruiting
labor, to collect debts or enforce contracts, to evade taxes or circumvent
courts, and to defend or assert titles to lands. Success or failure in the economic arena always depended on the relationship of the producer with
political authorities- local officials for arranging matters close at hand and
the central government of the colony for sympathetic interpretations of the
law and intervention at the local level when conditions required it. Small
enterprise, excluded from the system of corporate privilege and political
favors, was forced to operate in a permanent state of semi-clandestinity,
always at the margin of the law, at the mercy of petty officials, never secure
from arbitrary acts and never protected against the rights of those more
powerful.' (Coatsworth, J. H., 'Obstacles to Economic Growth in
Nineteenth-Century Mexico', *American Historical Review*, 83: p. 94, as
quoted in North, D.C., 1990, p. 116–7).

21. North (1990) p. 112. Path dependence points to the nature of constraints from the past imposing limits on current choices and therefore making the current choice set intelligible (p. 135).
22. Ibid.
23. North (1990) p. 122.
24. Motyl (1998) p. 11.
25. Birch (1999) Table 14. In September 1998, people were asked in a survey 'Some people consider that Ukraine should have a market economy. Other people think that Ukraine should restore a planned, state socialist economy. Using the scale on this card, where would you place your position with regard to this question?' The scale ranged from 1 to 5, 1 meaning strong support for market economy, 5 strong support for a planned, state socialist economy. Only 18.1 per cent of interviewed indicated strong support (1), and 9.1 per cent gave a 2 ranking. The average ranking overall was 3.2 indicating an inclination to support a centrally planned economy.
26. Rose and Haerpfner (1998) p. 25. The mean for Central and Eastern European countries was 53 per cent and 38 per cent.
27. Hishow (1999) p. 15.

Bibliography

Administrative Reform in Ukraine Special Issue of Ukrainian Law Review, Vol. 1, Nr 4 (Kyiv: Ukrainian–European Policy and Legal Advice Centre, 1999).

Äslund, A., 'Ukraine's Turnaround', *Foreign Policy*, No. 100, Fall (1995) 125–143.

Aston, T. H. and Philpin, Ch. E. *The Brenner Debate – Agrarian Class Structure and Economic Development in Pre-Industrial Europe* (Cambridge: Cambridge University Press, 1985).

Atta, D. Van, 'Households Budgets in Ukraine: A Research Report', *Post-Soviet Geography and Economics*. December. Vol. XXXIX, No. 10 (1998), pp. 606–16.

Atta, D. Van, *Background Notes on the Agricultural Concept Papers*, CPER Briefing Papers, 1 January 1999.

Atta, D. Van, Neubert, D., Plakhotnik, I., *Barter's Effects on Ukraine's Agricultural Economy*, CEPR Number 24 (1998a).

Atta, D. Van, Zoria, S.,Betlyi, M., Shanin, A., *The Ukrainian State Grain Order*, CPER-CARD Ukraine Reports, Number 1, 20 February (1998b).

Bagratian, H. and Gürgen, E. *'Payment Arrears in the Gas and Electric Power Sectors of the Russian Federation and Ukraine'*, IMF Working Paper, December 1997.

Baker, D., *'Dairy Policy in Ukraine'*, CPER Staff Analyses, No. 34, 1998.

Balmaceda, M. M. 'Gas, Oil, and the Linkages between Domestic and Foreign Policies: the Case of Ukraine', *Europe-Asia Studies*, Vol. 50, No. 2 (1998), pp. 257–86.

Beetham, D. *Bureaucracy* (Milton Keynes: Open University Press, 1987).

Ben, T. and Sychenko, V. 'Methods of Determination of a Level of Monopolism on the Markets of Industrial Production' (in Russian), *Ekonomika Ukraini*, No. 3, March (1999), pp. 37–45.

Birch, S. 'Representation in Ukraine: Evidence from the 1998 Elections', paper presented at the BASEES conference, Cambridge, 27–29 March 1999.

Boss, H. 'Ukraine's Economy in Sectoral and Regional Perspective', *WIIW Forschungsberichte*, No. 202, October (1993).

Braithwaite, J. and Hoopengardner, T. 'Who are Ukraine's Poor? in Cornelius, P. and Lenain, P. (Eds),1997, pp. 61–81.

Bremmer, I. and Taras, R. (Eds) *New States, New Politics: Building the Post-Soviet Nations* (Cambridge: Cambridge University Press, 1997).

Brenner, R. 'The Agrarian Roots of European Capitalism', in Aston, T. H. and Philpin, Ch. E. (Eds), 1985, pp. 48–78.

Burawoy, M. 'The State and Economic Involution: Russia Through a China Lens', *World Development*, Vol. 24, No. 6 (1996) 1105–17.

Castells, M., *End of Millennium. The Information Age: Economy, Society and Culture, Volume III* (Blackwell: Oxford, 1998).

Clarke, S. 'Privatization and the Development of Capitalism in Russia', *New Left Review*, No. 196, November/December (1992), 3–29.

Clement, H. *et al. Strukturwandel und Probleme der realwirtschaftlichen Anpassung in der Ukraine* (Munich: Osteuropa-Institut, 1996).

Clement, H., Knogler, M. and Sekarev, A., *Die Ukrainische Aussenwirtschaft vor dem Zusammenbruch?* Osteuropa Institut München. Working Papers, No. 166, December (1993).

Conrad, J., 'Kleine und mittlere Unternehmen in der Ukraine. Entwicklungshemnisse under Förderungsmassnahmen', in Hoffmann, L. and Siedenberg, A. (Eds), 1997, pp. 193–208.

Cornelius, P. K. and Lenain, P. (Eds) *Ukraine: Accelerating the Transition to Market* (Washington: IMF, 1997).

Cramon-Taubadel, S. von and Koester, U. 'Die Wettbewerbsfähigkeit der ukrainischen Landwirtschaft', in Hoffman, L. and Siedenberg, A. (Eds) 1997, pp. 127–44.

Crowley, S. 'Between Class and Nation, Worker Politics in the New Ukraine', *Communist and Post-Communist Studies.* Vol. 28, No. 1 (1995).

Crozier, M., *The Bureaucratic Phenomenon* (Chicago: University of Chicago Press, 1964).

Csaki, C. and Lerman, Z. *Land Reform in Ukraine; The First Five Years.* World Bank Discussion Papers, No. 371, 1997.

Custine, Marquis de, *Lettres de Russie* (Paris: Gallimard, 1975).

Deutsche Bank *The Soviet Union at the Crossroads, Facts and Figures on the Soviet Republic*, Economics Department, Deutsche Bank, Frankfurt, 1990.

DIW, *Zur Internationalen Wettbewerbsfähigkeit der Metallhütten in der Gemeinschaft Unabhängiger Staaten (GUS).* Deutsches Institut für Wirtschaftsforschung. Heft 177, 1998.

Duchêne, G. 'Ukrainian Economy in mid-1998: a State of Emergency', *Ukrainian Economic Trends,* May (1998) 4–9.

Eckstein, H., Flera Jr., F. J., Hoffman, E. P., Revlinger, W. R. *Can Democracy Take Root in Post Soviet Russia?* (Oxford: Rowman & Littlefield Publishers, 1998).

Elster, J., Offe, C., Preuss, U.K., *Institutional Design in Post-Communist Societies* (Cambridge: Cambridge University Press, 1998).

Estrin, S., Rosevaer, A. 'Enterprise Performance and Corporate Governance in Ukraine', *Journal of Comparative Economics*, Vol. 27, No. 3 (1999) 552–58.

Etkind, A. and Gozmann, L., *The Psychology of Post-Totalitarianism* (London: Centre for Research into Communist Economies, 1992).

European Bank for Reconstruction and Development, *Transition Report 1997* (London: EBRD, 1997).

European Bank for Reconstruction and Development, *Transition Report 1998* (London: EBRD, 1998).

Evans, P. *Embedded Autonomy: States and Industrial Transformation* (Princeton: Princeton University Press, 1995).

Fallon, P., Hoopengardner, T. and Libanova, E. 'Poverty and the Ukrainian Labor Market', in Cornelius, P. K. and Lenain, P. (Eds), 1997.

Ferge, Z. 'And What if the State Fades Away. The Civilising Process and the State', *IWM Working Papers*, No. 7 (Vienna: Institut für die Wissenschoft vom Menschen, 1997).

Fine, B., 'The Developmental State is Dead – Long Live Social Capital', *Development and Change*, Vol. 30, No. 1 (1999) 1–14.

Fleron Jr, F. J. 'Congruence Theory Applied: Democratization in Russia', in Eckstein, H. *et al.* (Eds) 1998, pp. 35–69.

Gaddy, C. G. and Ickes, B. W. *'Beyond a Bailout: Time to Face Reality About Russia's 'Virtual Economy'* (Washington: The Brookings Institution, 1998).

Gärtig, T., 'Anmerkungen zur Wirtschaftliche Entwicklung der Ukraine', in Hausmann, G. and Kappeler, A. (Eds), 1993, pp. 311–17.

Gibson, J. L. 'Political and Economic Markets: Changes in the Connections between Attitudes towards Political Democracy and a Market Economy within the Mass Culture of Russia and Ukraine', *Journal of Politics*, Vol. 58, No. 4 (1996) 954–84.

Gibson, J. L. 'Putting up with Fellow Russians: An Analysis of Political Tolerance in the Fledgling Russian Democracy', *Political Research Quarterly*, Vol. 51, No. 1 (1998a), 37–69.

Gibson, J. L. *Social Networks and Civil Society in Processes of Democratization*, Studies in Public Policy, No. 301 (Glasgow: CSPP, 1998b).

Giddens, A., *The Third Way. The Renewal of Social Democracy* (Cambridge: Polity Press, 1998).

GLS Research, GA-PBN, UFE Foundation, Government of Ukraine and USAID, *The Economic Reforms in Ukraine: Opinion Survey of 1600 Ukrainian citizens April/May 1997*. Kyiv, 1997.

Gould-Davies, N. and Woods, N. 'Russia and the IMF', *International Affairs*, Vol. 75, No. 1 (1999), 1–23.

Gregory, P. R. and Stuart, R.C. *Russian and Soviet Economic Performance and Structure* (New York: AddisonWesley Longman, 1998).

Grödeland, A., Koshenchkina, T. and Miller, W. L. 'Alternative strategies for coping with officials in different postcommunist regimes', *Public Administration and Development*, Vol. 17, No. 5 (1997) 511–28.

Gros, D. and Steinherr, A., 'Banking Reform in Eastern Europe with Special Reference to Ukraine', in Hoffman, L. and Siedenberg, A. (Eds), 1999, pp. 193–217.

Gummich, A. 'Die Reformentwicklung in Osteuropa – Lehren fur die Ukraine', in Hoffman, L. and Siedenberg, A. (Eds) 1997, pp. 25–43.

Gummich, A. and Voss, J. 'Auslandische Direktinvestitionen in der Ukraine – Nutzen, Hemmnisse und Lösungsansatze', in Hoffman, L. and Siedenberg, A. (Eds), 1997, pp. 232–48.

Hague, J. Rose, A. and Bojcun, M. 'Rebuilding Ukraine's Hollow State – Developing a Democratic Public Service in Ukraine', *Public Administration and Development*, Vol. 15, No. 4 (1995) 417–33.

Hare, P. M., Ishaq, M. and Estrin, S. 'Ukraine: The Legacies of Central Planning and the Transition to Market Economy', in Kuzio, T. (Ed.),1998, pp. 182–95.

Harris, N. and Lockwood, N. 'The War-making State and Privatisation', *Journal of Development Studies*, Vol. 33, No. 1 (1997) 597–633.

Hausmann, G. and Kappeler, A. (Eds), *Gegenwart und Geschichte eines neuen Staates* (Nomos, 1993).

Havlik, P. *et al.*, *The Transition Countries in 1999: A Further Weakening of Growth and Some Hopes for Later Recovery*, Research Reports, No. 257 (Vienna: The Vienna Institute for Comparative Economic Studies, June 1999).

Havrylyshyn, O. 'Ukraine: looking East – looking West', *The Harriman Review*, Vol. 10, No. 3 (1997).

Heets, V., 'Once More about Components of Economic Growth in Ukraine' (in Russian), *Ekonomika Ukraini*, No. 12 (1998), 4–16.

Hellman, J. S. 'Winners Take All. The Politics of Partial Reform in Postcommunist Transitions.', *World Politics*, No. 50, January (1998), 203–34.

Hilton, R. 'Feudalism in Europe: Problems for Historical Materialists', *New Left Review*, No. 147, September/October (1984) 84–95.

Hirschhausen, C. von, *Industrial Restructuring in Ukraine: from Socialism to a Planned Economy?* Discussion Paper No. 144 (Berlin: Deutsches Institut fur Wirtschaftsforschung, 1996).

Hirschhausen, C. von, Lunina, I. and Vachnenko, T. 'Die Energiewirtschaft der Ukraine – Bestandsaufnahme und Reformbedarf zur Unternehmisierung', in Hoffman, L. and Siedenberg, A. (Eds), 1997, pp. 144–62.

Hirschhausen, C. von, 'Gas Sector Restructuring in Ukraine: Analysis of Import Dependence, Price Formation and Socio-Economic Effects', in Hoffmann, L. and Siedenberg, A. (Eds), 1999, pp. 391–408.

Hirschman, D. 'Development Management versus Third World Bureaucracies: A Brief History of Conflicting Interests', *Development and Change*, Vol. 30, No. 2 (1999), 287–307.

Hirszowicz, M., *The Bureaucratic Leviathan. A Study in the Sociology of Communism* (Oxford: Martin Robertson, 1980).

Hishow, O., *Die Russische Wirtschaft nach dem Abschied von den Reformern. Wirtschaftspolitische Stagnation und Schuldenfalle.* Berichte des Bundesinstituts fur ostwissenschaftliche und internationale Studien, Nr 22, 1999.

Hoffman, L., 'Ein Stabilitätspakt für die Ukraine', in Hoffman, L.and Siedenberg, A. (Eds) 1997, pp. 57–67.

Hoffmann, L. and Siedenberg, A. (Eds) *Aufbruch in die Marktwirtschaft: Reformen in der Ukraine von innen betrachtet* (Frankfurt/New York: Campus Verlag, 1997).

Hoffman, L. and Siedenberg, A. (Eds), *Ukraine at the Crossroads* (Berlin: Physica Verlag, 1999).

Hofstede, G., *Cultures and Organizations* (London: HarperCollins Publishers, 1994).

Holdar, S., 'Torn between East and West – the Regional Factor in Ukrainian Politics', *Post-Soviet Geography*, Vol. 36 No. 2 (1995) 112–32.

Holmes, K. R., Johnson, B. and Kirkpatrick, M. *1997 Index of Economic Freedom* (New York: Dow Jones, 1997).

Hölscher, J. 'Zur Formierung markwirtschaftlicher Ordnungen in Zentralosteuropa', *Konjunkturpolitik*, Vol. 44, No. 4 (1998) 393–422.

Huber, P. and Wörgötter, A., 'Observations on Russian Business Networks', *Post-Soviet Affairs*.Vol. 14, January–March (1998) 83–91.

International Labour Office, *The Ukrainian Challenge: Reforming Labour Market and Social Policy* (Budapest: Central European University Press, 1995).

International Monetary Fund, World Bank, OECD, EBRD, *The Economy of the USSR* (Washington DC: World Bank, 1990).

International Monetary Fund, *Ukraine – Recent Economic Developments*. Staff Country Report, No. 97/109, Washington, October 1997.

International Monetary Fund, Ukraine – Recent Economic Developments. Staff Country Report, No. 99/32, Washington, May 1999.

Johnson, S., Kaufmann, D. and Ustenko, O. 'Household Survival Strategies', *Ukrainian Economic Review*. Vol. 11 No. 3 (1996), 112–16.

Jowitt, K. 'Soviet Neotraditionalism: The Political Corruption of a Leninist Regime', *Soviet Studies*, 35 (1983) 275–97.

Kakwani, N. 'Income inequality, welfare and poverty in Ukraine', *Development and Change*, Vol. 27, No. 4 (1996) 663–91

Kapuscinski, R. *Imperium* (London: Granta Books, 1994).

Kaufmann, D. 'Diminishing Returns to Administrative Controls and Emergence of the Unofficial Economy: a Framework of Analysis and Applications to Ukraine', *Economic Policy*, Vol. 19 (1994) 159–215.

Kaufmann, D. 'The Missing Pillar of a Growth Strategy for Ukraine: Reforms for Private Sector Development', in Cornelius, P. and Lenain, P. (Eds) 1997, pp. 234–75.

Knabe, B. 'Die System-Mafia als Faktor der sowjetisch-russischen Transformation. Teil 1: Vorbereitung under Durchführung des Systemwechsels', *Berichte des Bundesinstituts für ostwissenschaftliche und internationale Studien*, No. 47 (1998a).

Knabe, B. 'Die System-Mafia als Faktor der sowjetisch-russischen Transformation. Teil II: Die Instrumentalisierung des organisierten Verbrechens', *Berichte des Bundesinstituts für ostwissenschaftliche und internationale Studien*, No. 48 (1998b).

Koester, U. and Striewe, L., 'Huge Potential, Huge Losses – The Search for Ways Out of the Dilemma of Ukrainian Agriculture', in Siedenberg, A. and Hoffmann, L. (Eds) 1999, pp. 259–71.

Konings, J. and Walsh, P. P., 'Disorganization in the process of transition', *Economics of Transition*, Vol. 7 No. 1 (1999) 29–46.

Koropeckyj, I. S. *Development in the Shadow – Studies in Ukrainian Economics* (Edmonton: Canadian Institute of Ukrainian Studies Press, University of Alberta, 1990).

Koropeckyj, I. S. *The Ukrainian Economy* (Harvard: Harvard University Press, 1991).

Koropeckyj, I. S. *The Ukrainian Economy – Achievements, Problems, Challenges* (Harvard: Harvard University Press, 1992).

Kuzio, T. *Ukraine Under Kuchma: Political Reform, Economic Transformation and Security Policy in Independent Ukraine* (New York: St Martin's Press, 1997).

Kuzio, T. *State and Nation Building in Ukraine* (London: Routledge, 1998a).

Kuzio, T. (Ed.), *Contemporary Ukraine: Dynamics of Post-Soviet Transformation* (Armonk, New York: M. E. Sharpe, 1998b).

Landes, D. *The Wealth and Poverty of Nations. Why Some Are So Rich and Some So Poor* (London: Abacus, 1999).

Ledeneva, A. V. *Russia's Economy of Favours. Blat, Networking and Informal Exchange* (Cambridge: Cambridge University Press, 1998).

Lerman, Z. 'Land Reform and Farm Restructuring in Ukraine', *Problems of Post-Communism*, May/June (1999) 42–55.

Levine, R. M. and Bond, A. R. 'Prospects for Ukrainian Ferrous Metals in the Post-Soviet Period', *Post-Soviet Geography and Economics*, 39, No. 4 (1998), 151–63.

Lindler, R. 'Innen und aussenpolitische Bedingungen des Systemwechsels in Ukraine und Belarus', *Aussenpolitik* 46(4) (1998), 365–75.

Lindner, R. Kucma's Stuhl wackelt. Transformationsstau und Interessendivergenz in der Ukraine', *Osteuropa*, Vol. 48, No. 8–9 (1998) 920–37.

Lovei, L. and Skorik, K. 'Commercializing Ukraine's Agricultural Potential', in Cornelius, P. K. and Lenain, P. (Eds) 1997, pp. 198–209.

Lovei, L. and Skorik, K. 'Energy Sector Reform in Ukraine: Mid-term Report' in Siedenberg, A. and Hoffmann, L. (Eds) 1999, pp. 333–52.

Lukas, Z. *Agriculture in Transition: Widening Gap Between the CEEC's and Russia and Ukraine.* WIIW Forschungshefte, No. 258, June 1999.

Lunina, I. 'The Relations Between Central and Local Budget in Ukraine', *Ukrainian Economic Trends,* October 1997.

Lunina, I. and Vincentz, V., 'The Subsidisation of Enterprises in Ukraine', in Siedenberg, A. and Hoffmann, L. (Eds) 1999, pp. 119–131.

Lyakh, A. and Pankow, W. (Eds) *The Future of Old Industrial Regions in Europe. The Case of Donetsk Region in Ukraine* (Warsaw: Foundation for Economic Education, 1998).

Makogon, Y. 'Privletsenie innostranix investitsii I svabodnie ekonomitsietskie zoni', in *Problems of Development of Foreign Economic Relations and Attraction of Foreign Investments,* Donetsk State University, 1999, pp. 15–19.

Markwick, R. D. 'What Kind of State is the Russian State – if there is one?' *The Journal of Communist Studies and Transition Policies,* Vol. 15, December 1999.

Marples, D. R. *Ukraine under Perestroika. Ecology, Economics and the Worker's Revolt* (New York: St Martin's Press, 1991).

Melnyk, Z. L. 'Ukraine and Soviet Economic Development'. *The Ukrainian Quarterly.* Vol. XXIX, No. 1 (1973) 43–60.

Messner, D. *The Network Society. Economic Development and International Competitiveness as Problems of Social Governance* (London, Portland: Frank Cass, 1997).

Miller, J. R. and Wolchik, S., *The Social Legacy of Communism* (Cambridge: Cambridge University Press, 1994).

Miller, W. L., Koshechkina, T. and Grödeland, A. 'How Citizens Cope with Communist Officials: Evidence from Focus Group Discussions in Ukraine and the Czech Republic', *Political Studies,* Vol. 45, No. 3 (1997) 597–625.

Miller, W. L., Grödeland, A. S. and Koshechkina, T. Y. 'Confessions of Justified Sinners: Why Postcommunist Officials accept Presents and Bribes'. A paper presented for the BASEES Conference, Cambridge, March 1999.

Ministry of Economy, World Bank, International Center for Policy Studies, *Ukraine: Restoring Growth with Equity. A participatory Country Economic Memorandum,* Kyiv, 1999.

Ministry of Statistics of Ukraine, *Ukraine in Figures for 1996* (Kyiv: Naukova Dumka, 1997).

Möllers, F. 'Foreign Direct Investment in Ukraine – Experiences Taken from Reality' in Hoffmann, and L. Siedenberg, A. (Eds) 1999, pp. 138–61.

Möllers, F. and Siedenberg, A. 'The Interplay between Monetary Policy and Reform Policy in Ukraine', in Hoffmann, L. and Siedenberg, A. (Eds) 1999, pp. 58–80.

Motyl, A. J. *Dilemmas of Independence: Ukraine after Totalitarianism,* Council on Foreign Relations, 1993.

Motyl, A. J. 'Making Sense of Ukraine' *The Harriman Review,* Winter, Vol. 10, No. 3 (1997a) 1–5.

Motyl, A. J. 'Structural Constraints and Starting Points, the Logic of Systemic Change in Ukraine and Russia', *Comparative Politics*, July, Vol. 29, No. 4, (1997b) 433–49.

Motyl, A. J. 'State, Nation and Elites in Independent Ukraine', in Kuzio, T. (Ed.), 1998, pp. 3–16.

Motyl, A. J. and Krawchenko, B. 'Ukraine: From Empire to Statehood', in Bremmer, I. and Taras, R. (Eds.), 1997, pp. 235–276.

North, D. C. *Institutions, Institutional Change and Economic Performance* (Cambridge: Cambridge University Press, 1990).

OECD *Foreign Direct Investment in Ukraine* (OCDE/GD (97) 166) (Paris: OECD, 1997a).

OECD, *Framework for the Measurement of Unrecorded Economic Activities in Transition Economies* (Paris: OECD, 1997b).

O'Loughin, J. and Bell, J. E., 'The Political Geography of Civic Engagement in Ukraine', *Post-Soviet Geography and Economics*, Vol. 40, No. 4 (1999), 233–67.

Orsmond, D. W. H., 'Agenda for Fiscal Reform over the Medium Term', in Cornelius, P. K. and Lenain, P. (Eds) 1997, pp. 22–40.

Ott, A. *Wie hat die reale Macht in der Ukraine?* Berichte des Bundesinstituts für ostwissenschaftliche under internationale Studien, No. 31, 1997.

Perrotta, L. 'The Higher Up Don't Want To And The Lower Down Cannot – Analysis of Focus Groups Village Community Study. *CPER, Staff Analysis.* Issue 49 (1998).

Piirainen, T. *Towards a New Social Order in Russia – Transforming Structures and Everyday Life* (Dartmouth: Aldershot, 1997).

Pryor, F. L. and Blackman, M. 'The Ukrainian Industrial Sector in 1996 and 1997; Insights from the Rapid Enterprise Survey' *Ukrainian Economic Review*, Vol. III, No. 4–5, 1997–98 (1998).

Putnam, R. *Making Democracy Work: Civic Traditions in Modern Italy* (Princeton NY: Princeton University Press, 1993).

Rose, R. *Getting Real: Social Capital in Post-Communist Societies*, Studies in Public Policy, No. 278, Glasgow, 1997.

Rose, R. *Getting Things Done with Social Capital: NRB VII*, Studies in Public Policy, No. 303, Glasgow, 1998a.

Rose, R. *Getting Things Done in an Anti-modern Society: Social Capital Networks in Russia.* Studies in Public Policy, No. 304. Glasgow, 1998B.

Rose, R. and Haerpfner, C. *New Democracies Barometer V*, Studies in Public Policy. No 306, Glasgow, 1998.

Ruigrok, W. and Van Tulder, R. *The Ideology of Interdependence.* Thesis, University of Amsterdam, 1993.

Selm, G. van and Wagener, H.-J. 'Former Soviet Republics' Economic Interdependence', *Osteuropa Wirtschaft,* 1 (1993) 23–39.

Shen, R. *Ukraine's Economic Reform: Obstacles, Errors, Lessons* (Praeger Publishers, 1996).

Shlapentokh, V. *Public and Private Life of the Soviet People* (Oxford: Oxford University Press, 1989).

Shlapentokh, V. 'Early Feudalism – The Best Parallel for Contemporary Russia', *Europe-Asia Studies*, Vol. 48, No. 3 (1996) 393–413.

Sieburger, M. *Regionale Aspekte des Transformationsprozesses der Ukrainischen Wirtschaft – Die Gebiete L'wiw, Odessa und Donezk*, Berichte des Bundesinstitut fur ostwissenschaftliche und internationale Studien, No. 38, 1993.

Simon, G. *Welchen Raum läßt die Geschichte für die Modernisierung Rußlands?* Berichte des Bundesinstituts für ostwissenschaftliche und internationale Studien, No. 19, 1998.

Smith, G. and Wilson, A. 'Rethinking Russia's Post-Soviet Diaspora: The Potential for Political Mobilisation in Eastern Ukraine and North-East Estonia', *Europe-Asia Studies*, Vol. 49, No. 5 (1997) 845–64.

Smith, H. *The New Russians* (New York: Random House, 1990).

Smolansky, O. M. 'Ukraine and the Fuel Problem: Recent Developments', *The Ukrainian Quarterly*, Vol. LII, No. 2–3, Summer–Fall (1996) 125–9.

Solchanyik, R. 'The Politics of State Building: Centre-Periphery Relations in Post-Soviet Ukraine', *Europe-Asia Studies*, Vol. 46, No. 1 (1994) 47–69.

Solnick, S. *Stealing the State: Control and Collapse in Soviet Institutions* (Cambridge, Massachusetts: Harvard University Press, 1998).

Srubar, I. 'War der reale Sozialismus modern? Versuch einer strukturellen Bestimmung', *Kölner Zeitschrift fur Soziologie und Sozialpsychologie*, Vol. 43, No. 3 (1991) 415–32.

Stark, D. 'Privatization in Hungary – from "Plan to Market" or from "Plan to Clan"', *Eastern European Politics and Societies*, Vol. 4, No. 3 (1990).

Statistical Yearbook of Ukraine for 1996 (Kyiv, State Statistics Committee of Ukraine, 1998)

Statistical Yearbook of Ukraine for 1997 (Kyiv, State Statistics Committee of Ukraine 1999).

Striewe, L. and Cramon-Taubadel, S. von, 'Grain Production in Ukraine: Missed Opportunities and the Need for Immediate Action', in Siedenberg, A. and Hoffmann, L. (Eds) 1999, pp. 292–309.

Subtelny, O. *Ukraine – A History* (Toronto: University of Toronto Press, 1994).

Sundakov, A. 'The Machinery of Government and Economic Policy', in Cornelius, P. and Lenain, P. (Eds) 1997, pp. 275–89.

Sundakov, A. 'Transition Crisis: Is Crisis Management Delaying Transition?', in Siedenberg, A. and Hoffmann, L. (Eds) 1999, pp. 111–19.

Sundakov, A., Ossowski, R. and Lane, T. D. 'Shortages Under Free Prices: The Case of Ukraine in1992', *IMF Staff Papers*, Vol. 41, No.3 (1994) 411–34.

Szporluk, R., 'Reflections on Ukraine after 1994: the Dilemmas of Nationhood', *The Ukrainian Review*, Vol. 7, No. 7–9, March–May (1994).

Sztompka, P. 'Cultural and Civilizational Change: The Core of Post-Communist Transition', in Hausner, J., Pedersen, O. K. and Ronit, K. (Eds) *Evolution of Interest Representation and Development of the Labour Market in Post-Socialist Countries* (Warsaw: Cracow Academy of Economics/Friedrich Ebert Foundation, 1995) pp. 57–73.

TACIS EDUK 9402, *Addressing the Social Impact of Restructuring Enterprises in Ukraine. Socio-economic Public Opinion Poll*, 57–73, October 1996, pp. 57–73.

Tanzi, V. 'Public Governance in Transition', in Cornelius, P. K. and Lenain, P. (Eds), 1997, pp. 225–34.

Tedström, J. *Industrial Conversion in Ukraine: Policies and Prospects. Report on the USSR*. 23 August 1991.

Thiessen, U. 'Aussenwirtschaftliche Aspekte des Transformations- und Entwicklungsprozesses in der Ukraine', *DIW Vierteljahrsheft*, No. 2 (1996), 221–9.

Thiessen, U. 'Schattenwirtschaft in Osteuropa: Das Beispiel Ukraine', *DIW Wochenberichte*, No. 15 (1997a) 334–40.

Thiessen, U. 'Aussenwirtschaftliche Aspekte des Transformations- und Entwicklungsprozesses der Ukraine', in Hoffman, L. and Siedenberg, A. (Eds) 1997b, pp. 67–87.

Thiessen, U. 'Zur Schattenwirtschaft: Schatzmethoden, Schatzung und Konsequenzen fur die Wirtschaftspolitik', in Hoffman, L. and Siedenberg, A. (Eds) 1997c, pp. 67–87.

Tolstov, S. 'Legalisation of the 'Shadow Economy': National Traits of the Transition Period', *The Ukrainian Review*, Vol. 44, No. 3 (1997) 30–5.

Tretiakov, S. V. 'Sotsjialnie problemi Donetskovo regiona, ix resjenie na sovremenom etape', in *Problems of Development of Foreign Economic Relations and Attraction of Foreign Investments*, Donetsk State University, 1999, pp. 4–6.

Vardomskij, L., Vjatkina, N. and Savostina, L. *Probleme der strukturelle Transformation des postsowjetische Raumes*. Berichte des Bundesinstituts fur ostwissenschaftliche under internationale Studien, No. 19, 1997.

Vincentz, V. and Hirschhausen, C. von 'Price Policies and Subsidies in the Energy Sector of Ukraine' in Siedenberg, A. and Hoffman, L. (Eds) 1999, pp. 377–91.

Vinogradskaia, A. 'The Development of Small Enterprises' (in Russian). *Ekonomika Ukraini*, February (1999), 36–41.

Ukraina u tsifrax (Kyiv: State Statistics Committee of Ukraine, 1997).

Warner, K., The World Economic Forum of Geneva, The Harvard University Center for International Development. *The Global Competitiveness Report 1999* (Oxford: Oxford University Press, 1999)

Weissenburger, U. and Hirschhausen, C. 'Zum Strukturwandlung und der Industriepolitik in der Ukraine', in Hoffman, L. and Siedenberg, A. (Eds) 1997, pp. 109–27.

Willerton, J. P. *Patronage and Politics in the USSR* (Cambridge: Cambridge University Press, 1992).

Wittfogel, K. A., *Oriental Despotism – A Comparative Study of Total Power* (New Haven and London: Yale University Press, 1957).

Wittkowsky, A. 'Political Elites of Ukraine in Upheaval – Reforms and Structuring of Interest Groups',*Osteuropa*, Vol. 46, No. 4 (1996) 364–80.

Wittkowsky, A. 'Nationalstaatsbildung in der Ukraine: die Politische Okonomie eines 'historisches Kompromisses'', *Osteuropa*, Vol. 48, No. 6 (1998) 576–94.

Wolczuk, K. 'In Search of a Role': the Ukrainian Legislature in the Political System of Ukraine', paper presented at the BASEES conference, Cambridge, 27–29 March 1999.

World Bank *Land Reform and Farm Restructuring in the Ukraine*, Discussion Papers (Z.Lerman *et al.*) Washington D.C.,1994a.

World Bank *Income Inequality, Welfare and Poverty: an Illustration using Ukrainian Data* Washington D.C., 1995.

World Bank *Ukraine Coal Industry Restructuring Sector Report*. Washington D.C., 1996a.

World Bank *World Development Report 1997. The State in a Changing World* (Oxford: Oxford University Press, 1997b).

World Bank *Ukraine: Public Investment Review,* Washington D.C., 1997c.

World Bank, *World Development Report 1999–2000. Entering the 21st Century.* Washington D.C., 1999.

Zimmerman, W., 'Is Ukraine a Political Community?' *Communist and Post-Communist Studies,* Vol. 31, No. 1 (1998) 43–55.

Zucker, L. 'Production of Trust: Institutional Sources of Economic Structure, 1840–1920', in B. M. Staw and L. L. Cunnings (Eds), *Research in Organizational Behavior* (JAI Press, 1986, pp. 53–111.

Zon, H. van, Dillon, B., Hausner, J. and Kwiecinska, D. *Central European Industry in the Information Age* (Aldershot: Ashgate, 2000).

Zon, H. van, Batako, A. and Kreslavska, A. *Social and Economic Change in Eastern Ukraine – the Example of Zaporizhzhya* (Aldershot: Ashgate, 1998).

Zon, H. van, 'The Mismanaged Integration of Zaporizhzhya with the World Economy: Implications for Regional Development in Peripheral Regions', *Regional Studies,* Vol. 32.7 (1998) 607–18.

Zon, H. van, *The Future of Industry in Central and Eastern Europe* (Aldershot: Avebury, 1996).

Zon, H. van, *Alternative Scenarios for Central Europe* (Aldershot: Avebury, 1994).

Zviglyanich, V. 'The State and Economic Reform in Ukraine: Ideas, Models, Solutions', *Ukrainian Quarterly,* Vol. LH, No. 2–3, Summer – Fall (1996) 122–42.

Periodicals and newspapers

BBC Monitoring, Summary of World Broadcasts (BBC/SWB) Weekly Economic Report, part Former Soviet Union

The Day, newspaper, in English and Russian (Den) (http://www.day.kiev.ua/DIGEST/archiv.htm)

Eastern Economist, weekly, Kyiv

Economist Intelligence Unit (EIU), Country Reports Ukraine; Country Profiles Ukraine.

Ekonomika Ukraini

IntelNews, Business Journal, weekly Kyiv

Kyiv Post, weekly, Kyiv (http://www.thepost.kiev.ua)

Radio Free Europe/Radio Liberty Research (http://www.rferl.org/newsline/search/index.html)

Russia Today (http://www.russia today.com/rtoday.php3)

Ukrainian Economic Review, published by International Ukrainian Economic Association, Philadelphia.

Ukrainian Economic Trends, Monthly, Ukrainian-European Policy and Legal Advice Centre, Kyiv. (http:www.ueplac.kiev.ua/sitemap.html)

Zerkalo Nedeli (The Mirror, in Russian), Kyiv.

Chronology

1986
April 1996   The worst nuclear power station accident ever in Chernobyl.

1989
September 1989   The anti-reform Voldomyr Shcherbytsky is removed from his post as First Secretary of the Communist Party of Ukraine, that he had occupied since May 1972.

1990
January 1990   Almost one million people form a human chain from Lviv to Kyiv to commemorate the 1918 declaration of independence.

March 1990   The Rukh-led opposition wins nearly a third of the seats in elections to the Supreme Soviet.

October 1990   Prime Minister Masol, who had held the post since 1987, replaced by Vitold Fokin.

1991
August 1991   Failed coup in Moscow. Ukrainian parliament declares Ukraine independent.

December 1991   In a referendum, 90 per cent of the population votes for the independence of Ukraine. The Soviet Union falls apart. Leonid Kravchuk elected president.

1992
January 1992   Currency reform in Russia. Introduction of 'coupons' as parallel currency in Ukraine. Law on form of land ownership.

March 1992   Privatization begins.

September 1992   Prime Minister Fokin and his cabinet resign.

October 1992   Leonid Kuchma appointed as prime minister. Substantial cuts in gas deliveries from Russia.

November 1992   Kuchma gets extraordinary powers from parliament for a period of 6 months. Ukraine leaves ruble zone. Introduction of karbovanetz as provisional currency. Start of privatization of large state enterprises.

1993
January 1993   Parliament rejects economic reforms. The decree on privatization of land withdrawn.

May 1993	Parliament rejects prolongment of extraordinary powers for prime minister.
June 1993	Government announces 8–10 fold increase of rents and electricity. A miners strike begins in Donbas with far-reaching political claims.
July 1993	Ukraine decides to renounce the possession of nuclear weapons.
September 1993	Ukraine gives nuclear weapons to Russia. Parliament accepts resignation of Leonid Kuchma as prime minister. Successor is Jefim Zviahilsky.
December 1993	Annual inflation exceeds 10 000 per cent.

1994

January 1994	Agreement between Ukraine, Russia and the USA that aims at the destruction of all intercontinental missiles on Ukrainian territory.
Early 1994	The European Union and Ukraine sign agreement for partnership and cooperation.
March/April 1994	First free parliamentary elections. Communist fraction, supported by Agricultural Party and Socialist Party, becomes largest.
June 1994	Vitaly Masol becomes new prime minister. Leonid Kuchma wins presidential elections with 52 per cent of vote. Kuchma enters office one month later.
July 1994	Six thousand enterprises are put on the list of enterprises that cannot be privatized.
October 1994	President Kuchma proposes plan for comprehensive economic reforms: liberalization of prices and trade, acceleration of privatization and financial reform. Private ownership of land accepted. Most export quotas and licences abolished.
November 1994	Liberalization of prices and abolishing of subsidies for many products.

1995

January 1995	Citizens get privatization vouchers.
February 1995	Second phase of price liberalization: further price increases for municipal services.
March 1995	Prime Minister Masol resigns. Y. Marchuk becomes new prime minister. International donor institutions promise assistance to the amount of US$3 billion dollars for 1995, including 1.5 billion stand-by loan from the IMF.
April 1995	Parliament accept budget that foresees reduction of budget deficit to 3.5 of expected GDP and fullfils herewith IMF conditions.
June 1995	President Kuchma agrees with parliament speaker Moroz that president has the right to nominate ministers without approval of parliament, to implement economic reforms by decree and the right to dissolve parliament.

November 1995	Ukraine becomes member of the Council of Europe.
December 1995	Indicative export prices removed.

1996
January 1996	IMF postpones payment of fourth tranche of stand-by agreement related to lack of progress with privatization and budget consolidation.
April 1996	Ukrainian government signs memorandum with G-7 about closure of the nuclear power station in Chernobyl.
May 1996	Y. Marchuk dismissed as prime minister.
June 1996	Constitution of Ukraine accepted.
July 1996	Pavel Lazarenko appointed as prime minister.
September 1996	Introduction of new currency, Hryvna.
December 1996	International financial institutions promise US$1.5 billion dollars for support for economic reform.

1997
May 1997	Presidents Kuchma and Yeltsin sign Treaty of Friendship and Cooperation.
July 1997	V. Pustovoytenko appointed prime minister.

1998
March 1998	In parliamentary elections left-wing parties consolidate their strength. Election again failed to produce any consistent majority.
Sept/Oct 1998	Financial instability increases sharply in the wake of Russia's rouble devaluation.
September 1998	Ukraine signs a US$2.2 billion Extended Fund Facility with the IMF.

1999
May 1999	Parliament passes a bill limiting the independence of the National Bank of Ukraine.
June 1999	IMF backed Ukraine renegotiation of ING-Barings loan worth 163 US$million.
October 1999	IMF postponed payment of portion of Extended Fund Facility.
November 1999	Leonid Kuchma re-elected as president.
December 1999	Viktor Yushchenko appointed prime minister.
January 2000	Pro-reform majority formed in parliament.

Index